AGAINST THE CURRENT

Against
— the —
Current

THE REMARKABLE LIFE OF
AGNES DEANS CAMERON

BY CATHY CONVERSE

TOUCHWOOD EDITIONS

Edited by Cailey Cavallin
Cover design by Tree Abraham
Interior design by Colin Parks

LIBRARY AND ARCHIVES CANADA CATALOGUING IN PUBLICATION

Converse, Cathy, 1944-, author
Against the current : the remarkable life of Agnes Deans Cameron /
Cathy Converse.

Issued in print and electronic formats. ISBN 978-1-77151-270-1 (hardcover)

1. Cameron, Agnes Deans, 1863-1912. 2. Cameron, Agnes Deans, 1863–
1912—Travel. 3. Women—British Columbia—Biography. 4. Women
school principals—British Columbia—Biography. 5. Women authors,
Canadian (English)—British Columbia—Biography. 6. Women travelers—
Arctic Ocean—Biography. 7. Women travelers—British Columbia—Biography.
8. British Columbia—Biography. I. Title.

FC3823.1.C36C66 2018   971.1'03092   C2017-906611-0   C2017-906612-9

The publisher acknowledges the financial support of the Government of Canada
through the Canada Book Fund and the Canada Council for the Arts, and of
the Province of British Columbia through the British Columbia Arts Council
and the Book Publishing Tax Credit.

This book was produced using FSC®-certified, acid-free papers, processed
chlorine free, and printed with soya-based inks.

PRINTED IN CANADA AT FRIESENS

22 21 20 19 18   1 2 3 4 5

For Malcolm and Max:
Be bold. Forge your own path.
Stand apart if necessary.

It is possible that when the history of British Columbia comes to be written, the name of Agnes Deans Cameron will be inscribed therein as the most remarkable woman citizen of the province.

—VICTORIA *Daily Colonist*, MAY 14, 1912

CONTENTS

PREFACE

During Canada's 150th anniversary in 2017, Agnes Deans Cameron was recognized among the 150 most outstanding British Columbians in the history of the province. She appears next to extraordinary names like Captain George Vancouver, naval officer and explorer; Jeanette Armstrong, PhD, writer, educator, artist, and activist; Emily Carr, artist; Rosemary Brown, OC, OBC, politician, activist, and educator; Frank Calder, MLA and activist in aboriginal land claims and founder of the Nisga'a Tribal Council; and David Suzuki, CC, OBC, FRSC, scientist, broadcaster, and environmental activist. It is a well-deserved honour for a woman who spent her life going against the current.

Agnes Deans Cameron was a teacher, innovator, activist, internationally renowned author, journalist, lecturer, and traveller. During her lifetime, she was talked about as the most remarkable woman citizen of the province. She was not boastful and never clamoured for attention, but she was ambitious and had an insatiable curiosity along with a strong sense of self-determination. She made good use of her talents, becoming one of the most famous writers in Canada in her time and gaining an international reputation. Her celebrity garnered attention in hundreds of newspapers from Canada, the United States, and England. Her writing and stories appeared in small, tucked-away papers like the *Canebrake Herald* in Uniontown, Alabama, and star-quality publications like the *Toronto Globe* in Canada and the *London Times* and *Guardian* in England.

She was equally well known across Canada for her service in education. As president of the Dominion Educational Association she pushed for professionalism among teachers and their respective administrations. She knew how to be heard and, although it was not in her nature to seek a public fight, she never backed down when she, or her students, or teachers were being treated unjustly. On several occasions she took on the Department of Education and school board when she thought they had lost touch with their purpose or found their vision wanting.

I was first introduced to Agnes Deans Cameron years ago when Roberta Pazdro wrote a chapter for *In Her Own Right: Selected Essays on Women's History in B.C.*, a book Barbra Latham and I edited in 1980. The events that shaped Cameron's life, her integrity, her courage, and her intelligence piqued my interest. I was drawn to the fact that she was a strong woman who wrote her own script and could make the very best out of the very worst. This was someone who I considered had a lot to offer and could provide perspective and insight into our past. As a woman, I also felt that she could teach me about confidence and how to deflect the arrows that threaten to slay us the moment we dare to step apart from the norm. Some of the elements in her life intersected with my own. We were both teachers, both passionate about British Columbia, both writers, and while she spent time on rivers in scows, I plied the waters in kayaks. For the time being I tucked her story into the recesses of my mind and went on to explore and write about other remarkable women and their contributions to our country. Agnes Deans Cameron, however, never let go of me. For years she followed me around revealing small bits about herself. An article about her would appear in a magazine;

she popped up in a calendar paying tribute to women who made significant contributions to Canada. Her image was stitched into a tapestry that toured the country. She made brief appearances in books about early travellers, educators, and famous writers.

There finally came a point when I could no longer ignore her story. And so she took me on an incredible journey, which I shall treasure until I too become part of the past. Together we explored the beginnings of the Province of British Columbia, and I learned what it was like to be a young teacher in the infant stages of public education. She took me to the World's Fair in Chicago and on a tour about the city, on a ship to Honolulu before tourism became a popular pastime, to the opening of Happyland Park in Winnipeg, and into the great lecture halls of London. She wagged her finger at countries that wrote about Canada as a wasteland, locked in by ice and snow and devoid of cities, culture, and amenities. She was plucky—I liked that. She left me in the dust when she biked up a mountain in California and pedalled 160 kilometres over rutted paths to win the coveted title of the first female centurion for Western Canada. She showed me that history sometimes winds back on itself when we fail to heed its lessons. I read of the noisy scuffles between early bicyclists and pedestrians and the problems they caused to horse and driver; apparently, no one ever walked away from such an encounter satisfied. It is very familiar fare as the same issue blankets our news today. I suffered through the Point Ellice Bridge disaster with her and could not fail to notice how many of the same construction concerns and administrative issues plague the current rebuilding of a similar bridge in Victoria. I read with fascination her many articles on Red Fife wheat, experimental farms, and plans for expanding immigration to populate the immense regions of Canada's Wheat Belt. She covered the great river systems of Western Canada, noting early indications of Canada's vast supply of oil and gas. If it could be harnessed, she said, Canada, coupled with its exports of wheat, would become an economic powerhouse. As she visited the schools along the Athabasca and Mackenzie Rivers, I learned of the stories told by the Grey Nuns of Montreal about their early forays into the northwest and the poverty they and their orphaned charges felt as they grappled with the difficulties of surviving in a challenging environment. She honoured the strength of the people of the Western Arctic and often talked to audiences of their success in adapting to a very harsh environment. Though she could not totally escape her European bias of thinking of progress as a need to control, she warned against the exploitation of not only the environment but Indigenous people as well. While her trip down the Mackenzie occurred before residential schools and resettlement programs shamed our country, and before mining and oil extraction and climate change began to leave scars on the land, her mere presence was indicative of the British hegemony that would eventually force its institutions and culture upon the Indigenous people, which, over time, would destroy their culture and supplant their way of life, disconnecting them from their land and heritage.

Although Agnes Deans Cameron was born in Victoria, she was part of the cadre of middle-class British imperial colonists whose ideas of nation building, progressivism, land ownership, culture, religion, and history superseded all others. Initially British Columbia was a multicultural and multilingual society. On the streets of Victoria, Hastings Mill, Gastown, and many other communities, Indigenous languages could be heard alongside Chinook (the lingua franca of trade), French, Spanish, English, Cantonese, and German. Mixed racial groups were not uncommon. James Douglas, the governor of the Colony of Vancouver Island, was born in Demerara (Guyana) of a Barbadian Creole mother and a white Scots father. His wife, Amelia Douglas, referred to as the "Mother of British Columbia," was Cree, Irish, and French. However, as colonization gained in tempo, identity seemed precarious for everyone. Policies of separation and dominance gained a foothold among the British colonists, all of which must have had an effect on shaping the values and goals of the young Agnes Deans Cameron.

Though she fought for equality in pay and opportunity, joined groups to promote professionalism in education, and worked to further immigration through her writing, she did so as an Anglo-Protestant British woman. Though her viewpoint represents Western liberal modernism, her story is important precisely because she gives us insight into the way that early British Empire colonists saw Canada: as a place of economic and social opportunity. It is also valuable to learn of the struggles that she, as a woman, faced within that system. While the book she wrote later in life, *The New North*, is rife with many cultural biases, in an indirect way she exposes the commonalities shared by all peoples in Canada: our resilience, self-determination, sophistication, and love of place. She teaches of the necessity to be bold—to stand apart if necessary. She loved Canada and worked hard at promoting the country as a vibrant, humane, and progressive nation. If she could take a walk into the twenty-first century she would love the polyglot that we have become and would proudly acknowledge our successes and innovations, but she would be disappointed to learn of the continuing isolation and treatment of many of those outside the governing group who are pushed aside from those opportunities. Some things would be very familiar to her. The rancorous politics in her home province, which have been more or less a constant since Confederation, still entertain. She would be saddened to find that many of the issues that troubled her during her time as a teacher are still ongoing today. If she stepped into a classroom she would probably say we could do better with respect to teaching children to be creative thinkers and would have little patience for any technology that took children away from developing analytical skills. The continuing disputes between educators and officials would dismay her but might also make her feel both vindicated and justified for fighting so hard for teachers' and students' rights in her time. On the other hand, she would be irate with the casual acceptance of opinionated information that masquerades as fact and decry anyone who dared to act upon such unsubstantiated information as deceitful or lazy in her or his thinking. I fear we would all feel the sting of her pen as she took to the media to chastise us for losing our moral obligation to our children and society.

I urge you to heed the invitation extended by Felix Penne in a tribute he wrote to Agnes Deans Cameron upon her death: "Shoulder your pack, get out into the trail, follow this bold, adventurous spirit into 'the wild.'"

Introduction

The greatest hindrance to success is self-distrust, and a lack of originality.

—AGNES DEANS CAMERON

Sleep does not come easily on this mid-June night. Agnes Deans Cameron and her niece Jessie Cameron Brown, also known as "The Kid," are restive in their makeshift beds. The rain is relentless. Large droplets of water drip down the sides of their improvised shelter and seep into their clothing, making them feel even more miserable. They have not bathed or changed their clothes for the past four days. They nestle deeper into the ropes that serve as their bunk. Their campsite is the stern of a scow somewhere on the Athabasca River. It's a "hot hole," Cameron says. To make matters worse they are set upon by hordes of large, ferocious, dive-bombing mosquitoes. All night long they hear their incessant high-pitched buzzing as the females aim their needle-like probiscises at any exposed bits of skin in their search for blood.

"With cymbal, banners, and brass-bands he comes in cohorts to greet us," Cameron complains. They pull their jackets over their heads. "In the morning we are a sorry crowd, conversation is monosyllabic and very much to the point. It is the first serious trial to individual good-humour. When each one of your four million pores is an irritation channel of mosquito-virus it would be a relief to growl at somebody about something. But the sun and smiles come out at the same time, and, having bled together, we cement bonds of friendship."[1]

◆ ◆ ◆

The year was 1908. Cameron and Jessie were following the route of the early explorers and fur traders who travelled down the Athabasca and Mackenzie Rivers to the Arctic Ocean.[2] They were on a voyage of discovery. Cameron was a journalist and promoter of western and northern immigration. Her purpose was to explore the lands and communities along the great river systems of the north that, outside of the original inhabitants, had been known only to a handful of explorers, traders, prospectors, and missionaries. Canada in its grand design for developing the country was hoping to increase its population along the Peace, Athabasca, and Mackenzie Rivers, but was having trouble selling the northwest as a colonizing destination. Potential immigrants saw the land as hostile, cold, and barren. Cameron, who had penned many articles about Canada's western grain growing areas, wanted to show that the land beyond the Wheat Belt was vibrant and filled with opportunity. Explaining the motive for her trip she said, "Well, the Wheat Belt fascinated me, and I wrote about it in many leading American journals."[3] What was missing, she said, was information about the Fur Belt. It was the territory of the far north, from which skins and furs came down, that captured her attention. "I conceived the idea of travelling from Chicago to the Arctic Ocean, to see for myself that great land beyond the Wheat Belt which, now sparsely populated by hunters, trappers, and Indians, will in my opinion, one day teem with prosperous millions."[4] It would take them six months to travel sixteen thousand kilometres using rail, stagecoach, scow, steamer, and dugout canoe to reach the Arctic and come back. She had no idea on that sizzling hot Sunday in mid-May, when she and Jessie found themselves standing on a train platform in Chicago with a typewriter, a camera, and their gear waiting to embark their journey, that this trip would catapult her onto the front pages of newspapers and the oratorical stages of Britain, the United States, and Canada. She could not have known that her name would be forever inscribed as a great Canadian nationalist, and that she would be lauded as one of Canada's greatest writers of her time.

Cameron and her niece were on a trip few non-Indigenous women had undertaken. There had been other white women, wives of missionaries and trappers, who had travelled the liquid highway to communities north, but they had gone to stay, and none had gone so far. She had come a long way from the calamitous events that befell her just two years earlier. In 1906 the Department of Education in British Columbia revoked her teaching certificate and suspended her from her job as a teacher and as principal of South Park School for a period of three years. At the same time her eighty-four-year-old widowed mother, to whom she was devoted, died and the house that she had called home from birth was expropriated to make way for a thoroughfare. Life as she had known it had all but vanished. With no means of support, she found herself deeply in debt from her fight to retain her teaching certificate and her home. She was bereft but not undone. Her mother, who had been a forward-looking and positive sort, wrapped her children in a bubble of cheerfulness and stability. She always encouraged them to look for the best in people and when calamities befell them or doubts crept into their consciousness, they each knew the advice they would get from their mother: "We must just try to do the very best we can," she would tell them.[5] So Cameron picked herself up, dusted away the negatives, and contemplated her next move.

◆ ◆ ◆

Cameron was a bright and precocious child, vital and curious, and constantly seeking out information. She had an independent streak like her father and was not bound by the dictates of the day. As a young girl of thirteen, when many her age were wondering what life had in store for them, Cameron was decisive about her path in life. She was too young to contemplate marriage and family, but she somehow knew that she alone was responsible for her future. She set herself the task of managing her career track and developed a plan to bring it to fruition. It came as no surprise to any in her family that when she finished school she started training as a teacher, one of the few occupations open to women at the time. Her direction and the certainty with which she approached her studies were a natural outcome of her upbringing. The Scots traits of individual achievement, self-restraint, hard work, literacy, and self-confidence were laced throughout Cameron's family. She was raised by a mother who herself had been a teacher, as well as her mother before her. "Of Scottish parents, I was born in Victoria, Vancouver Island. Like most over-sea girls, I was brought up to do something and to earn my own living, and I did so as a school-teacher."[6]

Chapter One

THE LURE OF GOLD

*This was new land, and it could not be developed by
men who would always loll in the comforts of home.*

—DUNCAN CAMERON

Cameron's mother, Jessie Anderson Cameron, had been teaching in Fifeshire, Scotland, when her brother wrote to her sending money for her passage to join him in Sacramento, California. He had been part of a large outward migration of Scots sailing to North America, joining thousands of others hoping to make their fortunes in the goldfields. Jessie was twenty-seven at the time and verging on spinsterhood. She had nothing to lose and being an adventurous spirit the prospect of life in a far-off land was enticing. She agreed to go to her brother and left her teaching job sometime in 1851.

Getting to California was difficult. For those who staked their future on a dream it was a long and perilous journey that could take between six to eight months and cost anywhere from one hundred to six hundred dollars. There were several ways to get to the goldfields. Some of the "forty-niners," as they were called, sailed to the east coast of the United States, then followed the California Trail west. Although it was the safest route, many were unprepared for the long trek and died of starvation or exhaustion. Others sailed down to South America to cross the Isthmus of Panama. Once landed, they took the newly built railway the first eleven kilometres but had to trek the next ninety-three kilometres through jungle to reach the Pacific Coast. Along the way the travellers had to contend with robbers, poisonous snakes, mosquitoes, and alligators. Diseases like yellow fever, malaria, and cholera felled even the strongest. From Panama, they often had to wait months before getting passage on a ship to San Francisco. The more popular route, likely the one taken by Jessie, was to sail directly from Liverpool or Southampton to San Francisco, via Cape Horn. It offered its own dangers and many lives were lost to illness or shipwreck. From San Francisco, it was relatively easy to book passage on a steamer running into Sacramento.

Whatever Jessie had envisioned her new home to be, what lay before her was not the advertised picture of palm trees and streets paved with gold. Sacramento was an overcrowded boomtown filled with tents and hundreds of hastily constructed framed buildings. It was the Wild West where vigilante justice reigned and lawlessness, drinking, gambling, and murder were common. Sacramento was predominately a man's town. Few women, other than entertainers and prostitutes, stayed there. Money was so spotty and unpredictable that among the handful of women who followed their husbands, many found it necessary to supplement their income by taking in washing and doing extra cooking for the miners, in many instances earning more money than their spouses. Perhaps Jessie had done the same.

For single and respectable women like Jessie there was ample opportunity to find a husband among the townsmen. Before long, a restless, adventure-seeking Scot—who, like her brother, had come to the goldfields to make his fortune—began courting her. Duncan Cameron was smitten with Jessie and lest another ask for her hand, he quickly offered her a proposal of marriage. Less than a month before their wedding a disastrous fire broke out in a hat shop in the commercial district. It quickly swept through the town destroying over sixteen hundred buildings and causing five million dollars' worth of damage. The town lay in ruins, but despite the devastation around them they went ahead with their wedding and on Sunday, December 12, 1852, Jessie and Duncan were married. Two weeks later Sacramento was under several metres of water after rain and floods swept through the town. Determination, fortitude, and courage were needed to survive on the frontier.

After several months of disruption, the town began the process of rebuilding itself. The *Sacramento Union* was filled with articles about the entrepreneurial spirit that was evident among the survivors. In time, the Camerons relaxed into their normal rhythm and Duncan went back to his mining pursuits. It was not long before three sets of tiny feet were stomping around their modest house, each child clamouring for attention. William George was the first-born, Charles Napier arrived two years later followed by Margaret Helen, who died in infancy, and in 1858 Barbara joined the family.

Despite the hardships there was an unbreakable sense of optimism that permeated the town. Although many disappointed miners had their dreams dashed against the vagaries of luck, eighty-one billion dollars' worth of gold had been taken from the ground. By 1854 Sacramento became the state capital. The city was expanding, offering all kinds of opportunities for a hardworking family like the Camerons, but Duncan was an adventurer at heart and running a business was not something he wanted to do. The Sacramento gold rush was coming to an end and Americans were becoming quite vocal about foreigners picking over the remnants. As luck would have it there was exciting news on the gold front. In

1857, gold had been discovered in the Fraser River and four years later Billy Barker had struck gold in Williams Creek. The rush was on for the new "El Dorado." Duncan had done reasonably well in the goldfields, enough to take care of his growing family, but it was time to move on.

Shipping companies were unprepared for the thousands moving north. San Francisco ship owners ready to cash in on the exodus resurrected derelict ships from the scrap yard. The ships were inherently unsafe, but riches beckoned and it was a risk thousands of miners were willing to take. In the winter of 1860 the Camerons packed up their family and boarded one of the wooden side-wheelers that travelled between San Francisco and Victoria.[1]

It was a short jaunt up the coast and after a week at sea they left the rolling seas of the Pacific and entered the more sheltered water of the Strait of Juan de Fuca. As the deep ocean swells began to settle, those who had struggled with endless bouts of seasickness were grateful for the change. The scenery was breathtaking. On one side stood the magnificent snow-capped mountains of the Olympic Peninsula and on other side was a wild and rocky coastline outlined with trees that appeared to go on forever. The air was damp and a cold wind bit into the travellers. Though the Camerons had spent years in the dry warmth of California there was a familiarity about this weather—it was not unlike that of Scotland. Nonetheless, they pulled their wraps tightly around them. Within a few hours a beacon appeared on the horizon signalling their nearness to Victoria. The light at Race Rocks had just been completed. Many a ship had made it to this point only to be caught in the strong current and dashed against the shoals. For the Camerons it turned out to be a sign of home, as they learned that all the granite used in its construction was brought from their home country.

As they entered the well-protected harbour they saw a small settlement that was in the hurried and chaotic process of change. What once was a sleepy fur-trading outpost was now a lively town filled with businesses catering to miners who were occupied with obtaining licenses and stocking up on gold pans, shovels, pick axes, clothing, and food for the goldfields. Victoria served as the legal entry point, and prospective miners from all over the world descended on the town in the early days of gold being discovered. Within one week alone the population of Victoria rose from five hundred to thirty thousand.

As soon as the ship docked the family gathered their belongings and left their cramped quarters. It must have felt good to stand on solid ground. They disembarked onto a small wooden wharf in an area called Esquimalt. To get to Victoria they had to walk a few miles along a muddy road that led past saloons and unsavoury characters. Lined up along the side of the road were women, hoping to entice the arrivals to part with some of their gold in exchange for sexual favours. The children huddled closer to their parents.[2]

When they arrived in town they were overcome with the nauseating smell of sewage; animal waste from chickens and horses had been left to rot in the streets. As they passed by a grocer they noticed a dog relieving itself on a full basket of potatoes. The shopkeeper looked at them and shrugged. The town, such as it was, appeared rough and raw. The streets were wide and riddled with muddy potholes, a by-product of the hundreds of horses and carts that carried people daily to and from their destinations. Simply getting across the street became an exercise in sheer determination. Traffic was chaotic and boot-sucking mud grabbed at everyone who tried to get to the other side. It was so bad at times that it was rumoured that one proprietor had someone shoot an arrow across the street whenever he wanted to talk to the business opposite his store.[3] Victoria was not unlike Sacramento when the Camerons first arrived. The family had seen this all before and knew that it would quiet down and develop into something more livable, given time.

Victoria seemed to be a statement of contrasts. Speculators were everywhere. Land prices increased in price by seventy-five percent over a nine-month period and the cost of bread, butter, and tea was seen as shocking. Greed hung its shingle on the post of many establishments. Next to hastily constructed wooden structures that housed brothels and sleazy hotels were banks, a book and stationery store, and a post office, all sturdily built from brick. Shops were filled with tempting sweets. French spermaceti candles commanding three times the price of other candles were on offer, and luxurious lingerie made from processed Bengal silk could be purchased with the takings of the miners' gold. Culture was pushing through the veil of the rough and tumble, as gala parties bloomed and the Victoria Philharmonic Society played its first concert in 1859.

In the meantime, the family of five needed to find a place to live and Duncan was anxious to reach the goldfield while it was still lucrative. They heard of a new residential site that had just opened across the bay from Victoria. Historically James Bay had been part of the territory of the Swengwhung people, but in 1850 James Douglas, chief factor of the Hudson's Bay Company, signed treaties with several Indigenous groups securing their land with the promise they would be able to continue their traditional way of life and hunt on the unoccupied lands. Ownership of the land, however, was misconstrued by the HBC and over time such "promises" were all but forgotten by the colonists. After the signing of what became known as the "Douglas Treaties," the HBC proceeded to subdivide some of the area into town lots, leaving large tracts of land reserved for use as farmland. A newly built wooden bridge made the trip between James Bay and Victoria an easy commute. "Across James Bay," as people came to call the area, became a desirable place to live, particularly after Governor James Douglas built the colonial administration offices overlooking Victoria Harbour. Because the buildings looked like a mix of Chinese pagodas and Italian villa birdcages, they became known as the Birdcages.

The Camerons built a modest house on the corner of Birdcage Walk and Superior Street. Now known as Government Street, Birdcage Walk ran right into the Camerons' front yard. The area had a peaceful country look to it. Tucked between the town and the ocean, their property was surrounded by gentle hills and expansive fields of farmland. Over time Birdcage Walk became a very trendy development where large Italianate houses were built for bankers, civil servants, and professionals. Across the street from the Camerons was the home of the premier, John Robson, and behind them was a field that backed onto Carr Street, where the quirky artist Emily Carr lived with her family.[4] The Camerons often used to see the Carr girls and chat with them over their white picket fence. It was a pleasant life in James Bay. In her later years, Jessie told an interviewer how much she loved her home and that she often sat for hours watching the comings and goings on her busy little street[5]

As soon as the family was settled, Duncan purchased a mining license, as all prospective miners were required to do. It cost one-pound sterling for the rights and privileges of operating as a free miner for a period of one year. He then packed his gear and bade his family goodbye and left to work the Fraser River, hoping like the other miners to strike it rich. In between his return trips home, Jessie Clara Cameron was born, and on December 20, 1863, her baby sister, Agnes Deans Cameron, snuggled deep into her mother's arms for the first time.

Once the easy gold had been taken out of the Fraser River the miners moved on to the Cariboo. Where Duncan went after the Fraser is a matter of speculation, but he did spend time on Vancouver Island mining gold on the Leech River. The Colonial Secretary's Office issued a proclamation on August 8, 1862, offering one thousand pounds for discovery of gold on the island. There was a proviso; the money, which came from fees collected for licenses issued from working a particular track of land or gold field, must be equal to the amount of the reward and the extracted gold had to be equal in value to at least ten thousand pounds within six months of the issue of the licence. It was a gamble, but so was the life of a miner. Duncan's neighbour, Peter Leech, had been a Royal Engineer and was currently working for the Vancouver Island Exploring Expedition, a private enterprise set up to look for mining prospects on the island. In 1864 Duncan joined Leech on a trip to explore the Cowichan River and Cowichan Lake. Leech and his party soon discovered gold in a river that would become known as the Leech River. The rush was on. Over three thousand miners headed to the Leech River. Most of the gold was extracted within the year, but some mining continued up until 1876. It was not a rich vein, not like the major gold finds in the interior of the province, but over one hundred thousand dollars' worth of gold was taken from the bars and crevices that lined the bedrock of the river.

Duncan was rarely home, much to the disdain of his family. They wanted him to settle down and perhaps find another occupation, but their requests were always rebuffed. They needed the money, he told them, and he was not prepared to work at some monotonous job in Victoria that would lead to complacency. The heart of progress was to be found in the richness of the mountains and riverbeds, he said, and not by men who "would always loll in the comforts of home."[6] While he never made large sums of money, he earned enough to keep his family comfortable. He did try his hand at other jobs. Over the years Duncan was listed in the city directory as having the occupation of miner, contractor, receiver, and farmer.

While mining was taking hold on Vancouver Island, the major gold rush in the Cariboo was over. Thousands of miners, discouraged and broke, left British Columbia. The effect was strongly felt throughout all the gold-rush towns, but most poignantly in Victoria. The city fell into an economic slump. Unfinished buildings were abandoned, immigration stopped, and property values fell. Speculators and businesses that depended on mining revenue for their continued growth felt hard done by. However, some heaved a great sigh of relief for they could now afford to buy property and a house, and the price of commercial goods would be sure to return to within reason. The high cost of living had been particularly hard on those who had not made their living by mining.

Ever since the *British Colonist* published the first edition of its newspaper in December 1858 there had been a scorching debate about Victoria's boom and bust economy.[7] The paper, not yet settled into objectivity, chided the city for depending on mining and land speculation as their main source of revenue. It was the way to financial ruin, they wrote: "While, however, we have been over-estimating the value of real estate and the thousand-and-one copper and gold schemes, we have been underrating the very source of wealth which above all others would add to the stability of the colony and counteract the injurious fluctuations of mining speculation. We have persistently ignored our agricultural resources, and while sending large sums out of the country to provide for our own and British Columbia's consumption, we have been depending for our returns on a desperate lottery. All this is wrong in principle and ruinous in practice."[8] The argument, although not as true today as it was in 1865, still wavers between extraction and invention. Dependency on raw resources has always been a staple of the economy of British Columbia.

Chapter Two

THE EARLY YEARS FOR CAMERON
AND FOR PUBLIC EDUCATION

*Notice is hereby given that the High School will
be opened Monday morning the 7th instant, at
9 o'clock AM . . . All pupils who have passed the
examination . . . are expected to enroll themselves
at the commencement of the session.*

—JOHN JESSOP, SUPERINTENDENT OF EDUCATION

Agnes Deans Cameron grew up surrounded by a family who paid
a great deal of attention and respect to education. There was never
any question that all of Jessie and Duncan's children would be sent
to school. Education, reading, curiosity, responsibility, and making
one's way in the world were part of the ethos of the household.
When Cameron's sister Barbara was of school age public education
was not available. Families who could afford it sent their children

to England to study or enrolled them in one of the small private schools in the city. The more popular schools were Angela College for Young Ladies, Mr. Edward Mallandaine's Select School for Children, and Mrs. Wilson Brown's Church Bank House Academy for young ladies, the school Barbara attended. Her classmates were children of well-known personalities in the city. Dr. Helmcken, Speaker of the Legislative Assembly, sent his daughters to Mrs. Brown's Academy, as did Allen Francis, United States Consul, and Thomas Williams, Registrar of the Supreme Court. The courses they provided gave the students a foundation in modern languages, music, drawing, and the use of globes. There was no further program of formal education beyond the basics.[1]

For the future evolution of British Columbia, a public education system free to all youngsters was considered an important part of the process that was essential for establishing a moral, literate, and productive citizenry. Early education had been a haphazard affair, geared to only a select few. For some that was the natural order of things. British Columbia had only become a province in 1871; it was young and there were seemingly more important issues that needed attention. Before any consideration could be given to education the government had to first sort out their politics, craft an identity, and decide on their direction and goals. Besides, they argued, the government could not afford the luxury of offering anything free to anybody, especially the poor. Pressure for a public school system continued unabated. A vigorous tug of war for the public purse ensued. The self-appointed spokesperson for the cause was Amor De Cosmos, editor of Victoria's first newspaper, the *Daily British Colonist*, politician, and premier of the province, who waged a spirited campaign in support of having schools set up throughout the province. Finally, in 1872, the government initiated a Public School Act allowing for the creation of a board of education and superintendent of education. Cameron was nine at the time and, in all likelihood, was not drawn to the ongoing political sparring over the future of education. The next few years were busy ones for education in the province. For the new board, there were many hurdles to overcome. Forty schools were built and teachers needed to be hired to staff the schools. First among their concerns was the lack of trained teachers. Among the fifty new teachers hired only one had any professional teaching qualifications. The general perception among the public was that anyone could teach provided they had some schooling, however little. Teaching was viewed as a temporary occupation taken up by young women and men who were desperately in need of an income. It was an easy way to make some money, at least until a better offer came along.

John Jessop, the first superintendent of education, knew the lack of qualified teachers would be a serious drawback to the effectiveness of education. Until the population in British Columbia increased sufficiently to have teacher training colleges or normal schools, he suggested that high schools could operate as training institutes for teachers. The problem was there were no high schools in the province. With considerable effort and lobbying on Jessop's part, the first high school opened in Victoria in 1876. There was a great deal of interest in attending the high school and admittance was highly sought after. To ensure they received the very best applicants, a series of rigorous examinations were set up in twenty-one centres across the province.

For Cameron and her sister Jessie it was an opportunity not to be missed. On the day of the exam, perhaps a bit nervous and a little unsure of what was to come, they sat down at their desks waiting for the signal to begin. The test was not easy. The questions had been developed by the superintendent of education along with input from local politicians, scholars, and professionals within the community. This was the first time such a test had been compiled for the province, so procedures for determining the reliability and validity of the questions had not been measured, and for the students there was no precedent from which to study. Cameron breezed through the easiest questions, which simply tested recall, a big component of early education. There were also many questions that queried the applicant's basic understanding of the major principles of a given subject. To separate out the average student from the gifted there were many questions that not only required them to analyze a given situation, but also to solve an issue they had not met with before. When Cameron picked up her pencil her first question required her to prove the spherical nature of the earth. She also had complex fractional equations to calculate, oceans, cities, and political boundaries to name, and rules of grammar to discuss. Her concentration never wavered, but toward the end she was not quite so excited about pontificating on Euclid's postulates, theorems, or axioms. When the marks finally came out, fifty-eight percent failed. Agnes Deans Cameron and Jessie Cameron were among those who passed. Cameron came in thirteenth, and her sister was fifteenth.

On August 7, 1876, both girls were excited to be among the twelve girls and twenty-two boys from across the province accepted into the first high school to begin their training as teachers. The competition was going to be challenging. John Newbury received ninety-two percent on his entrance exams and Miss Anderson received ninety percent; the average grade was seventy-two percent. Samuel Maclure, who eventually became one of British Columbia's most famous architects, was a classmate of Cameron's. Cameron was a very determined young lady; she was naturally curious and always wanting to know more.[2]

Rather than a build a new school, the Department of Education repurposed the old Colonial School House. It was situated on the School Reserve in an area of ten acres that began at the head of Yates Street. Despite its rustic mien it was fitting that this old whitewashed, two-room log building would serve as the first high school, for it also had been the first public school in the province. It would now house a dedicated and more serious group of students, intent on a future professional career.[3] The inside of the high school was furnished with only the barest of necessities; a pot-bellied stove stood in the middle of the classroom, small desks were neatly lined up row by row, a slate blackboard covered the front of the room, and a terrestrial globe was pushed off in a corner. To separate the room into compartments, a dusty green curtain was hung from the ceiling. Although gone was the boisterous sound of younger, energetic elementary school children, the building was imprinted with their memories.

Around eight-fifteen every morning Cameron left for school to be there before the bell was rung at nine o'clock. It was a pleasant walk. She followed a well-worn path that took her through the woods until she came upon an open stand of stately Garry oak trees, heralding the entrance to the School Reserve. It was a walk she enjoyed, particularly in the spring, when the glen showcased masses of sturdy blue wild flowers. She liked to listen to the calls of the nuthatches, sparrows, and towhees as they flitted about the woodlands in search of food for their little ones. It gave her time to think about what she was to do with the coming day, like writing a new story for the semi-monthly newspaper put out by the Hyacinth Club. Perhaps she should include a riddle to spice things up a bit or add a jocular twist to her story. Her teacher always impressed upon his students the importance of being witty and amusing. Cameron loved working on the newspaper but she would also have enjoyed joining the debating club. She would have revelled in the opportunity to debate and discuss the issues of the day, but the Lyceum Club was for boys only. Unfortunately debating was not seen as an appropriate pursuit for young ladies. It was something she accepted, but grudgingly.

The curriculum was extensive. Cameron studied English, geography, botany, physiology, philosophy, astronomy, chemistry, algebra, Euclid, Latin, Greek, French, map drawing, and music. Part of her training included a regular daily practicum teaching the younger children next door in the new Boy's and Girl's School. The new school was not glamorous like some of the other Gothic-style buildings in Victoria. It was plodding and practical, but as plain and unassuming as it was on the outside, the interior and its amenities rivalled the best of any on the entire Pacific Coast.[4] When it was finished the superintendent of education very proudly commented, "Some of the school edifices in San Francisco are more pretentious in appearance; but none of them have such extensive and beautiful grounds, or such magnificent views of city, country, and surrounding waters."[5] The construction of the new school was indicative of a growing acceptance of the need for public education, particularly as it was built while the city was still struggling with an economic recession that began with the end of the gold rush.

The Girl's School was on the second floor. Cameron liked the spacious classrooms; it was a relief from sitting in a cramped room of the small schoolhouse all day. Some of the rooms in the new school could seat up to eighty people. The ceilings were five metres high and the rooms were well lighted. To feel comfortably warm in the winter was a treat. New hot air stoves heated the larger class-rooms and a well-stocked fireplace kept the smaller rooms cozy. The children loved the revolving seats that attached to their desks and they were forever getting into trouble for rotating them back and forth, but what child can resist such temptation no matter how much it annoys their teacher?

Spending part of each day teaching was a great opportunity for Cameron to learn how to prepare lessons for the children. It was challenging but at the same time exciting to be able to put what she had been learning into practice. Cameron quickly realized that to be an effective teacher she had to consider the whole child; their relationship with their parents, their social circumstances, and their way of learning. She wanted to teach children how to reason and not to be mere robots that would parrot back information when asked. One of her favourite exercises was to find out what her students thought and the processes they used to query their world. She would ask, "Suppose this morning an all-wise man were to enter our classroom. What six things would you ask?"[6] She was always surprised by the cleverness of their answers. At every opportunity, she encouraged her children to question and explore. She loved it when a student would come to her with a question like, "Why is it that we don't slip off the earth?" or "If you jumped off the world, and went straight on, where would you go to?"[7] She also learned that simply having an education oneself did not equip one to handle the complexities inherent in the learning process. In this she was ahead of many of her cohorts who saw education as merely imparting knowledge. It was an ideology that would set her repeatedly on a path against the supervisors and school board later in her teaching career.

Within days of the schools opening, Cameron and her classmates began to prepare for a visit from Lord Dufferin, the Governor General of Canada, and his wife, the Countess of Dufferin. It was not hard to get caught up in the excitement; the entire city was preparing for their visit. Visitors came from all over British Columbia to witness the event. The streets were lined with bunting, flags, banners, wreaths, and evergreens. The government building was illuminated and a triumphal arch was constructed so that when the Dufferins passed under it they would hear the national anthem sung by three young girls who were cleverly positioned in the niches. In the Inner Harbour the ships of war were dressed and a cannon salute was planned as the Governor General landed. Everything down to the smallest detail was attended to. For the safety of His Excellency, citizens were asked to stay on the sidewalks and to not leave their buggies unattended.

One of the more outstanding events was the showing of First Nations peoples from the coast. Coming from as far away as the Queen Charlotte Islands, the Haida were joined by the Heiltsuk, the Haisla, the Nuu-chah-nulth, and the Kwakwakw'wakw. After paddling many long miles, they entered Victoria's Inner Harbour in an impressive assemblage of large ocean-going canoes. It was a sight to behold as chiefs, dressed in their full regalia, stood at the bows of their canoes presenting a powerful show of pride.

British Columbia was in the process of developing and an official visit by such esteemed guests put Ottawa's stamp of approval on the young province, but behind the fireworks, concerts, and diplomacy was a more pointed reason for their presence. Ottawa had been increasingly concerned over the unstable politics and the continued threats of secession from the Dominion from its far-flung western province. Some of the big names from the old guard of colonial civil servants, like Justice Matthew Begbie, Henry Crease, and Amor De Cosmos, the second premier of the province, were well known in Ottawa as continued resisters to Confederation. British Columbia was fast becoming the enfant terrible of the Dominion and needed to be brought into line.

British Columbians' discontent was understandable. They had little economic connection to the Dominion and almost no cultural or psychological affiliation with Ottawa. The Bank of British Columbia had its headquarters in San Francisco, not in Ottawa. If anything, the new province looked to Britain and San Francisco as stronger allies in their future destiny. Also, because of its largely transient population, British Columbia had not settled down to the business of nation building. Politicians were more focused on self-interest and less concerned with economic and cultural stability. This fact made for endless fractious debates that stemmed from egotistical, self-seeking individuals who changed political affiliations as often as they doffed their hats. Ottawa was rightly concerned that they could lose British Columbia to the United States.

Part of the Dufferins' six-week itinerary included a visit to the Boy's and Girl's School to meet with the top academic students from all over the province. The occasion was the presentation of three medals, one silver and two bronze, to be awarded to the students with the highest graduating average.[8] While acting in the position of Governor General of Canada, Lord Dufferin worked to push Canadian ingenuity and excellence in education to the forefront. In 1873 he instituted the Dufferin Medal, which later became known as the Governor General's Academic Medal, which today is one of the most esteemed awards that can be earned by Canadian school students.

Students from across the province were invited to join the mayor, politicians, and dignitaries for the ceremony. Cameron along with the rest of her high school class had worked hard at preparing for the event. As their Excellencies entered the room a hush descended over the crowd. The children knew they dared not utter a sound, scuffle a foot, or twitch even one muscle. Six hundred children sang the national anthem with all the sweetness and fervour they could muster. It was the duty of the superintendent of education to make the introductions. Protocol demanded perfection and getting the Governor General's name correct was a bit of a tongue twister. Jessop stepped up to the podium and began; "To His Excellency, the Right Honourable Sir Frederick Temple, Earl of Dufferin and Governor-General of the Dominion of Canada." He then talked about the progress that had been made in the province in education and the value of honouring excellence. Lined up on the stage were the three students receiving their awards. John Cowper Newbury, a student in Cameron's class, was the recipient of one of the bronze medals.[9]

On the second day of school the Board of Education had to deal with a complaint made by one of the parents over the issue of introducing religious doctrine in the classroom. The public school system was set up to be non-sectarian, free of church dogma and governance. For those who wanted their children to have a Christian education there were church schools they could attend. No less at stake was whether British Columbia was prepared to keep church and state separate or to allow overlaps. While there were those who demanded that Protestant dogma be injected into the public school system as a counterpoint to what they saw as an increasingly immoral society, most parents were content with the secularism in their public schools.

This was not something any new employee wanted to face before they had time to establish themselves and their reputation. The principal of Cameron's school was the Reverend Alexander B. Nicholson, who came highly recommended. He seemed a good match and the superintendent of education was confident that he had hired the right man. Even the *Daily British Colonist* wrote a report praising the selection: "We are clearly of opinion that Mr. Nicholson will be found 'the right man in the right place,' and that he will imbue his scholars with a love of learning, as well as all that is good and noble in youthful age."[10] Nicholson unfortunately did not have time to bask in such celebratory praise. A maelstrom of letters hit the newspapers over the issue of religious teaching in the school.

Every morning Nicholson began the school day with a recitation of the Lord's Prayer, then read an excerpt from the Bible, and asked God to bless the children in his charge. Although he would have preferred to provide an interpretation along with the readings, he refrained. He was aware that the School Act of 1872 stated that all public schools must be conducted upon strictly non-sectarian principles and that no religious dogma or creed be taught. Nicholson had been a Presbyterian clergyman prior to taking up his job as principal, but to show his commitment to the school board he relinquished his position in his church. Nicholson was aware that many public schools within the Dominion and in the United States allowed prayer and Bible reading, but though he thought pure secularism impoverished the human spirit, he felt confident that he was acting within the parameters set by the Public School Act. But not all agreed with Nicholson's daily recitations.

Shortly after school began letters to the editor in both the *Daily British Colonist* and the *Daily Standard* poured in. Two in particular illuminated a basic weakness in the legislation. One writer, who supported Nicholson, wrote of the lack of clarity of the act: "to teach a 'creed' or a 'dogma' is one thing, but to ask God to bless the children of a school or to aid the teacher in his efforts to cultivate and expand their youthful minds, is a very different thing."[11] Another, opposing religious instruction on any grounds, argued, "The importation of prayer into the curriculum of the High

School cannot be tolerated without sapping the foundation of our school system. Therefore it must be discontinued." At no time was there ever any discussion about Nicholson's abilities as a school principal. The same writer further stated that, "Mr. Nicholson clearly is not disqualified as Principal of the High School. But in conducting any religious service whatever within the schoolbuilding [*sic*] he has very properly fallen under public censure."[12]

As the two letters indicate, there was confusion as to the meaning of "non-sectarian." It was easy to get lost in that definition. One interpretation was that it meant "non-denominational" while for others it implied "non-religious." The difficulty was that with respect to school prayers the Board of Education had vacillated between these two meanings. Confusing the issue was the fact that the School Act specified that one of the duties of the teacher was to ensure students behaved according to the highest moral standards, which were Christian based. This was reinforced in the textbooks, which had a Protestant Christian orientation. Yet the 1865 School Act stated that all books of a religious character, teaching denominational dogmas shall be strictly excluded.

The issue did not seem to fade as quickly as the Board of Education had hoped. The solution, they decided, was to amend the Public School Act of 1872 to exclude all clergy from holding any position, voluntary or otherwise, in a provincial public school. The intent of the amendment was to also restrict religious exercises in schools to the public recitation of the Lord's Prayer and the Ten Commandments, showing the inherent difficulty of defining non-sectarian.

Nicholson had given up a great deal to become principal of Victoria High School. He was upset and perplexed as to the charges levelled against him. He thought he had done everything asked of him by the School Act. The Board of Education and the position of Superintendent of Schools were only four years old at the time. Their jobs were not neatly defined and, above all else, they needed to be seen to be doing their due diligence, despite weaknesses in the legislation. Nicholson had no option but to step down from his position. In his letter of resignation, he focused on the confusion with the Department of Education's meaning of secularism. He claimed that he had opened and closed the high school with the forms the board recommended to be used by public school teachers, and did not regard such devotional exercises as inconsistent with secular education. "The clause 'strictly secular' to which you direct my attention, is not, to my mind, sufficiently clear to decide the exclusion of any reference whatever to religious ideas in the process of education," he wrote. "In one sense it excludes, in the other it includes the bible and devotional exercises. I would state that, acting under the instructions of the Board as contained in Appendix B, Public Schools Report, and considering those regulations as in force until repealed by a new decree of the Board, I have opened and closed the High School with the forms recommended to be used by Public School Teachers."[13] His resignation was accepted by the Board of Education on September 12, 1876. The back-story gossip was that the Board of Education had always wanted Stephen Daniel Pope, a graduate of Queen's University, to fill the position of principal. It came as no surprise then when Pope was appointed as Nicholson's replacement. Nicholson was the first of many to become the victim of a system that was ruled by secrecy, impulsiveness, and petty jealousies.

At first all seemed to go well after Nicholson's resignation. The students and parents as well as the Board of Education were well satisfied with their new principal, Stephen Daniel Pope. But within the first year Pope was faced with having to discipline one of the students for using insolent language and refusing to apologize. His response was to suspend the student, who in anger threatened Pope and said that he would rue the day he suspended him. A similar thing happened the second year and that student too was barred from class.

Suspension was a normal course of action to be taken in such situations. The rules and regulations were quite clear on the subject:

"For gross misconduct, or a violent or willful opposition to authority, the teacher may suspend a pupil from attending school, forthwith, informing the parent or guardian of the fact, and the reason of it."[14] Where Pope overstepped his authority was in failing to obtain the necessary permission of the school trustees, as was outlined in the 1874 Public Schools Report. Both sets of parents complained to the Board of Education saying that it was Pope who should be disciplined, not their children. They said he was unprogressive and that he was often seen at school in an intemperate manner. Such allegations were outrageous, Pope claimed. The board sat quietly, hoping the issue would fade. Pope was furious. Without their support, he informed them, he was not prepared to carry on with his duties and stayed home, causing school to close for summer holidays earlier than slated. Rather than considering the allegations, the superintendent and the board took what they thought was the easy route and fired him, stating that his lack of attendance meant that he had retired. Interestingly, both of the boys' fathers belonged to the same temperance organization as the superintendent of education.

The controversy did not go away. For weeks there were articles appearing in both the *Daily British Colonist* and the *Daily Standard*, the first attacking his behaviour and the latter criticizing the Board of Education and the superintendent for failing to look into the truth of the matter and dismissing Pope on a whim. By the end of the year the superintendent of education and the entire board of education were forced to resign by the newly elected premier of the province, George Walkem. Both Pope's and Nicholson's experiences were evidence of the insularity, mean spiritedness, impulsive nature, and political partisanship that characterized the early growth of education, a precursor to the continuing instability of a system that was and remains to this day heavily politicized. The dispute only temporarily affected Pope. He was rehired by the new superintendent, Colin Campbell McKenzie, to teach at South Saanich school and went on to become a highly respected administrator in the education system of the province.

At the end of her first year, Cameron began studying for the government qualifying teaching examinations. The tests covered each subject studied in school. She did not have to take all the tests at once, only those she felt ready to tackle. The exams would be challenging but even if she passed she was too young to receive an appointment as a teacher. For that she had to wait until she was sixteen. The exams set for early July were to be administered at the Legislative Assembly in the Parliament buildings. There were two different tests, one for the boys and another easier test for the girls. Many of the topics and questions were assigned by one's gender. Cameron had to pass tests in geography, grammar, rhetoric, composition, mythology, botany, physiology, natural philosophy, astronomy, chemistry, arithmetic, and music. She would also face questions testing her knowledge of Latin, Greek, and French. On the other hand, she did not have to worry about studying Euclid, mensuration, algebra, or bookkeeping. These topics were added to the boys' examinations. It was almost an insult for her because she enjoyed those courses and was as equally adept with the subjects as the boys.

As Cameron entered the testing room she felt confident but had no idea what to expect. She started with history and English literature, each of which took three hours to complete. As she began her history exam one of the questions she had to ponder over was on the topic of the Long Parliament. She was asked to recall when the Long Parliament in England was first summoned and then name the principal acts they passed before the commencement of the English Civil War. For the natural philosophy exam, she had to describe hydrostatic pressure and explain the principle on which it acts as well as delineating the parts of a steam engine and how it works.[15] When she sat down for the arithmetic portion of the exam she read with some surprise instructions for the "Gentlemen" to omit the first six questions. Apparently, those questions were considered too simple for the boys to bother with. Gender differences were also set for English composition; the boys wrote essays on science and peace and the girls on the element of beauty in nature and on manners. Further on, she was asked to provide her opinion of the results of the campaign for women's rights. She would have much preferred the question that her seatmate Samuel Maclure received. The boys were asked to write an essay on the influence that the discovery of gold in California and Australia exerted on civilization. This would have been a perfect topic for Cameron, as her family had been pioneers in the goldfields and it was likely that she often heard conversations around the house about the business of gold mining. Such gender differences did not sit well with the boys either. There had been complaints that the young ladies had an undue advantage over the young gentlemen. They rightly reasoned if they were to teach in the same schools and address the same topics then the examinations should reflect that. The Board of Education, often two steps behind the current ethos or practices of the day, decided that for future examinations there would be no differences. Lady applicants should take note and direct their studies accordingly, they warned.

Cameron had to wait an agonizingly long week before she received her results. She answered forty percent of the questions correctly, which put her slightly above the average. Five candidates failed the examination, one failed to complete, and only one student received a First Class Grade A certificate, which was valid for three years. Cameron's marks earned her a Third Class Grade A certificate, valid for one year. If Cameron had been old enough her results would have been sufficient to allow her to teach in a public school where at least one other teacher was employed, typical of rural postings. If she wanted to teach in an urban school where several teachers were employed, her certificate would only allow her to act as an assistant. To teach in an urban centre and forgo yearly retesting in favour of doing so every four years, she would either need to attain eighty percent on the examinations or be a graduate of a university. There were only a few teachers in the province who had graduated from Queen's University in Kingston or McGill University in Montreal. It was not until McGill opened an affiliate program in Victoria in 1903 that students could attend university locally. It was not a step that Cameron ever took.

At the end of the summer break Cameron went back to school. She was a voracious reader and loved learning. One of her goals was to win the Governor General's Silver Medal. She remembered the first presentation of the Dufferin Medal and set her sights on achieving such a prize. She thrived in a competitive environment. She demanded much and set her standards high. While she never did win the medal, she achieved the distinction of attaining the third highest score in the province.

Chapter Three

THE YOUNG TEACHER

*And, oh, if you are a parent or a teacher, don't strive to
fashion your children into one stereotyped pattern. A
child's individuality is the divine spark in him. Let it burn.*

—AGNES DEANS CAMERON

In 1879 Cameron was finally able to put her years of training into
practice. As a newly minted teacher she applied for a position at
Angela College. It was a good first job for her. Her school was about
a ten-minute walk from her house. Angela College was a private
school that was connected to the Church of England.[1] It was well
known in the community for promoting a British upper-class education, where manners and propriety were important elements in
the curriculum. Admission was usually gained through one's family
connections. The irony was that among the pupils were girls whose
fathers had lobbied for free non-sectarian schools; a few even held
positions on the school board. Dr. William Fraser Tolmie enrolled

his daughter. Tolmie had been the chief factor of the Hudson's Bay Company and served as the first chairman of the General Board of Education from 1865 to 1867. He was also a member of the Provincial Board of Education from 1872 to 1878. Other notables who sent their daughters to the school were Dr. Israel Wood Powell, a politician and member of the General Board of Education, and the person responsible for introducing the motion in the legislature for the Public School Act; Edward Graham Alston, barrister, politician, and the inspector-general of schools; Thomas L. Wood, acting solicitor general of the Colony of Vancouver Island and member of the Board of Education; and William J. Macdonald, magistrate in the Legislative Council and also a member of the Board of Education.

At the top of Church Hill, at 923 Burdett Avenue, Angela College competed with Christ Church Cathedral for an unparalleled view the city and Victoria's Inner Harbour. Built in 1865, Angela College was a distinguished-looking two-story, neo-Gothic structure with an octagonal tower that set it apart from its surroundings. Its construction broadcast that Victoria was emerging as a city of importance. At the opening ceremonies, the governor of Vancouver Island, Arthur Kennedy, spoke on the significance of such an institution for the colony. According to a reporter with the *Daily British Colonist*, Kennedy told the crowd that the new school would provide proper education and training to those women who would become the future wives and mothers of the coming generation. Kennedy received applause when he said, "No race of useful people could descend from any but good and virtuous mothers."[2] Justice Needham added that the building would be an important reminder of the determination of a young society: "When the edifice now being raised had crumbled into dust, and when the touching emblems were brought forth coming generations would bless those who were long before gathered to their fathers."[3] Behind the accolades was an unspoken concern that the new school, with its steep gabled roof and eye-catching coped mouldings, might go the way of so many of its predecessors.

One of the problems with the early private schools was stability; they survived only as long as their clientele were willing to support them. Angela College had been temporarily closed for two years before Cameron began teaching there. Others, like Miss Faussette's Roseville Academy, and Miss Brown's, the school Cameron's sister Barbara attended, eventually closed their doors.[4]

On that first day as Cameron opened the front gate of her yard and climbed up the steeply graded Church Hill, she was thankful the fall rains had not yet begun, as they always made the hill a muddy, slippery mess. Excited as she was she must have felt a slight twinge of apprehension. So many thoughts must have been running through her mind: Who were her students? What would they be like? Could she, as a sixteen-year-old, maintain discipline? Would the transitions between subjects run smoothly? What if she couldn't answer a student's question? Would she get along with the principal, Mrs. Mason? There had been a history of principals and teachers leaving Angela College shortly after they began. Would that happen to her?

When she entered her classroom, she found a prettily wrapped gift from the students—a lovely gesture, she thought, until she opened the package and found the remains of a dead mouse. The students squirmed in their seats trying hard not to laugh. It seemed it was a student tradition reserved for new teachers.

Those first few steps up the entryway into Angela College opened a door for Cameron that would forever change her life. She was ambitious and hardworking but could never have envisioned that she would come to be highly thought of across the country as a progressive educator and a consummate professional, that she would be the first female school principal of a public school in the province and would become a driving force for educational standards, as well as a champion for gender equality in wages. If she had known that her devotion to her profession and to her students, and her untiring work toward educational reform, would be the cause of constant friction between herself and the arbiters of education, eventually resulting in a public hearing and the suspension of her teaching certificate, would she have opened the door so eagerly?

Cameron taught at Angela College for two years but she was anxious for a greater challenge and wanted to move into the public school system. Teaching jobs for young women were more plentiful in rural areas. Men who joined the teaching profession were more likely to be placed in urban areas ahead of women, irrespective of seniority. Cameron applied for a posting. Her application was accepted and she was assigned a teaching position at Port Augusta, a rural area farther up Vancouver Island.[5] Transitioning from a private academy to the public school system was an important move for her. British Columbia was becoming less sectarian, less exclusive, and less British. The fight for a free, non-denominational public school system had been brawny, and while religious schools were recognized as an important part of the education system there was little appetite for any further support of them.

Teaching in a rural area was difficult. Rural schools were often isolated, the classrooms were cramped, and attendance was sporadic. Some teachers found themselves alone and lonely and their lack of experience and preparation for a rural setting did not equip them to handle the adversities they would face. Teachers were expected to be pillars of the community and have excellent negotiating and managerial skills. The success of their school depended on the teachers' ability to maintain local support and enthusiasm for a school program that was often at odds with rural life. Understandably teacher turnover was high, many viewing their rural experience as a temporary but necessary step to obtaining a position in a small town or an urban area. If there were behavioural problems with any of the children, the teacher was often blamed. There was an incident at one school in which a nine-year-old boy had "interfered with little girls" on his way home. The boy was expelled from school by the school trustees, which angered the boy's father. He placed the blame on the teacher, saying it was her responsibility to stop the other children in the class from annoying his son. The teacher managed to keep her position but she was held at fault nonetheless.

It was a heavy burden for a young girl not long out of school herself and yet Cameron revelled in the task that was set before her. This was the first time that she was on her own. She was not far, a day's travel by steamer from Victoria, but far enough that she had to rely on her resilience and emotional strength to see her through. At the time the only way to get up the island was by boat, but there were rumours that the government might build a rail line linking Victoria to the rest of the island. In 1871, when British Columbia entered Confederation, the government promised that a rail line would connect Vancouver Island to the rest of Canada. The hope was that it would be extended up the coast from Victoria.[6] It took sixteen years before a line made it up as far as Shawnigan Lake and another eighteen years to finally reach Comox in 1905.

The boat to Port Augusta left Victoria once every two weeks. Adventure and excitement overrode any pestering doubts Cameron may have had. Her trip from Victoria took her along a magnificent and densely forested coastline; the seas were rich with salmon, hundreds of sea birds bobbed on the water, and to everyone's delight the dolphins put on a short display of bravado as they crisscrossed in front of the bow of the boat. The shoreline was scattered with worn and rounded granite boulders that held secrets from thousands of years of contact with the sea, while black bears snuffled among the rocks looking for food. It was a stirring experience for the young school teacher and one that only whet her appetite for more travel. But behind the pristine beauty was a different reality. Through the mass of densely packed shrubs and trees, prospectors, surveyors, settlers, and land speculators were slowly altering the landscape. With their compasses, slide rulers, telescopes, saws, and axes they were laying waste to the cedars and firs that had stood tall for hundreds of years. They were looking for coal, and minerals, and land for farming. The Comox Valley where Cameron was heading was rich in minerals; it also offered open land that had ideal soil as well as the perfect climate for farming. With land prices rising in Victoria settlers had to look for property beyond the city. As Crown land was opened a single man could pre-empt forty hectares of land and a family could claim sixty hectares, with four additional hectares added for each child. Settlers came from all over to farm and mine.

By the time Cameron arrived in Port Augusta, the town had three hotels, three churches, a store, a school, a butcher shop, a few blacksmiths, wagon-making shops, and a jail. It was a small town of three hundred permanent residents, with sailors and seafarers periodically swelling the population. The main naval base was in Victoria but in 1876 the Royal Navy set up a training site at Goose Spit at the far end of the harbour at Port Augusta. Governor James Douglas encouraged the move as he thought there were too many restive sailors milling around Victoria. It would be a good idea, he said, to have an outpost. Preferably farther away from the city, where they would not be seduced by the bars and ladies of the night.

A ship's arrival at Port Augusta was always a busy time. The wharf, particularly in the summer, resembled a farmers' market. All around stacks of crates and boxes filled with farmers' products stood ready to be delivered to communities in Nanaimo, Cowichan, and Victoria. The most popular food items from the Comox Valley were butter and beef, reserved by the best tables on the island for Sunday suppers.

As Cameron, now eighteen, disembarked from the ship she walked up the long wood-planked wharf, described by one resident as looking like a spider because of the array of crossed tresses that served as its underpinnings. At the head of the pier, on her left, was the Elk Hotel framed by a picturesque picket fence. The verandah was filled with guests taking advantage of the attractively set tea tables that overlooked the harbour. Across the street was Joseph Rodello's newly built store, the Cariboo and Fly. Not veering from her path, she continued up to the top of the hill and past a large group of spreading maples, then turned west. She continued past a large field covered in stumps and grass where James Robb and his son were busy scything hay. They were too occupied to look up so did not notice that their boarder was passing by. Farther along Cameron came upon a large barn and the Robbs' homestead. She had finally reached her destination. Port Augusta was too small to have a teacher's residence so she needed to board with a reputable family.

The Robbs were among the original settlers who had come from Scotland to take advantage of the offer of a large parcel of land, something that was not available to them in their home country. Recognizing the richness of the area they pre-empted over a hundred hectares of forest and bush. Working hard, James and his son cleared some of the land, which they developed into a thriving and prosperous farm. They then built a dock for the boats they knew would come and divided the waterfront into small parcels to sell when the town began to expand. By 1884 the Robbs had put some of the lots up for sale for the unheard-of price of three hundred dollars.

The school, which served the Comox Valley, was built on Mission Hill. In 1872 the Rev. George Hills, Bishop of Columbia, provided a quarter-hectare piece of property for the school. The building was constructed for a cost of 519 dollars. The resulting school was a wooden one-room structure about sixty-six square metres, typical of rural schools. There was just enough room for a blackboard, desks for the students, and the pot-bellied stove, but not much more. Cameron was taking over from Mr. Crawford who had been with the school since it opened. She had twenty-six students—twelve boys and fourteen girls. She would be paid fifty dollars a month, standard for a new teacher with her level of certificate. Her salary, which was public knowledge, proved to be a bone of contention for at least one resident in the community.

The malcontent was a bush surveyor who worked for less pay and whose job was tenuous even in the best of times. He felt that for a woman, and one so young, to earn more than he went against the natural order of things. The new schoolmarm was "lucky . . . to be earning six hundred dollars a year," he protested.[7]

Cameron's classroom would have been a tight squeeze if all the children who were registered with the school district had attended class every day, but at most there were only about nine or ten children sitting at their desks at any one time. Schools were not particularly popular with the parents in most rural areas; they failed to see the point of an education that had little value for their way of life. Farm families needed their children to help in the fields and around the home. Simply getting to school added to the mix of reasons as to why school enrollment was low. The conditions of the roads and bridges, and inclement weather in the winter made it impossible for even the very best teachers to maintain regular enrollment. Teachers may have understood the reasons students failed to show up for class, but they found the lack of regular attendance disruptive and believed that it prevented students from learning their lessons. As early as 1873 the Department of Education made enrollment compulsory for children aged seven to fourteen. Such an edict was met with little success. So, the following year, in a misguided attempt to enforce the legislation, teachers' pay became dependent upon attendance. It put a huge burden on the teachers and did not succeed in altering the attendance record. It was an issue that would continue well into the twentieth century.

Superintendent of Education C. C. McKenzie was aware that it might be difficult for those children who lived far away from the schoolhouse to attend school regularly. The situation created a problem for him. How was he supposed to enforce compulsory attendance in light of the very real barriers against such an edict? The Port Augusta school cost the government 1,123 dollars per year, a small sum in the overall picture of spending on schools in the province, but when considered in cost per child, the amount was in some cases twice that of other schools. In 1879 McKenzie formally cautioned the school in Comox that daily attendance was low; the legal limit to maintain a school, he reminded Cameron's predecessor, was ten students. It was a number Cameron was all too aware of. She knew that she would have to work hard to obtain those numbers.

Before Cameron began teaching at Port Augusta the rules and regulation for teachers' duties and comportment had been fairly relaxed. Some teachers, perhaps more so in rural areas, were not always prompt on the start and closing of the school day. The superintendent of education found that teachers absented themselves when they pleased and frequently failed in their duty to report students' progress to anyone. In the Eighth Annual Report on the Public Schools of the Province of British Columbia, 1878–1879, the superintendent of education wrote, "On the whole I cannot forbear from saying that the utmost carelessness and indifference exist among teachers as to whether the statistical and other information they supply is at all accurate, and if their zeal educationally is to be gauged by the amount of it they display in their communications with the Education Office, the Province has need to demand of its servants a thorough reformation in both." When Cameron stepped into the classroom teachers were under the direction of a new set of rules that clearly laid out their duties, a move that she would agree with wholeheartedly.

Each morning she had a vigorous six-kilometre walk to the school, along an estuary and over a rickety bridge and up a steep hill. At exactly nine-thirty on August 7, 1882, Cameron opened the doors to welcome her students for the fall term. She had been in the schoolroom early that morning making sure everything was in order. Teachers were required to be at the school at least fifteen minutes before the beginning of class. While that may have been adequate for an urban classroom, it would not have given Cameron time to ready her classroom, which was a more rustic affair. As a teacher, she was responsible for ensuring the room was clean, the desks and chairs were lined up, and the register was laid out. She posted each day's timetable, which included the order of the day's exercises and the time devoted for each subject. In the fall, when rain and chill pummelled the schoolhouse, she lit the stove to have a warm classroom ready for her students, who in many cases walked miles to attend. She gave her students a fifteen-minute break in the morning and an hour for lunch. At three o'clock every afternoon she dismissed her class for the day. As the only teacher, she was responsible for overseeing the daily maintenance of the yards, outhouse, fence, and books and generally attending to anything that was amiss. She kept a register noting visitors and comments they may have posed and reported students' progress to their parents monthly. At the end of every month she dutifully wrote a report to the superintendent of education and the school trustees on the operation of the school.

She enjoyed her time teaching in Port Augusta and despite some parents' reluctance to send their children to school, the little schoolhouse became an important meeting place for the community. Cameron was well liked; she seemed to fit in with the community, although they did think her short haircut a bit peculiar. Before she realized it, December was upon them and she was busy readying her students for their examinations, which were scheduled to take place four days before Christmas. As soon as her duties were completed she closed the school for their annual two-week winter vacation. She would not be returning; she was moving to another school in the New Year.[8]

As she was packing her things to leave for Victoria, the harbour was hit by a severe storm. The waves heaped up into stacks and the wind sent spindrifts flying. The force of the surf was so powerful that it smashed several new pilings on the pier. Anxious passengers thought that they might be spending Christmas waiting on the dock. It was a great relief when the weather cleared and everyone stepped aboard the venerable old steamer *Wilson G. Hunt*, which would take them to points south.[9] With better weather on their side, the ship made it into Victoria on Christmas Eve.

When Cameron arrived home the city streets were decorated and ready for Christmas. The shops throughout the town were fêted with long garlands of cedar and fir entwined with red ribbons. Stores were filled with large assortments of novelties, toys, dolls, and games for the children. Meat vendors vied with each other in their selections and decorations. They brought in Christmas beef fattened on quality grass from the mainland; mutton and lamb from Salt Spring Island, reputed to be the finest in the province; rabbit, bear, and Berkshire hogs from Mr. Bryant's on the Saanich Peninsula; and poultry from the farm of Mr. Wale. Pheasants, turkey, geese, and partridges, festively adorned with flags, ribbons, and holly, hung in the windows. The churches were the centre of the celebrations and were beautifully appointed for the holidays. Christ Church Cathedral, which looked over all others, was elaborately framed with celebratory wreaths and swags. Its large windows and carved doors were outlined in evergreens, and the pillars of the nave were twined with holly and ivy. From the street, the choir could be heard practicing selections from Mendelssohn and J. S. Bach. It was hard not to get caught up in the cheerful atmosphere, but as Presbyterians Christmas for Cameron and her family was a simpler and quieter affair.

At eleven o'clock Christmas morning Cameron and her family attended the services at St. Andrew's Church. Most of the women dressed in corseted suits and high-necked dresses in somber creams, greys, and greens. The service was a simple affair but the jubilant voices of the choir rang throughout the church, giving joy to the congregation as they welcomed the birth of Jesus. As part of their tradition, St. Andrew's dedicated the proceeds from the Christmas collection to the poor of the city. It was a practice carried on by many of the church groups and businesses in the city. Christmas in Victoria was a time to reach out to those in need. While some gave alms to the poor, others in the city donated their time to cook traditional Christmas meals for those less fortunate, a custom that is carried on to this day. Sitting down to a meal of roast-beef, turkey, plum pudding, candies, and nuts was a welcomed treat for those who spent their days begging on the streets. Even inmates residing in the city jail were accorded a nice, hearty Christmas supper, finished by cigars for all.

Schools reopened on the fifteenth of January. Cameron's new posting was in Granville, an industrial area located on Burrard Inlet on the British Columbia mainland. Granville was a small coastal enclave situated on the edge of British Columbia's logging frontier. It did not naturally draw people in. Settlers spurned Burrard Inlet, viewing the region as a geographical dead-end. Not until the Canadian Pacific Railway decided in 1887 to locate the western terminus of the great continental railway at Granville did the population expand beyond the early lumberers.

A few days before school Cameron took one of the ferries that ran from Victoria to Burrard Inlet. From afar the lush forests and snow-covered peaks of the North Shore mountain range offered a beautiful backdrop to the industry of Burrard Inlet. When she landed at Hastings Mill she was immediately greeted with a mélange of scents. The sweet smell of wet cut lumber competed with the putrid odour of wetland skunk cabbage, a plant loved only by small insects. She could see the peaked roof of the schoolhouse from the dock—it was just left of the lumber manager's house. In the foreground, leading up to the school, was a sizeable clear-cut swath of land with hundreds of large protruding stumps surrounded by a sea of mud, the refuse of intensive logging. Great billows of grey-white steam towered into the air from the "flower pot" burner, and the relentless clanging of machinery emanating from the mill added to the desolation and ugliness of the place. The harbour was filled with ships sporting tall masts and spars, loading lumber for various destinations around the Pacific, and as far afield as Chile, Australia, China, Great Britain, and Europe. British Columbia's hemlock, Douglas fir, spruce, and cedar were highly sought after around the world. In particular, the massive knotless cedars and firs, referred to as "Vancouver toothpicks," were perfect for ship masts.

Burrard Inlet was a community made up of a diverse group of people who were brought together purely for the economic opportunities British Columbia's rich timber forests offered. There were West Indians, Germans, Chinese, Filipinos, Mexicans, Russians, Peruvians, Indigenous people, Hawaiians, and Europeans. Hastings Mill was a seaport and a logging settlement populated mainly by transient single men. The workers lived on site in cottages and bunkhouses provided by the company. The mill executives were like paternal landlords, seeing to the needs of their employees and working to build the necessary supports in the community. To thrive as a business, the mill needed a skilled workforce beyond the loggers and fallers. To attract engineers, machinists, bookkeepers, accountants, and venture capitalists it was necessary to build a church and a school. On May 14, 1881, Bishop Acton Sillitoe held the first service in St. James' Anglican Church. Worshipers were happy to move out of the little schoolhouse that had served as their temporary base and into a real church. It was more than just a place of worship; the presence of the church represented permanence in an otherwise tenuous life and had the effect of creating a gentler settler society. It also served as an important marker by which the owners, managers, and skilled workforce could define their status in a rough and tumble mill town. Unfortunately, five years later during a hot windy day in early June, fires that were used to clear stumps spread out of control and levelled the new town of Vancouver and destroyed most of Hastings Mill, including St. James' church.

Despite the mélange of people, Hastings Mill was not immune to elitism and racism. While the unmarried employees of the mill lived together in the bunkhouses, Indigenous workers, who were thought of as the hardest workers by their bosses, lived separately from the rest of the community, as did the Chinese. The families of the mill managers set themselves up as the moral arbiters of the community and worked to inculcate high moral standards among the migrant workers. They lived apart from the workers, preferring to build their homes on a hill above the mill. Their social life included tennis parties, afternoon teas, sumptuous garden parties, and the occasional ball where the elite could display their wealth and stylishness. The managers and their wives were referred to as the gentlemen and ladies of Burrard Inlet and New Westminster. In truth, however, social class was more fluid and complex, continually reshaping itself as industrial capitalism grew and expanded.

The school opened on February 12, 1873, to twenty students. Although Hastings Mill built the school, as a public institution it came under the jurisdiction of the Department of Education. It turned out to be a great deal for the government, whose only initial cost was to furnish the necessary equipment. The sum the Department of Education paid for the start-up of the school at Hastings Mill was 575 dollars; the teacher's salary and periodic repairs to the schoolhouse were the only ongoing expenses.

The schoolhouse was rudimentary at best. The building itself was a one-room, whitewashed wooden structure with a pitched roof and tiny windows that let in just enough light. At fifty-five square metres it was a bit cramped for the forty-four students registered, but like all rural schools home chores and disinterest made for spotty attendance. Cameron generally averaged no more than thirty-two of her students at any one time. Her living accommodation was a tiny teacher's cottage attached to the back of the school that had just enough room for a bed and dresser and her books. A raise in salary of five more dollars a month more than made up for any inconvenience she felt.

Cameron's student population was evenly split between girls and boys, and the students came from all kinds of cultural and regional backgrounds. Who knows what Cameron thought of her multicultural and mixed-race classroom in Granville. Her main focus was always on student learning, and while she never spoke or wrote about her students negatively, she never publicly addressed the issue of the growing effects of racism in her writing, nor made any overt statements about the subject. However, she was quick to praise children who dressed and behaved according to British colonial standards and she worked diligently to instill the values of her heritage in her students. The school system she worked in was oriented toward urban, white, Protestant, Northern European values and departure from that represented a rift that needed to be fixed. Cameron was very much a product of that culture.

Unfortunately, it was common for white teachers to have negative opinions of non-white children, and they were picked out as different and in need of adjustment. They were sometimes punished more frequently and more severely than the white children and were shamed and humiliated for their background. In Moodyville, for example, one teacher whipped his Indigenous students mercilessly. In retaliation for one such beating, they snuck into his garden and hung dead snakes on the branches of his apple tree.[10] Other teachers were more sensitive to their students. Mrs. Catherine Cordiner, a previous teacher at Granville, wrote a letter to John Jessop, the superintendent of education, about a white student who mistreated an Indigenous boy. She thought she was stating her impartiality when she wrote, "I love the children, black and white, are the same to me. I am an impartial Teacher. Act conscientiously and as long as I am able to impart instruction to them they shall all have it in equality."[11] Another teacher in the nearby mill town of Moodyville said that her "mixed blood" students were laid-back and parochial but were very nice children.

On some weekends when Cameron was finished preparing for the coming week, she would walk the kilometre-long roughed-out path to Granville, known locally as Gastown. Gastown was named after a steamboat captain, "Gassy Jack" (John Deighton), who opened the first saloon in 1867. Gassy Jack earned his name because of his propensity to regale his customers with stories.[12] Over time Gastown would became the core of Vancouver, but in Cameron's day it was generally quiet except when the loggers came into town to drink and dance. The town had three hotels, a couple of saloons, one general store, and an assortment of merchants selling dry goods and general merchandise. There was one restaurant, a well-stocked butcher shop, and an intermittent doctor. Cameron avoided the loggers and the saloons but she liked exploring the area around the mill.

Cameron's term at Hastings Mill finished at the end of June. Excited to see her family she packed her belongings to return home for the start of the long summer break. She always seemed to arrive back in Victoria during the beginning of a festival or special event. This time the city was enjoying a beautiful sunny Dominion Day celebration, the twelfth such commemoration since British Columbia joined Confederation in 1871. Victoria was dressed for a party and everyone was out enjoying the various events. Flags were everywhere in sight. Firemen attired in their full-dress uniforms marched through the streets accompanied by a local Victoria band. The *Princess Louise*, which had been operating up the coast to Alaska and back, was in port to take people to Pedder Bay for an afternoon excursion. Saanich farmers hosted their annual Dominion Day picnic and at noon Lieutenant Shears commanded the firing of the salute at the batteries at Finlayson Point. Not all were in a festive mood, however. With large crowds tempers sometimes flared, as in the case of a very noticeable spat between two well-dressed women in the heart of downtown. With emotions raging one spit in the other's face and, as the *Daily British Colonist* reported on July 3, 1883, "applied an opprobrious epithet" to the woman.

The talk of the town, particularly among women's groups, was a lecture given the previous day by Frances E. Willard, president of the US National Women's Christian Temperance Union. Reverend Coverdale Watson, pastor of the Methodist Church on Pandora and Broad Streets, invited her to give a speech about her work for temperance. She was famous for her talks on not only temperance but also women's suffrage, equal pay for equal work, and women's rights. It was a well-attended event in the city and Cameron would most likely have attended. Willard had a long list of credentials that would have appealed to Cameron. She was a teacher and lobbyist. She had been president of Evanston College for Ladies and when the college merged with Northwestern University she was appointed as the first Dean of Women.

The church, described as inferior by some, was adorned with wreaths and sprays of sweetly scented flowers sending a delicious perfume wafting throughout the building. As people walked into the church they were greeted by a "Welcome" banner decorated in red, white, and blue flowers marking the British ensign on the right side and the Stars and Stripes on the left. The mayor welcomed Miss Willard and said that it was an honour and one of the most pleasing events of his life to be asked to present her. He congratulated her for taming the "curse of drink." As he shook her hand he said, "In the name, then, and on behalf of British Columbians, I give you a hearty welcome—a thousand welcomes, and may heaven speed you in your God like mission."[13] As Willard stepped to the podium she was breaking ground as the first woman to address an audience in this city from the pulpit of a church. It was all rather daring, and some thought her quite forward, although such feelings faded into the background when she began to speak. She was a commanding orator, often bringing her audience to tears when she spoke of the harmful effects of drinking. It was an important event that set women's groups on a directed course of action that would reverberate throughout the city and change women's relationships with their communities. Cameron would be part of that movement, particularly in matters that focused on education.

Cameron did not have much time to relax once she arrived home. She immediately began preparing for the exams she needed to take to renew her First Class B teaching certificate. Not everyone was guaranteed a pass simply because they were already teaching. Three out of eight teachers taking the same level of certificate as Cameron did not pass. In his annual report on the status of education in BC, the superintendent of education chastised those who failed saying that they relied on their abilities in the classroom and did not review their subjects sufficiently. There was an ongoing debate among some of the teachers about the need for examinations. They asserted that their certificates should be granted for life. It was not a feeling shared among the majority of the school trustees. Teachers continued to press their point. During discussions the following year the Department of Education relented somewhat and decided that holders of first-class certificates would be able to automatically renew their certificates. They said that the status of candidates had improved sufficiently to allow them to ease up on annual testing for certain certificates but pointed out that there was no room for "the drone" in the classroom. Those who had little ambition to excel would not find a place.

What exactly did "little ambition" and "drone" mean? This set off a maelstrom of "spleen venting" in the press between the teachers and the Department of Education. It was all too subjective the teachers said. As clear parameters for teaching standards were not established teachers feared that favouritism would be a motivating factor in deciding which teachers would get their certificates renewed. It was true that the early history of the Department of Education had been administered in such a manner, but as one anonymous individual pointed out, educational matters were managed differently now. "The real enemies of our system are those who, to gratify their spleen, are constantly raising false reports and making groundless and malicious charges against others who are honestly and zealously endeavoring to push onward and upward. Happily, these vindictive mischief makers are being gradually compelled to 'take back seats,' where continued indulgence of their ruling passion will be comparatively harmless."[14]

The 1880s were an exciting time for teachers in the province. This was a time of growth in education, and educational qualifications were at the forefront of most agendas. Grievances with school boards, pay issues, poor working conditions, and high teacher turnover would not be discussed until the 1890s. As attendance at public schools increased, so too did the number of school trustees. The balance between male and female teachers was now fairly even, although all school principals were male. Salaries ranged from a high of one hundred dollars a month to fifty dollars a month, dependent upon a teacher's certificate and years teaching. Seven new school districts were created at Canoe Pass, Mount Lehman, Port Moody, Shawnigan, South Comox, Spallumcheen, and Stave River. There was still the problem of the lack of teachers with professional training. A normal school (what today we'd call a teachers' college) was desperately needed, but until that time Stephen Daniel Pope, the superintendent of education, invited teachers to a meeting to discuss the idea of establishing a professional organization.[15] His intent was to create a body whose stated aim was to help improve teaching skills, increase professional knowledge among teachers, and act as a regular conduit for educational policy. The result was the Victoria Teachers' Association, which in 1885 became the first professional association of its kind in the province. Cameron was keen on furthering professionalism among teachers, and not only played a significant part in its development but became a regular contributor to the association. Over time the Victoria Teachers' Association became a significant building block in teacher solidarity and years later transformed into the British Columbia Teachers' Federation.

After having successfully renewed her teaching certificate, Cameron applied for a position at the Girl's School in Victoria. She was hired as the third assistant in the fourth division. Her salary continued at fifty-five dollars a month, in contrast to that of the first and second assistants, who received seventy dollars. Three hundred and twenty girls were registered in five divisions. Cameron was thrilled to be teaching in the school where she first trained as a teacher. Since she had last set foot in the school, registration had outpaced available space, so a new wing had been built onto the school. The first few days at work were busy ones for Cameron. Her mind was on the many things she had to do: student names needed to be printed out ready for the first day, books arranged, room organized, paperwork completed—the list seemed endless. She was so focused on the tasks at hand that as she was on her way downstairs she lost her footing and went tumbling to the bottom, injuring herself in the process. Fortunately, nothing was broken but she was sufficiently injured for the incident to be reported in the news.

Six months into the school year Cameron's father died. He had been away on a shooting excursion and had not yet returned home. No one took any notice as he was often away for days at a time. On January 29, a typical Monday morning, Cameron ate her breakfast and left for school. Unbeknownst to the family, during the previous night Duncan's horse had found its way back home. When Cameron's mother went out into the yard she noticed his horse standing in his stall, but there was no indication that its master was anywhere to be seen. Jessie had a terrible sense of foreboding; she knew that something was amiss. It was a long agonizing day and night before she learned of her husband's fate. His body was found the following day lying beneath his wagon. It appeared that he was thrown from his spring cart on the Gorge Road. He was not far from the Gorge Inlet, a popular spot for swimmers and picnickers, yet no one had seen him. The newly constructed road had been built over a ravine and had not settled down into a hard-packed surface. It was muddy and slippery, and rutted with gnarly roots. Apparently, Duncan was trying to ease his horse up the steep bank when the animal lost its footing and went off the road. Duncan was pitched from his cart and fell three metres into a hollow. He might have lived but the cart tumbled after him, crushing him. In a panic the horse broke loose from his harness and managed to get up the bank and continue home. The conclusion of the examiner was that Duncan died from of a concussion of the brain. Spring-cart accidents were not uncommon, and it was not unusual to read in the paper that someone had died because of a wagon flipping over. Although Victoria was well known throughout the northwest coast as having an excellent system of roads, many of the roads outside of the city were unstable and pockmarked with holes. Duncan Cameron, one of the early pioneers of Victoria, was dead at fifty-eight years of age.

When a message came for Cameron that morning she was stunned. She immediately left school and went to her mother. Three days later the family gathered together at their home for a small private ceremony. Around one-thirty in the afternoon they lined up behind the glass enclosed hearse as two sleek ebony horses, festooned in black ostrich plumes, shepherded Duncan's body from Birdcage Walk and through town to St. Andrew's Presbyterian Church. The ceremony began at two o'clock. The new organ dominated the back of the church and piped out familiar and comforting music, laying to rest that once dashing young man who had swept Jessie off her feet in the California goldfields so long ago. Sadness overtook them all but they were a stalwart family and would manage. Although Jessie had sons with whom she could live, Cameron stayed with her mother, supporting her and taking care of her until her death twenty-one years later at the age of eighty-four.

Cameron continued teaching at the Girl's School for a number of years, gradually working her way up to the Boy's School and then Victoria High School. She was logged into the Victoria school registry as teaching at the Girl's School until December 1889, at which time she moved to the Boy's School, teaching there until June 30, 1890. She began the fall term in 1890 teaching at Victoria High School. She was twenty-seven at the time.

Chapter Four

A VERY PUBLIC SCUFFLE

I try always to push on those who seem to
be hopelessly anchored in a grade.

—AGNES DEANS CAMERON

The year 1889 had been quiet and peaceful in Victoria, lending credence to its genteel reputation. However, underneath the reserved façade was a city in the midst of a building boom. Commerce and trade were extremely lucrative, making Victoria the place to be for social activities and business ventures. Over one million dollars was spent in the city on projects, 350 new dwellings were built, and still supply had not met demand. Hardly a shop, house, or warehouse was built before it was bought or leased. So many new faces appeared on the streets that the town seemed to lose its familiarity. The January 1, 1890, issue of the *Daily Colonist* included a piece about Victoria's past year and future prospects: "If human happiness can be gauged by the measure of prosperity, the year that has just gone out must be regarded as the happiest Victoria has known . . . Her mercantile establishments are amongst the soundest in the Dominion. Her harbour is the rendezvous of an extensive sealing and fishing fleet. Her manufactories are numerous and varied. Her homes are attractive and costly, and the Imperial Government has shown confidence in the permanency and appreciation of her position by establishing a naval station with a dockyard and dry dock at Esquimalt."[1] Victoria glowed in a Camelot-like ambience, although the beginning of the New Year, at least for Cameron, did not feel that way.

Despite the sunny prospects, the beginning of the new year saw Victoria in the grip of a deep freeze; a delight for crowds of eager ice skaters but not so for those who had to contend with a particularly virulent strain of influenza that was sending a great number of people to their beds. The Russian flu, which had killed over a million people worldwide, made everyone quite nervous. The people who were the most vulnerable were the city's frontline workers: the police force, firemen, physicians, and teachers. Without quarantines in place teachers had a duty to attend to their students, which they did willingly. Fortunately, the worst that happened were several mild cases of the mumps.

The year 1890 was also when Cameron hit the first public bump in her teaching career. One of the boys in her geography class was a particularly difficult student who had repeated problems with authority. He was quite a bit older than the rest of the boys in his division, since he had failed his grade on four previous occasions. Cameron always had her students' interests at heart and helped them work toward success, but at some point every teacher meets their nemesis. Herbert Burkholder had been a challenge for her from the start. She had set out her expectations for him as she had for all her students. Hoping to challenge him and at the same time give him a chance to experience success, she asked Burkholder to point out the mountains of Europe on the map. It was not a difficult request; the exercise had been part of everyone's homework the previous day and it was covered many times in the lower grades. Burkholder stood up and said that he didn't know the answer to the question. She replied, "[You] should be able to answer such a simple question . . . [you] must have learned it over and over again in the lower grades."[2] She then passed the question on to the next boy, telling Burkholder to keep his eye on the map and try to pick it up from Redfern. Burkholder deliberately looked away, ignoring the lesson and his teacher's request. She repeated the exercise three more times to try to help him, but he stood his ground. "I'll learn it after school. I won't look on the map now!" he said defiantly. A hushed silence descended over the class; there were no twitters or whispering among the students. Everyone knew that Burkholder had stepped over a line.

Submission to educational authority, which even took precedence over the family, was an important prescript the community viewed as essential for character development and shaping children into good citizens; ones that would believe in fair play, duty, and civic responsibility. Cameron could not let the incident go unpunished. Later, in retelling the story, she said, "I try always to push on those who seem to be hopelessly anchored in a grade . . . I told the boy that what I had asked him to do was reasonable and that I expected him to do it . . . This was the first shadow of disobedience in the class since I had taken charge of it, and the second time only in my ten years' teaching experience that a pupil had refused point-blank to do as I asked."[3] She gave him two minutes to change his mind and informed him that if he did not do as she requested she would get her whip. Time seemed suspended as the clock ticked off the seconds. Quiet gave way to a strained stillness among the class. What happened next was expected and acceptable per the rules and regulations set down by the superintendent of education. At the end of the two minutes, Cameron picked up her whip and said to Burkholder that he would be punished until he changed his mind. Entrenched in his insolence, he informed her that he would leave school before he allowed her to punish him.

The procedures governing such behaviour did not require teachers to consult with the principal before whipping a student, only that they record the punishment in the school register for later inspection by the school trustees. Still, Cameron consulted her principal, Mr. Halliday. She explained the situation to him and he agreed that the boy must do as he was told and take his whipping. With the authority of the principal behind Cameron, Burkholder quickly changed his mind and said that he would accept his punishment. He tentatively held his hands out as Cameron whipped him two or three times, but then he decided he'd had enough and ran from the room. Suspension was the next course of action. Although not taken lightly, suspension was an acceptable action for insubordination.[4]

The attitude in the public school system in the 1890s was that discipline and order were important to maintain a well-balanced learning situation and students were best helped and supported by a kind but firm and judicious teacher. Physical force and expulsion were seen as seldom necessary and were addressed in the annual report of the public schools: "The teacher who uses moral suasion effectively in the government of his school will accomplish the *best* results, not only in the moral training of the pupils but in their intellectual advancement."[5] There is no question that the whip or rod was used, but they were employed most often by lesser-trained teachers. The number of cases of corporal punishment was not recorded for 1890, but in 1894 there were 2,444 cases, out of a population of over thirteen thousand students. It seems that practice and ideology were at odds. It was recognized there were certain instances in which such actions were necessary, such as in cases of gross misconduct or a violent or willful opposition to authority, but only after calm and mature deliberation took place. In those cases where physical punishment was warranted, the regulations did not allow a student to be hit on the head and only a switch or suitable rod could be used.

Cameron wrote a note to Burkholder's parents explaining the situation. She pointed out that if they wished their son to be received at the school again, it was important to send him back with his apology in hand. Mrs. Burkholder met with Cameron and apologized for her son's unruly behaviour and thanked her for taking such an interest in him. She agreed that her son must be prepared to take the consequences of his behaviour. All was resolved amicably, or so everyone thought. The boy's father sent him back to school the next morning, but unbeknownst to him his son never appeared at school. When he was made aware of his son's truancy, Mr. Burkholder said that he would find his son and take him in hand for his defiance. He thanked Cameron for her leniency and willingness to take his son back and assured her he would personally bring the boy to school prepared to submit to whatever punishment was deemed necessary. Wednesday rolled by, then Thursday, and finally Friday. Burkholder had not returned to school. He absolutely refused to go back, and to bring the point home he ran away for a night. Everyone hoped the weekend would bring a resolve.

The case, however, was not so easily dismissed. While Cameron was enjoying the Victoria Day celebrations, Burkholder's father was busy lodging a complaint with the Victoria School Board. Why he changed his mind was never known, but those involved were taken by surprise. Unfortunately, once the issue was taken out of the hands of those immediately involved, the situation rapidly deteriorated. What was an unpleasant incident between one teacher, her principal, and a student instantly gained notoriety in the news and was referred to as "The Burkholder Case." Rumours and innuendoes were unstoppable and, as people are wont to do, many offered their opinion on the matter without having all the facts before them. Being a rationalist, Cameron thought that if she could explain what had happened to the public, people would see reason and the issue would evaporate. To that end she wrote several detailed articles in the local papers.

Mr. Burkholder also took to the newspapers. Writing in the *Daily Colonist* he declared that, "The Chairman of the Board of

Trustees stated that we, the 'parents,' expressed ourselves as satisfied. We are not satisfied with Miss Cameron's statement viz., that if the boy was 'touched,' fancy touching a pupil with a rawhide, every stroke of which almost lifting the teacher off her feet. She was asked not to strike on the head when doing so, and when she persisted in striking at random the boy showed his manhood by wresting the rawhide out of her hand, throwing it on the floor and quietly leaving the school room. Miss Cameron denies striking the boy on the head, and that is why I was anxious for an investigation . . . I was asked to bring back my boy to school; last Monday morning I did so with the distinct understanding that if Miss Cameron ever undertook to punish the boy in a like manner that the boy would repeat the praise worthy act, take the rod from her again and leave the room. The boy did not apologize, neither do I consider that he had any right to do so . . . I believe in upholding the teachers when in the right, but I think the time has fully come for a reformation in our public schools on the whipping question . . . it is whip, whip all the time."[6] Charles Hayward, the acting chairman of the Victoria School Board, supported Cameron's actions adding his view in a letter to the editor. "This matter, from its notoriety, has become so important in its bearings upon the discipline of the school, that there must be no mistake about the terms upon which the lad came back; and if Mr. Burkholder really believes what he has written, that there was no apology or expression of contrition, or that the pupils entertain an idea that the boy returns as a hero having performed a 'praiseworthy act,' then the apology and promises must be again given, and in such a way, as to leave no doubt upon the subject." He found that Mr. Burkholder's language and bearing toward Miss Cameron were unpleasant and, "by way of making matters still more disagreeable," he wrote, "he [Mr. Burkholder] insisted upon having Miss Cameron brought before the trustees. Both Mr. Wolfenden [Alexander Kabery Wolfenden, a secondary school trustee] and myself then told Mr. Burkholder that, basing our opinion entirely upon his version of the affair, we felt that the lad had received no more punishment than he deserved."[7] Cameron was more than willing to have the matter investigated by a full inquiry set before the school trustees, despite Burkholder's repeated statements that she was desperate to avoid an investigation. He also stated that Cameron said that if an investigation took place she would tender her resignation. Coming to her own defense, Cameron clearly articulated that "I more than once told both the secretary and the chairman of the Board that I courted the fullest inquiry. The statement that I 'said in Mr. Wolfenden's office that I would tender my resignation,' is untrue . . . How he in face of this can state in public print that I shirked inquiry I fail to see. I have spent the last ten years of my life in the school-room, and no one can truthfully say that I have ever lost control of my temper or addressed a pupil angrily."[8] The school board was of the opinion that the investigation asked for was unnecessary.

Hoping for a respite from the affair, Cameron followed her family into St. Andrew's Church for Sunday services on May 18. Their pastor, Patrick McFarlane McLeod, was a dynamic speaker who could easily rally his congregation. She was looking forward to his sermon. It would at the very least focus her attention elsewhere, or so she thought. He was a commanding man, standing tall at two metres; he had piercing blue eyes framed by a shock of white hair. Looking out over his flock, he began with a quote from Colossians 3:21: "'Fathers, irritate not your children, lest they be discouraged.' My reasons for calling your attention are first, that I have had occasion to observe that some of our young people seem to have grievously suffered through their environment during their earlier years . . . Second, I find a system of discipline prevailing in our public schools which is demoralizing both to teachers and taught." He then delivered a derisive sermon on the evils of whipping children in school. "I have no intention to say a word which might hurt the feelings of any conscientious teacher. Since coming to Victoria my attention has again and again been called to this subject, and I have spoken my mind very freely to trustees and teachers as opportunity has offered; but, as there appears to be no sign of any change in the discipline and as appeals to the trustees bring about no practical result, I wish, with all earnestness, to enter my protest here and now against this constant and unjustifiable use of the rod by some teachers . . . What right has a teacher that mocks at religion, that openly flaunts his or her irreligion before the world, to undertake the care of Christian children and to sit in judgment on their conduct? . . . When a parent or teacher allows passion to rule him in inflicting punishment he at once loses all moral power over the child, and if he has any conscience will feel degraded in his own eyes when his short madness is over."[9] By the time he was finished no one in the church that morning was unclear about his opinion on the matter at hand.

His sermon was printed verbatim in the newspapers a few days later. Such a public lashing would shake even the strongest and while Cameron may have felt uncomfortable during his address she did not shy away from his criticism. She responded with a letter to the newspaper: "Teachers don't enjoy doing this (the Reverend P. McLeod to the contrary notwithstanding), but sometimes it is necessary. Insubordination in a schoolroom, like resisting an officer in the execution of his duty, or like mutiny on board ship, is a serious offense and must be promptly and decisively met."[10]

McLeod claimed that he had no knowledge of the Burkholder situation when he delivered his sermon, but the examples he used were strongly suggestive of the case at hand. Later, in a verbal to and fro in the newspaper, he went further and accused Cameron of beating other boys to the point of drawing blood. While he was in the forefront of thinking in the city about the place of corporal punishment in the schools, his recounting of the details of the case were incorrect and the vitriol of his attacks on Cameron were unwarranted. The facts did not support his allegation. Others too weighed in on the issue. Dr. J. S. Helmcken, a well-respected public figure, past Speaker of the Legislative Assembly, and a person who was integral to bringing British Columbia into the legislature, responded by writing, "My feeling is that discipline in school must be had and preserved, and so it is absolutely necessary that discreet punishment should be a law . . . The teachers must be supported. If they be unfit, discharge them, but do not encourage insubordination. I have always heard of Miss Cameron being a good teacher, and cannot understand why she should be persecuted for simply, judiciously and effectively performing her duty, save that some one wants to get her place for some one else."[11]

Adding to the debate, the *Daily Colonist* addressed the value of good behaviour in public schools, starting from the standpoint that discipline was a necessary and good thing. What was unclear and debated for many years was the manner and parameters of that philosophy, as in the case of corporal punishment. Those advocating for physical punishment, like Cameron, felt that it imbued respect for the teachers and acted as a positive control in the classroom, while others thought that it led to learning difficulties and poor self-image. It was not until 1973 that an amendment to the Public Schools Act banned the use of any form of physical punishment in the classroom. In its place were set guidelines for early intervention as well as programs for de-escalating behaviour seen as threatening, strategies that were not available to Cameron eighty years earlier.

Because the entire case was fought in public the stakes became high for all involved. Burkholder was trying to protect his son; McLeod was fighting for a principle; Cameron for her integrity and reputation; and the school board and school principal for the importance of discipline in the classroom. There were so many articles about the Burkholder Case that readers begged the media to focus on some other issue. One fed-up letter writer wrote, "I most strongly protest against this driveling day after day in the papers on the subject of corporal punishment. Don't you think it has gone beyond the limits of reason on both sides? . . . A whipping will not do any boy harm . . . and the rising generation is being but very poorly brought up if it is so thin skinned that it cannot bear a little twitting."[12]

The matter was finally resolved when the boy came back to the school and apologized, albeit hesitatingly and with a gentle coaxing from Cameron. The Burkholder affair eventually faded from the public stage and was forgotten, though over a hundred years later, writers searching through the attic of historical ephemera have attached that event to most everything that is written about Cameron. Unfortunately, some applying current standards of teacher-pupil comportment have mistakenly branded Cameron as mean, callous, and disloyal to the children in her charge. To this and to her earlier detractors she would say, "For mine own part, I object. I don't think Nature intended me for an Ogre . . . I'd rather, oh, so much rather, assume the role of guide, philosopher and friend."[13]

Cameron loved working with children and thought that they were far more interesting than grown people. During a presentation she gave to a group of Canada-wide teachers at an annual Dominion Educational Association meeting, she said that if a teacher does not have the child as a focus, then the schoolroom is not where they belong. "Do we half appreciate, I wonder, what the children do for us daily? We talk of 'educating the child,' ignoring the fact that he does more for us than we are ever privileged to do for him."[14] Years later a student of hers wrote, "There are many of her former pupils who remember her for her criticism of outmoded ideas and her untiring work for school reform. It is the fortunate pupil who in the course of school days encounters a teacher who kindles a spark of learning. Agnes Deans Cameron did this for many of her pupils. Thankfully, I was one of them."[15]

Discipline did remain an important element in Cameron's educational comportment. That same student who praised Cameron was not easily let off the hook when she presented careless work. Ada McGeer sent an essay to one of Victoria's newspapers in response to a contest for best paper on the current play in town: *The Merchant of Venice*. A delighted Miss McGeer won the prize. The newspaper printed her essay, spelling mistakes and all. Cameron, rather than congratulating McGeer, castigated her in front of the class for failing to correct her spelling before entering her composition.

On the issue of discipline, Cameron did acknowledge the important relationship between the child and their parent. In an article she wrote she gave credence to the mother-child bond, saying that if she was a mother and not an "old maid" she would be loath to give up so much influence to the teacher. Yet from a teacher's perspective, because home discipline was becoming less tangible, it was important to preserve the balance of power. "The school-teacher must be inexorable," she wrote, "otherwise chaos in the body politic."[16] She never understood the parent who would place themselves between a child and the natural consequences of their own disobedience. They "are guilty of the cruelest folly," she said, "as there are few allowable deviations in the sterner school of the world." School and indeed life is not all about pleasantries. It is not always "one long sweet song." She believed that to become an engaged person and citizen and take one's place in the world requires work and discipline. "There are hard duties in citizenship and I contend that the habit of always expecting to be pleased and interested while a child does not help the man or woman to do earnest work in hard places."[17] This thinking sometimes put her at odds with parents and earned her a reputation that was contrary to the devotion she had toward her students.

Chapter Five

NOTEWORTHY FIRSTS FOR PUBLIC EDUCATION IN BRITISH COLUMBIA

At the commencement of the year the Trustees were fortunate in securing the services of Miss Cameron as teacher of the third division.

—J. P. MCLEOD, PRINCIPAL OF
VICTORIA HIGH SCHOOL, 1891

At the beginning of July 1891, Cameron was moved to Victoria High School, making her the first woman in the province to teach in a high school. She was to teach in the third division at a salary of ninety dollars per month, ten dollars more than she had been earning at the Boy's School and twenty more than at the Girl's School. In comparison, the highest salary for permanent staff was a hundred dollars per month while the lowest was fifty dollars. Victoria High School was very pleased to have Cameron join their staff. The principal, J. P. McLeod, wrote in his annual report to the superintendent of education, "At the commencement of the year the school trustees were fortunate in securing the services of Miss Cameron as teacher of the third division. Not only did Miss Cameron do excellent work in the first and second divisions, but at both the Christmas and the Midsummer Examinations she succeeded in passing all her pupils into the second division."[1]

On Saturday, May 28, 1892, a resident of the city visited his doctor thinking he had the flu. His symptoms were vague—a fever, headache, and extreme fatigue. Dr. Helmcken sent him to the Royal Jubilee Hospital to be treated for a bladder complaint. Dr. Richardson, the hospital doctor who conducted the man's examination, recognized his symptoms as smallpox, a highly infectious disease. The virus has an incubation period of seventeen days; the patient had unknowingly become a conduit for the beginning of an epidemic in the city. The source of the disease was most likely a stevedore working cargo on a ship at a wharf in Vancouver. While the city had been down this route before, potential epidemics were mostly dealt with on an ad hoc basis. There was no social policy on infectious diseases at the time. Vancouver had been lobbying for a contagious disease hospital on Deadman's Island and Victoria had the Albert Head quarantine station, but it was not in operation at the time. Until they could get it up and running, smallpox victims were turned away from the hospital and sent home. Those who had the disease, and everyone in their house, were to be quarantined. To ensure compliance, guards were posted at the entrances to the houses. Clothing and bedding and anything else that had been touched by victims were either burned or soaked in chloride of mercury and then boiled. A second case of smallpox had appeared during the first week of June and then another on the fourth of July. By the twelfth of July there were forty-eight cases throughout Victoria. Fortunately, the school children were on their summer break; otherwise the rate of infection could have been much higher. This was the second time fear of an epidemic had gripped the community within a few years. When the epidemic died down the government established a Royal Commission to consider measures that could be taken to prevent the spread of disease and to prevent further outbreaks in the future.

By the fall term of the 1892–1893 school year Cameron had renewed her teaching certificate and was now earning one hundred dollars per month, a salary commensurate with her years of teaching and position in the high school. While the epidemic was over by the start of the new school year, attendance was noticeably affected. Initially students and their parents were understandably wary of another outbreak, but it did not take long for attendance to normalize.

As the epidemic receded into the background the citizenry began looking toward the future. A new parliament building was under construction and several manufacturing plants opened for business, giving the city a paper mill, cement works, and a new chemical plant. But the topic that captured people's attention was the opening of the World's Fair in Chicago. The daily news was full of articles about the marvels of the fair, outlining in detail a city built of white French neoclassical buildings surrounding a grand network of manmade canals; it was a wonder of the world, people proclaimed. There were descriptions of moving sidewalks, a Ferris wheel where people rode in cages that propelled them seventy-six metres into the sky, dishwashers and fluorescent light bulbs. Fifty foreign countries as well as forty-three states and territories were registered exhibitors. Over thirty million people, including a few from Victoria, took in the sights from May to October.

What surprises the World's Fair held, with its architecturally distinctive White City, large display of electricity, and advanced technology. It piqued Cameron's interest. She was always fascinated with learning new things and she had to see it for herself. After the closure of school for the summer of 1893 she packed her bags and set off by train to Chicago. The Canadian Pacific Railway (CPR) was advertising a trip from Victoria to Chicago in eighty-three hours, with round-trip fare of fifty dollars and five cents.[2]

She took with her a camera, which had been a trusty companion on many past adventures and would continue to be on those yet to come, and several notebooks to record her experiences. Not one to do something purely out of self-interest, Cameron decided to make an event out of her trip. She planned to write a series of eye-witness articles, illustrated with photographs. Upon her return to Victoria she put together a slide show using a magic lantern, a large bulky forerunner to the slide projector. Her first talk, scheduled for Tuesday, October 24, was quickly sold out. When she arrived for her presentation the lantern she requested was not available at the last moment so she had to make due with an unfamiliar projector. As a teacher, she was used to things going wrong and, although a little flustered, she compensated without anyone being the wiser. Her lecture was accompanied by a musical program in which Ciro Pinsuti's "The Bedouin Love Song" of passion and pain was sung along with the ballad "Wandering Minstrel." It was a highly successful presentation and all agreed that they had a lovely evening. Cameron gave several more such presentations around the city to great applause.

On the corner of Michigan Street and Park Road, now Douglas Street, not far from Cameron's house, bricklayers and stonemasons were busy at work constructing a new school. When completed, South Park School would bring the number of public educational institutions in British Columbia to 202. The number of children attending school had been growing steadily over the years, putting pressure on already overcrowded facilities. Fiscal budgets were tight and never left much money for new schools, so it came as welcome relief when the announcement came that construction of a new school was about to commence.

The design of South Park was typical of schools at the time, with towers, large stone quoins accenting the corners, and windows stacked one above the other in linear precision. An imposing large carved stone entrance highlighted the sweeping staircase. Almost immediately some people started complaining about the look of the school. A more architecturally distinct structure would have been better some said, something more suited to Victoria's status as the provincial seat of government. The architect, William Ridgway Wilson, who was well known for his Tudor Revival style, parried with an object lesson in design, explaining that there were but two courses open to the architect: "A comparatively plain building with simple but first-class construction and finish in every detail, or an ornamental building with construction and finish of the cheapest. It seemed to me that the former was the only proper course to pursue." He went on to write, "The question of style is so largely a matter of opinion in a plain building of this class, that I will not venture to present my views. I have only tried to clothe the plan with as pleasing an exterior as the funds would allow."[3] The teachers and students were not among the school's detractors. They had long awaited the opening of South Park School.

At the end of June, Cameron wrapped up her teaching at Victoria High School and prepared to join the faculty of the new school. When she stepped into South Park School on August 13, 1894, she did so not as the young neophyte she was so many years ago, nor as a battle worn teacher, but as the principal of the new school, making her the first woman in the province to hold such a position. She and her staff were delighted with what Wilson had built. In her first annual report to S. D. Pope, the superintendent of education, she wrote that the school was a model of practicality. "Its lighting, heating and sanitary arrangements could scarcely be improved. Tasteful surroundings must exert a refining influence on all, and especially so upon children. If we as teachers have failed in our work, the fault must be ours alone, for we have been given by the Trustee Board all needed accessories."[4]

Today South Park School operates an alternative school for elementary school children with a focus on environmental awareness and fine arts. It is charming amid its leafy home of oak trees and park-like setting. The finials, gabled roof, and red brick fit in with the mix of modern and historical that the city of Victoria has become. Tally-Ho carriages pulled by sturdy Clydesdale, Belgian, and Percheron horses pass daily in front of the school, taking visitors on their tour around the city, as they have done since 1903.[5]

Having been the first female high school teacher in the province and now the first female principal of a public school was not particularly important to Cameron, although she was well aware of her status and the power that it brought. Cameron was the first of the liberal equal-rights feminists. Her thinking was that women were equal to men and it was due to her hard work that she had made it to the top of her profession. Rather than spending time debating one's place, creating a positive and successful learning environment for her students and faculty and improving educational standards held more sway with her. "Look back over your own school days. Who was the teacher for whom you entertain the kindliest feelings, the one who most influenced your life?" she wrote. "It wasn't that teacher who held you off at arm's length, and in allopathic doses administered the school course to you straight. It was the one who got at your inner self and let you see a little bit of his own in the process."[6]

Chapter Six

MEANINGFUL EVENTS

There is a woman at the beginning of all great things.

—ALPHONSE DE LAMARTINE, QUOTED
BY AGNES DEANS CAMERON

Cameron's love of travel was never quenched. She had an insatiable curiosity, loved learning and exploring the world. She often took short trips to walk the streets and visit the museums of San Francisco, but in 1895 she ventured farther afield. After the end of the school year Cameron, along with eight other women teachers, two of whom were from South Park School, boarded the RMS *Minowera*, a Canadian-Australian ship, for an eight-day cruise to the Hawaiian Islands. Rather than a luxury cruise line, the *Minowera* was a multi-purpose ship that carried cargo, lumber, and mail, as well as passengers. It was an enjoyable trip. They were well treated with every comfort provided. Entertainment was quiet and self-organized; reading and walking the decks were pleasurable activities. Meals were formal affairs. For lunch they started with a soup followed by a fish dish of potted salmon and walnuts, complemented by a hot dish of stewed steak and braised tomatoes. There were also several cold choices: roast beef, Melton Mowbray pork pie, corned beef, pressed ox tongue, York ham, and various potted meats. After, they were served a choice of salads, and finished with tapioca custard and servings of cheese and fruit.

The days aboard the ship took on a slow tempo. Time seemed to stop for the women; it felt good to be able to play cards, read, and unwind. Just as they had grown accustomed to their relaxed schedule, the Hawaiian Islands came into view. The women took to the upper decks, breathing in the salubrious sea-scented breeze.

As they drew closer to Honolulu, the sight before them was breathtaking. Colours appeared more vivid. Varying shades of green outlined the rich foliage of the shoreline complementing the shimmering turquoise of the water. Up toward the hills they could see misty rainbows cavorting across the valleys. The plummy palms, sweet fruitiness of the frangipani trees, and the heavenly perfumed bouquets of jasmine and pikake scented the air. The weather felt sticky and warm, but the gentle sounds of the surf pulling against the finely ground shells of the white sand beaches beckoned to them. The only disadvantage, they would soon discover, once ashore, was the daily visitation of fleas, cockroaches, biting centipedes, and mosquitoes, which Cameron noted in a piece she wrote about her trip: "Our last waking thought was a blessing on the man who invented mosquito netting, and to the sad faraway hum of the disappointed insect."[1]

The purpose of their visit is not clear, but a newly established teachers' association in O'ahu most likely commanded their attention, along with spending their midsummer vacation in a tropical paradise. Cameron did say that they were enjoying a holiday "which we thought we had earned, and had our hearts tuned for pleasant impressions only."[2] Although tourism in Hawaii was still in its infancy, the previous year had drawn nearly six thousand visitors to its shores. The popularity of Honolulu as a destination took everyone by surprise and there were often more people than hotels. Though some were able to find accommodation in private homes, Cameron and her group managed to find room in the cottages of the Royal Hawaiian Hotel. Travelling to the Hawaiian Islands as a tourist was considered a luxury trip. The average cost including transportation, room and board, and rental of horses for getting about was over two hundred dollars. She did remark upon the prices in Honolulu reporting that: "Everything in Honolulu is dear with the exception of the native fruits."[3]

It was an interesting and historically memorable time for Cameron to be in the islands. Seven months before their arrival, Hawaii had been locked down under martial law. A group of six hundred royalists, opposed to the 1893 illegal overthrow of the Kingdom of Hawaii by pro-American forces, tried to take control and reinstall Queen Liliuokalani to the throne. When Cameron and her group arrived, Honolulu was fairly calm, but the atmosphere was noticeably unsettled. The flag of the Kingdom of Hawai'i was still flying over Iolani Palace.[4] Queen Liliuokalani was in residence at the time, imprisoned in a second-floor room for a year. Perhaps when Cameron passed by, the queen was busily writing "Aloha Oe," which came to be one of the islands' most beloved and recognizable songs.

It is not known how long the group stayed. Ships to and from British Columbia were not that frequent. However, they were most likely still in the islands on August 18, when Honolulu experienced its first case of cholera. By September 10 the city was divided into quarantined districts. By September 18 there were eighty-five confirmed cases. In any case, Cameron was home by the end of August, as she was recorded as attending the first meeting of the Ladies of the Maccabees in her capacity as finance keeper on September 10.

The Ladies of the Maccabees were one of the leading business groups among women offering not only social and self-improvement activities for women, but also disability, life insurance, and old age benefits for women and children when few others did. It was an organization that was close to Cameron's heart and she would not have missed it.

Cameron was still under the spell of the magic of Hawaii when she wrote a series of five pieces she titled "In Lava Lands" for the *Victoria Daily Times* on Honolulu. Her articles played well in Honolulu. Remarking on the recent trip, Honolulu's *Evening Bulletin* wrote: "Miss Agnes Deans Cameron, of the Victoria lady teachers' excursion, has a series of bright letters on Honolulu in the *Victoria [Daily] Times*. She pays much attention to Kamehameha Schools and the Bishop Museum."[5]

Cameron was now thirty-two years of age and still single. The average age for marriage at the time was twenty-two for a woman and thirty-two for a man. Marriage was viewed as an important state for women's economic survival and the fulfillment of women's lives, but it was not for everyone. While there was a growing acceptance of women choosing to remain single, there were still negative stereotypes conferred on unmarried women. Victoria was rife with unattached men of eligible age and sufficient property: three men for every woman. The popular thinking of the day, for both men and women, was that if a woman remained single she must be undesirable or unattractive, unable to woo the attention of men, or too picky. Unmarried women were commonly referred to as "old maids," a term that had negative connotations because staying single by choice transgressed society's expectations of womanhood. Yet some women who had "respectability" through their family standing, or whose income allowed them independence, chose not to marry. Young women like Kathleen O'Reilly, because of their families' fortunes, were economically independent. Even though she had several suitors, she turned them down. She loved her life, she said, and had no need to improve her social standing or gain economic viability through marriage. Others like Emily Carr and Agnes Deans Cameron had vocational aspirations that would not have been realized if they had married. Teaching was regarded as a suitable occupation for a woman and no one questioned Cameron's marital status. While the Cameron household was not wealthy by the O'Reillys' standards, her salary afforded her a comfortable lifestyle. When she became principal of South Park School she was one of the highest paid women in the city. Cameron continued to live in her family home and her income allowed her to support her widowed mother and her sister Jessie, who also remained single. She was enjoying her life, which offered a freedom that marriage would frustrate.

Did she ever know love? What of her sexuality? some have asked. In "The Avatar of Jack Pemberton," a piece of fiction she published, she wrote knowingly of the transcendence of love and the breathlessness that catches one unaware when two lovers meet. "Turning quickly, with every nerve-a-tingle, and taking her hand in mine, I looked into her eyes and told her the story which a man tells once and once only. I don't think either of us had realized till that moment that we loved, though each year our separate lives had been but an onward step approaching this union and all of our days and nights had led up to this moment when each knew that henceforth to the end of time our two lives must flow together—one rich full, complete stream."[6] She appreciated the male form and expressed it in her writings. While on a train trip to Winnipeg in 1904, she described a cowboy who had joined her party in Calgary as "big, bronzed and straight as an arrow. He talks as gently as a lady and as he passed through the 'diner' a flunky says in an undertone, 'Take off your hat.' His eyes are blue and steely, and we half-hoped for a fight, but with a curl of the lips the sombrero comes off with a graceful sweep, and we can only wonder what would be left of the flunky had he been deemed game worthy of those tightly drawn muscles of whipcord."[7] In her description of a Royal Canadian Mounted Policeman that she met she wrote, "What magnificent types are these men of the Mounted Police." "What Men Have Said About Women," an article she wrote in 1906, provides another look at her opinions on love and on marriage. In it she includes over a hundred quotes from philosophers and writers like Rousseau, Browning, Thackeray, and Dumas that focus on the strength of women, the issue of equality, but also love: "Two smiles that approach each other end in a kiss"; "Love embraces woman's whole life—it is her prison and her kingdom of heaven"; "Woman was made out of the rib, taken from the side of a man; not out of his head to rule him, but out of his side to be his equal, under his arm to be protected, and near his heart to be beloved"; "A man philosophizes better than a woman on the human heart, but she reads the hearts of men better than he"; "There is a woman at the beginning of all great things."[8]

Did she have a lover, was she intimate with anyone, did she have proclivities toward other women? While such questions are impossible to answer with any certainty, it is most likely that her reputation in the community and position as a school principal, as well as her commitment to her profession, were always forefront in her thoughts. Behaviour that would take her away from her direction was most likely never entertained. Perhaps a partial answer can be found in a talk that she once gave to an audience in London when she said that she had not had the privilege of growing up in a wealthy family and she realized at an early age that she had to be responsible for her own keep and that of her mother, she did not have the luxury to do otherwise. She was also strongly independent and many of her writings showed that she preferred to be mistress of her own fate.

The 1890s were also the era of the "New Woman" and Cameron fit into that mould perfectly. The concept of the New Woman was one who was independent, educated, uninterested in marriage and children; had opinions based upon her education; believed that women should be afforded the right to vote, receive the same pay in work as their male colleagues, have the right of entry to the professions and have the laws of the country recognize that women were equal citizens. This was not a new concept by any means. The issues of opportunity and equality have always been uppermost in many women's minds. Upper- and middle-class women saw it as their duty to protect their families and to involve themselves in shaping the laws and the direction of their communities.

One of the articles published in the *Daily Colonist* on the New Woman stated, "The most exemplary housewife nowadays does not sit down to count threads and neatly backstitch the necessary dozens of shirt fronts. Probably she takes up instead the daily newspaper and becomes interested in the government of her country, even, perhaps, to the extent of forming an opinion about it."[9] In another piece, the vice-president of the Council of Women of Victoria defined the New Woman as "One who is enabled, by her training and education, more worthily to fulfill the design for which she was originally created—to be a helpmeet to man and Queen of Home, her power to be shown in the skill with which she can arrange, rule and order that home, at the same time never forgetting that, though she 'has a personal work and duty relating to her own home,' she has also 'a public work and duty which is the expansion of that.'"[10] It was empowered femininity.

Outside of her job Cameron was involved with several women's organizations, as were many women of her status. Women's groups were the focus through which social change was wrought and Cameron belonged to several such groups, including the Council of Women of Victoria and Vancouver Island, the BC Women's Council, the Canadian Women's Press Club, the Ladies of the Maccabees, the YWCA, the Woman's Christian Temperance Union, and the National Council of Women of Canada. Women's groups had always been the backbone of reform in Victoria, but in the 1890s a vast network of women were creating national organizations to more effectively address many of the issues of growing urbanization and corporatism. They focused on work equality, collective bargaining issues, philanthropic work, social welfare, and voting rights.

The majority of women's organizations, and the women who led many of the social movements of this time, did not see themselves as being in competition with men. Women's natural place, they felt, was in the home, but because of their innate proclivity toward caring and nurturing they believed they could offer a different perspective from men. To be a better companion to her husband, a woman needed education and should be allowed to shape the destiny of her community. Women, they affirmed, were no less deserving of equal status than were men. While Cameron believed in many of the same goals she took umbrage with hiding behind the protectorate of the home.

Cameron came at the question of equality more by way of a rational, logical standpoint. To her, women were not inferior to men. She did not think that discussions of equality needed to be buried in arguments that used domesticity as the backdrop. Women, she said, should be given the same opportunities as men. Voting was one of those issues that she championed, although not as vigorously as others in the community. In an article she wrote on the topic of suffrage she said, "I remember as a school girl wondering why it was that the high school boys would have the right to vote when they became twenty-one, while the girls, although our general class record was better than theirs, would never be given that right. I am still wondering. The question is one of such simple justice that I wonder that anyone with a desire to be considered logical can be found to oppose it. Anyone with reason has a right to help in determining what laws shall govern him. Women have reason, and, therefore, should vote." To those who argued that voting was unwomanly and would make her less feminine and gentle she retorted with, "A vote is simply a recorded opinion. It is difficult to see how the mere recording of an opinion could lessen one's refinement." The logic was simple she said, "Women should have the right of suffrage because she is judged by law . . . Since I am man's equal *under* the law, then surely I should be his equal *before* the law."[11] Reflecting on her experience at the Chicago World's Fair, where she learned that there were three hundred different occupations engaged in by women, she argued that, "Having proved themselves competent to administer business affairs successfully, they naturally ask the reason that should prevent their participation in matters of deeper responsibility which affect the welfare of the whole body politic."[12] In the same article, she also pointed out that it is the laws voted on by men that decide women's property tax: "Is it the old wrong of 'taxation without representation.'" She had no doubt that women would eventually gain the right to vote because they should have it. "No taxation without representation" became a rallying cry for the suffrage movement.

Cameron continued to write and give talks in support of equality and on the importance of women's civic responsibility toward voting. By 1884 white women who owned property could vote in elections for school trustees, although they could not yet stand for election.[13] The following year, on March 6, 1885, Maria Grant, one of the forces in the suffrage movement and doyen of social causes, was the first woman elected to the school board. She and Cameron would later be at odds over school curriculum and testing policy, but for now it was a great win for women. Women would not gain the right to vote in provincial elections until April 5, 1917 and in federal elections on May 24, 1918.

Those opposed to women's suffrage often held that women, in the main, didn't want the franchise; it was only a few zealots who were creating a lot of noise, they claimed. While it was true that some men as well as women thought that they should keep their spheres separate, citing divine law, many women believed that for the sake of their families it was critical that they had a stake and responsibility in issues that directly impacted their families. In fact, women were the major force directing social reform throughout the British Empire and the United States. They tackled issues of crime, disease, alcoholism, and prostitution, and improved the lives of working-class women and the destitute. Women studied law, became astute at lobbying, and learned how to be strong administrators and fundraisers and in the process built the substrate for political action. Their goal was to obtain the franchise; they knew that if they could not vote in provincial elections, politicians would not listen to them.

As the influence of women's groups became more evident, it was apparent that to avoid working at cross-purposes a national organization representing all groups should be created. An announcement in the newspapers notified its readers that, on Friday, November 8, 1895, the regular meeting of the Victoria Teachers' Association would be postponed to allow women teachers to attend the first convention of the National Council of Women of Canada. There was much on the agenda that would impact education and a strong representation of teachers was thought to be beneficial.

The NCWC, an affiliate of the International Council of Women, was formed in 1893. The purpose of the organization was to bring together many of the women's groups whose members had been working and advocating for the welfare of women, children, and their communities. While the member societies kept their unique status and continued to operate independently, the NCWC provided a medium of communication and a powerful force for dealing with issues of common interest. It was to be a big event.

Twenty-nine member organizations from Victoria and Vancouver entered City Hall for the first annual conference. At ten o'clock, Her Excellency the Countess of Aberdeen and president of the NCWC opened the meeting with a silent prayer.

Cameron, along with three other teachers, attended as representatives of the Victoria Teachers' Association. The afternoon meeting was given over to resolutions presented by various representative groups. The Woman's Christian Temperance Union asked that the Local Council of Women petition both the provincial and municipal governments to establish a home for aged and indigent women as they had done for men. Cameron added to the proposal, suggesting that the home for women ought to be connected to the men's. "It would give all concerned a more comfortable, home-like feeling, there is no saying what happiness the combination might not be productive of—I heard of two inmates of the Hawaiian home, aged respectively 95 and 93, being happily married not so very long ago."[14] The resolution was adopted.

As for issues directly affecting education, several teachers from South Park School raised concerns over the protection and security of the young. They specifically requested that the organization condemn the lax attitude of police toward dealers who sold tobacco products to children under sixteen. They also wanted to stop the practice of some local businesses of hiring young boys to work as messengers for saloons and houses of prostitution and help to create a bylaw prohibiting the employment of young boys for night jobs.

Schools were having a serious problem with truancy. An act in 1891 made school compulsory, but there had never been any provision for enforcement. One of the school trustees, Mrs. Grant, suggested that a woman should be appointed to the position of truancy officer. She recognized that it was a move that might not receive popular support in the community, so in hoping to get her motion accepted she mistakenly pointed out that a woman could work for less salary than a man. Not surprisingly, there was a tremendous outcry among audience members. Cameron was particularly angry and quickly retorted, "Pay the work, not the worker . . . If a woman does a man's work give her a man's pay."[15] After a great deal of emotional discussion, a resolution to request the school board to actively enforce the compulsory clause of the school act was passed omitting, however, the request to have a female enforcement officer.

The most passionate debate was over the issue of adding kindergarten to the school system. The executive put forth a motion to petition the BC government to revise the school law to allow children under the age of six to attend the public schools. They pointed out that in the United States and elsewhere, young children were ready for school and benefited from beginning school at an earlier age. To not add kindergartens to their school programs, they said, would be morally irresponsible. The resolution presented read: "Whereas the school law does not of this province; and whereas it has been, and is being, proved in the States and elsewhere that for children of such tender years the kindergarten system is both morally and intellectually superior to any other educational method extant; Therefore be it resolved, that the Council of Women of Victoria and Vancouver Island do petition the government to forthwith amend the school law, making no restriction as to age, and to speedily establish kindergartens in connection with the public schools of this city and the province of British Columbia."[16] The benefit of kindergarten or lack thereof was an issue current in many teachers' conferences and educational writings. It was the kind of debate that had the undecided and perhaps less informed gravitating to the opinions of the speaker of the moment. Cameron objected vociferously to the proposed amendment. She was resolute in her opinion that the present educational system functioned admirably. It is not the case that kindergarten is morally superior to any other educational method, she instructed. Further who was to pay for the addition of kindergarten? She pointed out that as the province would not support a kindergarten then cities would have to levy an additional per capita tax to support it and, she said, it would be an added burden on the poor who would not be able to withstand the additional taxes. She simply did not see the need for it. She was also opposed to the wording, logistics, and intended outcome of the resolution. It was too vague, she said. It did not specify what actions were required to amend the school act. More important than creating kindergartens, she said, was the immediate need for a training or normal school for teachers in the province. Her comments certainly did not endear her to the drafters of the resolution, but they did add to a very lively debate and pointed out the need to be clear on goals and the specifics of intended outcomes without which nothing would get done or be accepted by any government body. Cameron was persuasive and the resolution was deferred to a later meeting.

The first of many annual meetings of the Local Council of Women came to a close sometime after five o'clock in the afternoon. It was exhilarating, refreshing, and worthwhile to be able to consolidate the knowledge and lobbying techniques from the various groups who were working for positive social change in their communities. As a united group they emboldened the various groups to hone their skills, strive harder, work more productively, and know that as a united group they could be successful.

In May 1896, the children at South Park School were gearing up for their final month of school. Cameron's niece, Jessie Cameron Brown, had been working hard to maintain her place on the honour roll. She was the top student in the school and was hoping to snag the coveted Governor General's medal for the year, which she disappointingly did not win. In the meantime, the city was abuzz with activities and revellers celebrating Queen Victoria's seventy-seventh birthday. Festivities were being held throughout the Commonwealth, but for the city that was named after the queen, the annual May 24 Victoria Day tradition held special significance. People came from Seattle, Port Angeles, Port Townsend, even as far away as Minneapolis, Minnesota, and Providence, Rhode Island. There were horse races, bicycle races, tennis tournaments, swimming, music, and public dances, to the delight of all. A favourite game was the greased pole and pig contest, although not necessarily for the unfortunate pig. One of the Navy ships would grease up a boom and place a pig in a crate at one end. The idea was to make it to down the boom, pull a string to let the pig out, then jump into the water to catch the animal and swim with it to shore.

The highlight of the day was a sham battle between the Navy and the Army. Some years it was held on Beacon Hill, but this year it was being staged at Macaulay Point in Esquimalt Harbour. To get to Macaulay Point people had to take a streetcar across a bridge and over the Gorge Waterway. The inlet was festooned with brightly coloured flags that stretched from shore to shore. A lucky few were invited to watch the boat races from the expansive lawns of the stately homes that graced the shoreline, while servants served strawberries and cream. The battle was in the early afternoon on May 26. To get a good viewing spot people started arriving as early as ten o'clock. By noon thousands of people lined the banks. Just as the battle was about to begin, the last few revellers hopped onto the streetcar to take them across Point Ellice Bridge. The streetcar was filled to capacity. There was only seating for forty, but people managed to crowd in the front with the driver. A few daring young boys excitedly piled on top of the car. Everyone was having fun and no one minded the tight squeeze. The conductor was working his way through the passengers and had collected 108 fares with more to go. As they entered the bridge Miss Smith leaned over to her sister and ominously said, "We are going into the jaws of death." Suddenly the bridge began shaking and then the flooring of the bridge flipped up, "like the blades of a jackknife," one passenger said. Electric Car Number 16 slid to the side and then the middle sections of the bridge collapsed and with it the streetcar. They hit the water hard. As the streetcar began sinking air pressure built up inside. As the last one to jump aboard, Mr. Englehardt was fortunately near the doorway when the pressure blew him out of the car. His friend, however, was hit with a beam on the back of the head and killed. Several other passengers were jettisoned out the windows. There were a couple of young girls in the front who were trapped under the ironwork from the bridge. Two horse-drawn carts crossing the bridge at the same time were tossed into the water, drowning the passengers, as was a bicyclist who was struck by metal as he fell to his death. Screams and cries for help were heard coming from all over the water. Onlookers were stunned.

Rescue operations started immediately. Most of the city's doctors rushed to the scene. Fourteen-year-old Eliza Woodil found herself thrown into the water. Amid the chaos she managed to rescue two young children and all three were plucked out of the water by one of the boats on the scene. Another boat found Sophie Smith and her sister. Sophie was unconscious and held up by her sister. It was a gripping scene as doctors worked on her for two hours as her sister stood tearfully by imploring them to bring her back. A deep sadness overtook them when they finally had to admit defeat. Captain Grant, whose residence was on the bank, immediately set up his house to act as a triage station and a place to lay out the deceased. Dismayed and horrified, people walked through the rows of bodies looking for their mothers, fathers, and children. Among the dead were a little boy who still had his knitted gloves on and an older gentleman whose hands were clenched tight. The day after the tragedy the entire city was wrapped in mourning. Church bells rang throughout the city as horse-drawn funeral carriages made a steady procession to Ross Bay Cemetery. Fifty-five people perished in the accident.

The bridge was never meant to sustain such weight. Those responsible had to be held accountable. Less than three weeks later, on June 12, the case went to court. A swift verdict was pronounced; the jury held the tramway company, Consolidated Electric Railway, responsible. It knowingly allowed the streetcar to be overloaded, they said. Consolidated Electric was not the only entity that shouldered the blame. The City Council of Victoria was found guilty of contributory negligence, because they did not maintain the bridge nor take steps to restrict bridge traffic to within safe limits. The provincial government was also reproached for not properly supervising the building of the bridge, which the court said was of poor design and construction. The city engineers were also brought in, but it was ruled that they were not at fault. They were said to be competent and were trying their best to maintain the bridge, but were so interfered with by government officials in the Department of Public Works, who lacked any knowledge of engineering and technical issues, that they were unable to carry out their duties.

Early in the 1890s a new phenomenon hit the province; it was the era of the bicycle and it took Victoria by storm. It was not the first time bicycles captured people's attention, but earlier versions were nothing more than short-lived fads. They were uncomfortable, difficult to ride, and dangerous, but changes in technology made the bicycle safer and easier to control. Once they were mass-produced they were within reach of the average wage earner. Victoria had always been sport oriented and the bicycle fit right in with cricket, yachting, baseball, horseracing, rowing, lawn tennis, and bowling, which were all popular pastimes. The newspapers published daily columns on upcoming competitions, particularly between Victoria and their American neighbours to the south. They even added a new section to their papers, which they called "The Wheel."

For most, the bicycle was seen as progressive, avant-garde, the newest item in cutting-edge technology, but there were those naysayers who worried over its potential influence on the morals of young people. Young couples might be tempted to engage in courtship away from family controls, they argued, and to see a woman straddling a bicycle was simply indecent. Whatever one's opinion, the bicycle left an immeasurable imprint on the city, becoming a strong cultural and economic force in its own right. It created opportunities for businesses specializing in new technologies and influenced everyday fashion. For women, the looser-fitting bicycle suit allowed them to get rid of constricting corsets and billowy skirts, which had effectively diminished their ability to breathe and restricted their movements. Advice from one of the cycling books suggested the appropriate clothing for women "both for service and appearance, is a skirt of medium length, not too full, and of fairly substantial material, with long leggings or gather to match the skirt. The bloomer costume seems to meet with much favour and has apparently come to stay. Some women think they ride better without corsets, but certainly tight lacing is unadvisable, if not absolutely out of the question."[17] The bicycle also helped shape laws governing transportation and allowed people the freedom to explore rural areas, which in turn translated into improved roads. Racing and touring clubs became popular and families flocked to Beacon Hill Park on the weekends to enjoy a ride. Bike paths were hastily cobbled together and seemingly overnight there were trails leading to Cadboro Bay, Gordon Head, Cedar Hill, Cordova Bay, and even out as far as Metchosin and Sooke.

Not everyone could afford a bicycle—prices ranged from forty dollars up to eighty-five dollars for the top of the line—but those who could, both men and women, took to the streets, eager if somewhat wobbly, riding their new bicycles. Initially there were no rules governing right of way or safety. Consequently, cyclists caused no end of trouble between themselves, pedestrians, and carriages. Horses were spooked and pedestrians were wary of crossing the street for fear of getting hit. Letters to the editors flooded in to local newspapers complaining of the near misses with bicycles on the streets of downtown. Cyclists were "inconsiderate," "thoughtless," and "careless," angered citizens wrote. But the bicycle was here to stay.

A simple machine with two wheels, pedals, gears, and a chain gave a tremendous sense of freedom to women. For the first time, they could easily get to any place they wanted to go on their own. The bicycle changed women's lives so significantly that it became a symbol used by suffragettes and the Women's Christian Temperance Movement. Susan B. Anthony, the famous women's rights advocate and key organizer of the International Council of Women, wrote about the significance of bicycles for women: "Let me tell you what I think of bicycling. I think it has done more to emancipate women than anything else in the world. It gives women a feeling of freedom and self-reliance. I stand and rejoice every time I see a woman ride by on a wheel . . . the picture of free, untrammeled womanhood."[18] The bicycle also brought an awareness of the health benefits of exercise and opened up to women the chance to increase their physical prowess. Women began competing with men in this new sport, which created a tentative equality between the genders. It fit comfortably with the image of the New Woman.

Beacon Hill Park was a great gathering place for cyclists and the city began hosting racing events showcasing well-known figures in the racing world. In one such event held on Saturday, June 7, the city arranged a demonstration bicycle race featuring Miss Jessie Oakes, the world champion female bicyclist. She was slated to race against Diamond, a speed demon of a racehorse owned by Mr. Campbell. The race was held at the Driving Park horse race track. There had been a few demonstration races prior to Jessie Oakes, but none reaching the fame of Oakes. The cable car company arranged to run extra trips to take people to the event. When Oakes, on her mechanical steed, lined up wheel to nose with Diamond, it was anyone's guess as to who would win. At exactly one o'clock the starter pistol went off. The track was exceptionally bad and Oakes was facing a head wind. Flying around the track, Oakes rode with her characteristic strength and managed to keep ahead of the seasoned racehorse as the crowd roared with anticipation. It was a tense race, but she crossed the finish line before her opponent, winning the day. From that time on news of cycling events, both local and international, began appearing in the news. Entrepreneurs, recognizing a business opportunity, rushed to be the first to set up bicycle shops.

Cameron was smitten by the new bicycle craze and took to it easily. She became a member of the Victoria chapter of the Wheelman's Club, an international touring and racing group, and participated in many of the city's bicycle events. She loved long-distance riding, often wheeling out to Sooke and back, a particularly difficult seventy-seven-kilometre round-trip trek. It was not long before she wanted a more difficult challenge. Sometime during 1897 she obtained a copy of *The Cyclers' Guide and Road Book of California* by George W. Blum, the undisputed bible for cycling in the state. It covered everything a rider needed for touring. There were articles on road conditions, maps outlining bike routes, distances between points, hotels offering reduced rates for wheelmen, bike maintenance for trail riders, and training ideas for getting in shape. California, her second home, would be a wonderful place to tour by bike, she thought. Her decision was made. As soon as her summer break began in July she would take a biking holiday in California.

She made all the necessary arrangements and once in California she joined a group of other like-minded cyclists. Her goal was to bike from San Jose to Mount Hamilton. Her destination was the famous Lick Observatory to see the world's largest refracting telescope. She dressed comfortably, looked her bike over, and fine-tuned her seat so her weight was placed more on the pedals and not on her saddle. Experience taught her that such an adjustment would to help with speed and most importantly prevent saddle sores. Starting in Sacramento, Cameron turned southwest into the Santa Clara Valley heading to San Jose to make the journey up into the Diablo Range to Mount Hamilton. It was an arduous thirty-one-kilometre ride up a hot, dusty, sinuous path. Her muscles screamed at her for what she was putting them through. She was relieved when the white dome of the Lick Observatory finally came into view. Once on top, the whole of the Monterey Peninsula opened before her. It was breathtaking in its panoramic view, and well worth the effort.

Coming back triumphant from her trip, Cameron wanted more. To say she was ebullient was an understatement. Touring was exhilarating, and it motivated her to take up yet another challenge. She set her sights on becoming the first female Centurion in the West. Centurions, sometimes called the Century Riders, were an internationally recognized group of amateur bicyclists that completed a one-hundred-mile course within a specified amount of time. Male riders had to complete a course within ten hours, women had fourteen hours, and tandem riders had twelve. The prize was not only winning the Arrow Pin, a highly coveted tiny metal bar embossed with a pair of wings and an arrow, but also belonging to an elite group of cyclists noted for their skill and endurance.

Cameron chose to ride tandem. She partnered with another member of Victoria's Wheelman's Club—L. A. Campbell, holder of the Western Canadian long-distance record with a time of six hours, fifty-nine minutes, and thirty seconds. Known as a very strong rider who could keep up a gruelling pace over long distances, he had the reputation of being one of the most sportsmanlike riders in the history of cycling in the West. Campbell had earned his Arrow a month before his ride with Cameron. They knew each other through teaching. Campbell was a well-respected teacher and happened to be an official referee for the Victoria Junior Association Football Club, of which Cameron was president. It may seem unusual for a woman to be head of a football club, but one of the boys' teams came from South Park School and was considered the team to beat.

The race was scheduled for an early six-fifteen start on Saturday, September 11, 1897. Their course was the Saanich Peninsula track. If they followed the usual route they would leave from City Hall in Victoria and report in at Wright's Hotel in North Saanich, before returning for a second round. That would bring them to a distance of eighty-six miles. The remaining fourteen miles would take the riders up Yates Street to Oak Bay Avenue, along the Beach Road to Beacon Hill Park, circling once around the park then riding back to Oak Bay by way of Quadra and Fort. Most of the races ended at Mount Baker Hotel, an elegant place to take stock of the day's achievement. Mount Baker Hotel was a popular resort in a majestic setting. It overlooked the Strait of Juan de Fuca and was directly in line with Washington's Mount Baker, the snow-capped sentinel of the Cascade Mountain Range.

By 5:40 in the evening they had been on the road for over eleven hours; fatigue was setting in. They had just one hour to complete the race and had to dig deep into their energy reserves. When they finally took their feet off the pedals and dismounted from their bike, their time was eleven hours, thirty minutes, and thirty-five seconds. A bit worse for wear, they had accomplished what they set out to do. They would have completed the race in a faster time but for a mishap along the way. They had pedalled the first sixty miles on an Adlake bicycle, chosen for its strength. It was when they switched to a lighter geared Crescent, an excellent racing bike that was deemed to be the fastest in the world, that they broke the front fork and were thrown from the bike. They were badly shaken and had a few cuts and scrapes but felt fortunate to have escaped serious injury. The clock continued to tick away as they spent precious time waiting for a remount. As they came into sight of Mount Baker Hotel they noticed the large number of supporters and media waiting for them. Congratulations were offered all around. In a ceremony held on October 23, Mrs. H. Dallas Helmcken presented both Cameron and Campbell, along with five others, with the coveted century Arrow Pin. It was a big day for Cameron. She was immensely proud of her achievement. She was entitled to wear her pins at all times, signalling her accomplishment. As record holders, both she and her partner put the West on the map for cyclists.

Cameron was at a wonderful stage in her life. As a teacher and school principal she had reached a prominent position in her career. Her ability with words, her skills at public speaking, her wit and sharp intellect garnered her many invitations as a guest speaker at conferences and for recitations at the theatres throughout the Dominion. Her income was sufficient to enable her to nourish her love of travel, which she often shared with Victoria audiences through her famous slide shows, talks, and writings. Her participation in her community was everywhere evident. Between 1897 and 1899 she added several more committees to her already growing resume of community work. She was an outstanding example for her students and to other women.

Change was happening quickly in Victoria; it was now a city of well over sixteen thousand people. City boundaries had been expanded; telephones, street lamps, and electric streetcar service were commonplace. Coal mining on the West Coast, along with increased trade with Asia and South America, brought prosperity not only to Victoria but also to the province as a whole. A rail ferry was promised to connect Victoria with Canadian and American transcontinental systems by the beginning of 1900. With extra money filling its coffers the city had undertaken a beautification project, hoping to become a summer resort of importance. The future looked bright, but Victoria had its underbelly too. There was an old saying that "on Johnson Street, from Government street down or up . . . if a man was drunk he'd roll out of one [bar] and fall into another one."[19] There were new opportunities for jobs, but those without education were being left behind. Child poverty was a growing concern, particularly as it left out in the streets impressionable young boys who sometimes found undesirable employment working for the many bars in the city.

Early in 1899 Cameron was approached by the newly formed Epworth League of St. James Methodist Church with the idea of providing academic instruction to young boys who had not had the opportunity to attend school or had dropped out to earn a living. It was a project close to her heart. The Epworth League was a pan-Methodist organization established for young people with the purpose of improving intellectual aptitude and piety among the urban young, and they had made education a priority. In March, Cameron along with three other teachers began a daily program teaching courses in writing, arithmetic, bookkeeping, literature, history, chemistry, and stenography. While most people would be drained and tired after a long day of teaching and tending to administrative duties, Cameron eagerly set out every evening from seven to eight-thirty to help those who had not the same opportunities as others.

The dawn of a new century brought forth an era of social activism and transformation. Efficiency, growth, remodelling, and scientific solutions were foremost in people's thinking. Social groups stepped up their activities and directed their actions toward creating healthier communities and ameliorating society's social ills. Schools, in particular, were considered an important instrument in creating a better society. In the 1900s teachers were looked on as having the ability to mediate class differences, structural differences, and social differences; to quell the rambunctious; and to be the preventers of crime and delinquency. Society ascribed to schools and teachers powers beyond their capabilities. This was the Progressive Era; it was modern, and education was seen as the way forward, but first education itself needed to be reformed. Personal development through education was still considered a valid pursuit, but more importantly schools needed to develop a curriculum that supported the emerging market economy. There was a growing interest in preparing children for managing the practical aspects of their lives and to give them the tools through education for a life of economic self-sufficiency. The Dominion government was actively lobbied by representatives of industry from organizations like the Canadian Manufacturers' Association and the Trades and Labour Congress, who wanted to have a countrywide policy on vocational training. They said that if Canada was to compete on a global scale the country needed more skilled workers.

A vigorous debate over the purpose of education ensued. Several important questions were at issue. All educators recognized that the prosperity of any nation needs intelligent, cooperative, active citizens, but should school focus on scholarship or act more as training ground for the industrial and commercial work life of the new society? Should the goal of education be to give students a toolbox of knowledge and skills to be able deduce, synthesize, imagine, and appreciate? What are the limitations of school? Manual training and domestic science became part of that discussion.

Across the country in Ontario, a remarkable woman by the name of Adelaide Hoodless began a campaign to teach young girls domestic science with the intent of improving the health standards of their families. There were so many instances of children dying needlessly from poor food preservation, deficiency of sanitary standards, and lack of pure milk and clean water. Hoodless herself had lost her fourteen-month-old child to a stomach complaint, most likely from contaminated milk. She felt morally bound to rectify the situation and would do anything she could to bring about change. Her speeches were heartfelt, wrenching, informative, and practical. She spearheaded the Women's Institutes, wrote a textbook on domestic science, worked with Lady Aberdeen to establish the Victorian Order of Nurses, and engaged the support of the National Council of Women of Canada. Education was a prominent item on the agenda of the NCWC, and Margaret Jenkins, a member of the Local Council of Women and a school trustee, was in step with the call for domestic science for girls.

The Local Council of Women put considerable effort into lobbying the school board to include domestic science in the curriculum. Knowing that the school authorities would be reluctant to spend the necessary funds to equip such a program, the Local Council of Women sweetened the plea with an offer of three hundred dollars to purchase the necessary equipment, if the board would see fit to hire an appropriate teacher. Cameron, who was a member of both groups, was irate and in this she stood alone within the organization. Her vociferous lack of support for including domestic science, or any other vocational program, as part of the curriculum put her at odds with everyone else and created a rift that had the organization later deny her support when she ran for the position of school trustee. Speaking on domestic science she said, "This Local Council of Women were all agog for domestic science. When I, opening my eastern windows which look toward the sun, saw the procession of cooking stoves and stew pans . . . heading for the schoolroom door, I lifted up a feeble wail for mercy. In this whole Council of women I found no friend. I was anathema and ultra-conservative. I was unprogressive and lazy. Did I not know that cooking was a good thing, a most necessary thing."[20] She knew that she was obstructive because she did not want to see education come to the state where every boy was taught to be a carpenter and every girl a cook.

As a delegate and member of the executive at the 1904 Dominion Educational Association, Cameron gave a talk on what she saw was the problem with the proliferation of non-academic classes in the public schools. She pointed out that the WCTU had succeeded in introducing a program on the effects of alcohol in the schools, the SPCA wanted to include the teaching of domestic animal health, and the sewing guilds were lobbying for practical courses in stitchery to be added to the school curriculum. She emphasized that spelling and arithmetic began to take a second seat to these new courses. "You can't open your school-room door for a breath of fresh air without letting someone with a mission fall in," she said.[21] Having a large number of children sequestered in classrooms makes it very tempting, she thought, for everyone who had a passion or was on a hobbyhorse to decide what should be included in the curriculum. As to the nature of the curriculum she said, "I want to clearly define my position with regard to these Bands of Mercy, Bands of Hope, WCTU's and SPCA's; this sewing, sawing and swimming, straw-weaving, rope-splicing, wood-splitting, cooking, and tonic sol-fa. Some of them I know to be good in themselves, and the rest may be. But this is not the question which confronts us. Five hours is a period of time with mathematical limitations. You can't crowd something new into it, without crowding something old out. Already the groundwork subjects have suffered of necessity. We have 'enriched' our course at the expense of thoroughness."[22] She also said, "In my own school ten percent of each week is given to physical and military drill, another ten percent is claimed at the Domestic Science and Manual Training Schools, Nature Study nibbles away its precious fraction."[23]

Yet in 1899 she stood at a lectern, as a director of the British Columbia Society for the Prevention of Cruelty to Animals (BCSPCA), supporting the inclusion of the study of the natural world in schools. "The lessons learned from the marvelous pages of books of nature will last when all our didactic lectures have passed away like a tale that is told," she claimed. "The great central facts of interdependence and altruism become living truths to the child as he recognized for himself the beautifully fitting links in the great chain of nature."[24] If learning was to be narrowed to courses that only focus on one's bankbook, she said, then it would become easier to lose the moral tone of our humanity; an opinion that modern day educators continue to press.

She made a plea for parents, school boards, and school trustees to have more faith in their teachers: "The teacher more than any other worker is at the mercy of theorists. No one gets more gratuitous advice than she does. Everyone you meet is willing to tell you how to do your work, they are just bubbling over with recipes of 'how to do it.' Parsons keep a regular supply of sermons for our use. City editors, when they run short of subjects for the Sunday sermonette, just turn their attention to 'these well-paid and certainly not over-worked teachers.' 'Children are riot patriotic,' they say, 'and the teacher is to blame.'" To bring her point home she recited a popular poem called "New Fangled Schools":

They taught him how to hemstitch, and they taught him how to sing,
And how to make a basket out of variegated string,
And how to fold a paper so it wouldn't hurt his thumb;
They taught a lot to Bertie, but he couldn't do a sum.
They taught him how to mould the head of Hercules in clay,
And how to tell the difference 'twixt the bluebird and the jay,
And how to sketch a horsie in a little picture frame;
But strangely they forgot to teach him how to spell his name.[25]

Cameron continued to press her point at a number of conferences and meetings she attended. She talked about the crowded curriculum, the rush to advance education at the cost to the students, and the need for cooperation between parents and teachers. She was a riveting speaker and her opinions put her on the national stage. Educators across the country knew of the illustrious Agnes Deans Cameron. A Miss Murry writing about the meeting of the National Council of Women of Canada in London, Ontario, in 1901 for the *Educational Review* was impressed with Cameron. She described her as a commanding figure with a striking personality, highly intelligent, full of energy, decisive, and yet sympathetic and warm-hearted. "She has independence of thought, good command of language and a peculiarly keen sense of humor, which was very evident in her paper."[26] There is no question that Cameron knew how to engage an audience and what better way to get your ideas across than to pepper your talk with humour, which she did with great relish.

Chapter Seven

A Troubling Time

*There is then an individual responsibility born with
each one of us, whatever our environment, a duty
to one's self from which we cannot get away.*

—AGNES DEANS CAMERON

On a chilly January morning, the city of Victoria awoke to the
sound of bells tolling throughout the city, announcing the death
of Her Imperial Majesty Queen Victoria, Queen of Great Britain
and Ireland, Empress of India. During the evening of January 22,
1901, the Prince of Wales sent a telegram to the Lord Mayor of
London that read, "Osborne, 6:45 p.m.—My beloved mother
has just passed away, surrounded by her children and grandchildren. Albert Edward."[1] Queen Victoria's death was not entirely
unexpected; newspapers had been keeping vigil for the past week
on the sudden decline in her health. Across the country meetings and social functions were postponed, business shut down.

Cameron sent the children home from school for a period of three days. A sombre mood blanketed cities across the nation as the country went into full mourning. Shutters covered windows, blinds were drawn in sympathy, and city buildings were draped in unaccustomed pennons of black. Flags from every flagpole were lowered to half-mast and would remain so until sundown on the day of the funeral, which was to take place on the second of February. People noted that the city was the quietest they had ever experienced. Victoria the Good was dead; her long reign of sixty-three years was concluded. With her death, the Victorian Age ended and the city lost its namesake.

In early February Cameron received notice of the death of her favourite uncle. She decided to take a month's leave of absence to attend his funeral in Sacramento, California. She arranged for Miss Speers to act as principal while she was away. The warmer, sunnier weather in California must have given her a boost, because when she arrived back in Victoria she blew in like a windstorm and marched headlong into a debate about gender discrimination in the payment of teachers' salaries.

At their weekly board meeting in April, the school trustees decided to approve a pay raise for male assistant teachers. Cameron was not concerned about her salary; as a school principal she was at par with other male principals, most of whom received one thousand eighty dollars a year. Across the county, however, women earned thirty percent less for the same level of certificate and experience as did men. In Victoria, the pay differential between men and women existed, but less so than in other school districts within the province. As more women entered the teaching profession the disparity of salaries between men and women began to widen. Cameron did not stand idly by. She and a group of women teachers gathered to discuss the issue. They did not have a problem with the increase, so long as the same applied equally to women teachers. What they did not like was a precedent for paying men and women with the same level of certificates differently. In her precise analysis and reading of the effects of such a move, Cameron stressed the point that it was grossly unfair, as many of the women teachers had spent years in training and preparation for their profession. They were committed and devoted, she said, and were in it for the long haul: "It is a vicious principle to establish any such basis of payment of salary as that of sex . . . it will be a most unfair discrimination and one which has never yet been recognized, though in many minor ways it has long been tacitly attempted to discriminate in favour of the men who teach in the city schools . . . many of the young men look upon teaching as merely a stepping stone to some other profession more attractive and remunerative."[2] The school board responded to the women saying they were interested in attracting more male teachers for boys and thought the best way to do that was to raise the salary level. Cameron countered their contention by saying that such a move to widen the gap would drive a wedge between teachers and likely result in keeping men out of the profession altogether.

In his report on the status of education for the province of British Columbia, the superintendent of education, Alexander Robinson, Esq., stressed that it was critical to have trained, skilled, and committed teachers. It would be foolish, he said, to employ inexperienced teachers, as it would shortchange the students and the community as a whole. Money had to be saved by some means and he thought paying women teachers less was the best avenue with the least complaint. Education for the province was a large budget item; 369,000 dollars was spent annually with nearly two thirds of that sum going toward teachers' salaries and incidental expenses.[3] By way of comparison, expenditures for the administration of justice for the province amounted to 120,000 dollars, and for government salaries 254,000. Costs were mounting.

It was a slippery slope Cameron said: "It is only a question of time till the school boards will say that they are merely the custodians of the people's money, and if they get equally as good service from the ladies for less money than from the gentlemen, they will be doing wrong to continue the employment of male teachers, and the latter will have to go."[4] Cameron was not naturally a defiant person, but while she did not relish such clashes she never backed down from a skirmish when she felt others' rights were being usurped. The school trustees were hoping to avoid just such a confrontation. The best way around it they decided was to have closed meetings on the issue. Trustee Belyea was not keen to have the issue debated by the public, particularly by those whose objective he felt was to get back at some members of the board. He placed Cameron in that camp.

The salary differential was an issue that would plague the trustees for some time. During an all candidates meeting in 1902 for those running for a position as school trustee, one of the questions put to them was, "Are you in favour of paying the same salaries to women teachers as are paid to men for the same service?"[5] Some waffled, one answered saying he for one did not believe that women could be as efficient in teaching boys as could male teachers, another wanted to see the number of male teachers equal to that of women. In the main, all the candidates agreed with the premise of equal pay for work of equal service but felt that in this case financial pressures necessitated a more creative application of the principle of equality.

The *Daily Colonist* was supportive of Cameron's plea to the board on behalf of women teachers. They pointed out that from her status as a school principal, and because she had the longest-serving record in the city schools, she was in a position to provide a fair and credible opinion. "From her personal experiences in striving for the recognition of the principle of equal rights as to salary, and position, and from having successfully reached the various positions once held exclusively by men, and for which she has proven herself well qualified, she has demonstrated that when she was given the same salary as a man would have received in the same position, the board has done the right thing in establishing the precedent which the ladies are now anxious shall not be over-ridden."[6]

Confrontation with the school trustees did not end with the issue of salaries. Toward the end of June, a dispute arose over a change in the year-end examination procedures. The superintendent of education wanted to substitute oral exams for the usual written ones. Cameron in her capacity as a school principal joined Mary Williams, the principal of the Girls' Central School in Victoria, to oppose the change. It had been within the province of the school principals, not the superintendent, to set the style of exams for their schools. They could see no benefit in changing the exam system to an oral one, particularly when no one had any idea as to what was required. It seemed to be another idea pulled out of the ether at the last minute by people who were not in the classroom daily. Both school principals were resolute in their refusal to make the substitution. When it came time for the students of South Park School and Girls' Central to take their tests, they sat down at their desks with pen and paper at hand and proceeded to answer the questions as they had in previous years.

The populace was tired of hearing about the inner workings of the school system. They were more focused on the deplorable road conditions on Government Street and the cost of replacing the temporary Point Ellice Bridge, and were especially fearful that the plague stemming from Hong Kong was only one boatload of goods and passengers away; they were not prepared to read about another school board fracas in the papers. As well, the trustees were growing weary of principals, particularly women principals, who did not know their place and who kept testing the edges of obedience and authority. So behind closed doors and without input from either principal, Mr. Belyea, one of the Victoria school trustees, advanced a motion to suspend Cameron and Williams. His opposition to women principals was well known and he particularly disliked women who operated from a sense of authority. The vote put Helen "Maria" Grant, the only female school trustee, on the spot. She was the first woman in Canada elected as a school trustee and was very conscious of her position. Through her work as the leader of women's suffrage in Victoria she proved herself to be strong, independent, and not easily intimidated. However, she felt that as she was on many of the same committees as Cameron, there might be a conflict of interest. Whatever her personal feelings about the two women, she backed away from the issue and absented herself when the motion was tabled. The Victoria Superintendent of Education Alexander Robinson, Esq., weighed in on the issue, accusing both principals of insubordination and suspending them for the rest of the term. The media, which had earlier been supportive of Cameron and Williams, cried shame on them for defying a constituted authority.

In June of the previous year, the Board of School Trustees had adopted a new set of regulations relating to the organization and conduct of schools. Both principals said that they were not aware of the change and had they known would have heeded the rules. In fact, Wilson was so apologetic that she was immediately reinstated; Cameron was not so easily intimated. She believed that running away from an issue was not the way to solve anything, and slipping into a comfortable regime of always deferring was lazy thinking and an abrogation of one's civic duty. In a paper she wrote for the *Educational Journal of Western Canada* in 1899, she talked about the idea of true citizenship saying, "We cannot stand aside from that of which we are a part and say we will take no interest in it . . . As citizens we have a duty to participate, a duty that we cannot relegate to others."[7] She pointed out that as a teacher and citizen it was imperative to nourish creative thinking, to help those who govern the various levels of a community to live up to their potential, to think independently, to act as a role model, to encourage the weakest to be strong, and to create an environment that would be wholesome and strong. Sometimes, she said, that means you stand apart and recognize that it is not always desirable to be in unison with the norm.

Cameron penned a letter to the Board of School Trustees in which she asked for a meeting to defend herself.

To the Board of School Trustees, Victoria:

Mrs. Grant and Gentlemen:

In reply to yours of yesterday, stating that I am guilty of certain infractions of the School Act, I wish to state that I have always striven to obey the law loyally and fearlessly.

And I would most respectfully ask that I be allowed to appear before the board and be confronted with the evidence on which I have been condemned unheard.

As this matter, through the newspapers and otherwise, has already gained a certain amount of publicity, I would further ask that such meeting be of an open nature.

I am, madam and gentlemen, very respectfully yours,
Agnes Deans Cameron
Principal of South Park School.[8]

Was this a simple case of two factions caught in a power struggle tinged with overtones of gender inequality? There was no question that the country was still a long way from seeing women as equal partners in the workforce. Men clearly commanded the power and held the significant positions within the education system and women who spoke from a sense of authority and confidence were typically repressed, but the lines were blurring and shifting. The suspension was more than a dispute over gender inequality or personal animosities. The issue went deeper than that.

Across the province there was a growing movement on the part of government to delocalize control over the schools. The government's thinking was that members of the local school boards, who were put in office by a small electorate, may find themselves representing partisan interests with biased agendas. Therefore, all decisions about education would be better served coming from a centralized authority. The Board of School Trustees strongly objected, and instead recommended in their 1899 school report that amendments be made to the School Act that would give the school boards more control over local school affairs. It was a debate that loomed large within education. Was it better to bring education into the protectorate of the provincial government, which represented the larger public interest, or to have a system that could respond to local needs? How much control should the various levels of educational directors and administrators have in shaping the course of education? How much control should individual teachers have in such matters?

The city superintendent of schools, Frank Eaton, weighed in on the issue, saying rigidity and uniformity in school administration was unprogressive and too restrictive. The inspector of schools, S. B. Netherby, agreed, pointing out that governing bodies operate best when they govern the least. "I have made it my aim to urge upon the teachers the necessity for independent methods founded upon the results of study and investigation."[9]

The problem was that the School Act was not particularly clear in outlining the responsibilities of the trustees and district superintendents in determining and administrating school policy. Cameron's quarrel was not in countermanding the School Act, but with the school trustees' interpretation. They maintained they had the right to change the methods of examination, but Cameron informed them that the School Act consigns control over such matters to the principal. As so much had been done behind closed doors it was time to go public with the issue. Picking up her pen she wrote a letter to the editor of the *Victoria Daily Colonist*:

> *My wish has ever been to keep the law in its fuller*
> *and deeper intent, and I am glad of the opportunity of*
> *expressing publicly to Mr. Robinson, superintendent of*
> *education, my honest regret if anything in my attitude*

*may have been deemed lacking in the respect due from
me to him.*

*My quarrel has been elsewhere. The School Act vests
(under certain rules and regulations) in the principal and
not in the city superintendent, the responsibility of grading
his school, and while I retain my position as principal,
I shall not evade that responsibility, nor relegate it to
another. Thanking you for the space given to this.*

*I am, very truly yours,
Agnes Deans Cameron,
Principal of South Park School*[10]

The superintendent of education responded immediately. In a
letter to her, which was subsequently published in the newspapers,
he accepted her argument and rescinded her suspension.

*Madam: On the receipt of your letter of the 26th inst.,
I beg to advise you that you are . . . restored to your
full legal status as principal of the South Park School
of Victoria. You will, therefore, proceed to finish the
grading of your school, keeping in mind that you
have scarcely two days left in which to accomplish
this work.*

*I beg to assure you that the city superintendent of the
Victoria Schools, what ever may have been his practice
in the past, will in the future recognize your status
as principal.*

*Believe me when I assure you that the events of the
last few days have not been of my seeking, and that
I have been compelled to perform what I believed at
the time was a duty, however disagreeable. I trust,
however, that our future relations will be of the most
cordial character.*

I have the honour to be, madam, your most obedient servant.

Alexander Robinson.
Superintendent of Education.[11]

Despite people's fatigue with the ongoing arguments within the education system, Robinson's decision was most likely swayed by public opinion, as both principals were extremely popular.

Cameron did not miss a beat. She went back into her classroom and readied her school for the coming summer holidays. The Victoria school trustees would have their pound of flesh, but not yet. For that they would have to wait.

Chapter Eight

AN UP-AND-COMING WRITER

*Christmas Eve in Victoria, Vancouver
Island, and a wild white night . . .*

—AGNES DEANS CAMERON FROM "THE
AVATAR OF JACK PEMBERTON"

Sometime early in 1903 Cameron began writing in earnest. She was a busy person so it is difficult to imagine how she shoehorned a budding writing career between her duties as a principal, her committee work, biking, community presentations, teaching night school, her travels, and taking care of her mother. Every spare minute of her day must have been accounted for, but talent always finds a way to creep into those unscripted minutes that normally slip by unnoticed. For a long time, something inside of her was tugging at her, pushing her to take up her pen and write; she felt compelled to express herself. Instead of scripting articles about trends in education or letters to the newspaper, usually in defense of her students, her faculty, or herself, she changed her focus and began composing her first short story, "The Avatar of Jack Pemberton."

She conjured up a tale about a theosophical reincarnation and a great love forged in the ether of an Arctic night. Sitting at her typewriter, being careful not to let her fingers get caught in the spaces between the little round key tops on the keyboard, she wrote her first paragraph: "Christmas Eve in Victoria, Vancouver Island, and a wild white night. Inside, eight friends have gathered from north, east and south . . . as they had done every year on this night for the last five years to share and reminisce over the past year. Two among them were chosen to share their stories. Jack Pemberton began telling of his strange story . . . in that thirteen days, when my body was neither dead nor alive, my Ego, my real self, was busy with the past. Like an open book a former existence spread itself out before me, and this life dropped off like a garment. Memory was a clear-cut etching and no line joined the picture of that life to this one."[1] As each word appeared on the paper she became more invigorated. It was not long before her characters took over and dictated the direction of the story. She was hooked.

When she finished, she sent her story to the *Pacific Monthly*, a magazine started in Oregon in 1898 that printed articles on literature, culture, travel, and politics. She was overjoyed when they published her little piece, particularly as she shared space with several well-known and impressive writers like Leo Tolstoy, Jack London, and Sinclair Lewis, who also had written articles for the *Pacific Monthly*.[2] She loved the thrill of writing, it energized her and she delighted in moulding words into a meaningful structure. From this time on she was never far from her typewriter. She began submitting articles to highly respected magazines in Canada, then in Britain and the United States. Among her most popular pieces were travelogues about British Columbia, Alberta, and the Pacific Coast. Readers could not get enough of her stories about the red serge uniformed Royal North-West Mounted Police. The *London Daily Mail* in Middlesex, England, published a daily column authored by Cameron.

She was an avid reader and loved nothing better than to share her findings with others by sprinkling her publications with the occasional book review. She was her own best critic and meticulous in her editing, so it came as no surprise when she became editor of the *Educational Journal of Western Canada*, a professional periodical to which she regularly contributed educational articles. She also published in the *Coast*, an illustrated monthly printed in Seattle. Her articles appeared in many of the top literary magazines at the time. *Everybody's Magazine*, which supported writers like Jack London, Anton Chekhov, Edna Ferber, Rudyard Kipling, A. A. Milne, and Arthur Conan Doyle, added Cameron to its roster of frequently published authors. Coming out of New York, the magazine had a readership of over five hundred thousand people. By 1907 she added the *Saturday Evening Post* to her list. It was one of the most widely circulated magazines in America. The name Agnes Deans Cameron was already familiar fare in Canada, but by 1907 she had forged a bond with readers in the United States and in Great Britain. Canada—and especially her home city—was proud of the success of their homegrown daughter; her accomplishments were often noted in newspapers across the country. She soon joined the newly established Canadian Women's Press Club and became a member of the United Kingdom Institute of Journalists.

Her growing international fame showed Britain that Canada had come of age. Until this time Britain had only a passing interest in its far-flung colonies to the west, even though three-fourths of the population of Canada came from the motherland. Canada was the place to which Britain sent their wayfarers. They emptied their workhouses and their orphanages and gathered their unemployed, and put them on ships in the hope that they would disappear into an untamed and wild land where bears and cougars reigned.

Wealthy families who had difficult or malingering sons sent them to Canada and paid them to stay away. If Britons thought about Canada at all they viewed it as uncultured; a feral land filled with privations, a place fit only for the hardiest explorers. It was an image coaxed along by travel writers hoping to tell a good story.

Good writing equals good storytelling; Cameron understood this. But writers who pandered to false images about the country of her birth could expect to feel the shake of her retorts, even across the expanse of oceans. In 1903 London published a school geography and atlas in the *Canadian Gazette* that was to be used throughout the Empire. It was a popular publication particularly among university academics and students studying at Oxford and Cambridge. When Cameron picked up the latest edition, the seventh, she was shocked to find it full of misinformation. She immediately sent a letter of corrections to the High Commissioner for British Columbia in England, the Honourable J. H. Turner, who happened to be the past premier of British Columbia. He read her letter at a meeting of the Canada Club that was being held at the Albion Tavern in Aldergate, England. The group was shocked by the inaccuracies. Turner passed the letter on to the publishers of the *Gazette*. Mistakes abounded. Canada was described as a country of "frozen wastes and swamps," ignoring the fact that Canada was considered the granary of the Empire. Ontario and Quebec were called "Canada Proper," leaving the rest of Canada's propriety in doubt. There were no cities mentioned at all in Canada, presumably because they did not exist, and when describing British Columbia only four towns were mentioned as being of any standing: Victoria, New Westminster, Yale, and Hope, completely ignoring that Esquimalt was the naval base for the British Navy and that Vancouver, with a population of thirty-five thousand, was a lively city and an important seaport for international shipping. The publisher, Relfe Bros. Ltd., replied to Cameron with a feeble explanation that they had not revised the Canada section for many years.

"Madam—Our attention has been drawn to several inaccuracies in our School Geography and Atlas . . . Unfortunately, publishers are, to a great extent, in the hands of their authors with regard to bringing books up to date. The latter are supposed to embody all the latest alterations in every edition, but we regret that this was not done in the book in question, the Canadian portion of which has not been revised since the book was first written, several years ago . . . As you have placed the shortcomings of the book before the public in the press . . . we immediately promised to have the matter rectified upon its being brought to our notice by Lord Strathcona. An errata slip has been inserted in the edition just ready, and for the next issue the Canadian portion will be entirely rewritten."[3] Cameron was also in receipt of letters from high officials in both England and Canada thanking her for her attention and corrections.

Cameron also took the British media to task for sloppy journalism. Invention and false perception seemed to fuel much of the writing about Canada. Some errors were quite humorous, but sadly showed a lack of understanding of Canada. British newspapers reported, for example, that Quebec, New Brunswick, and Maine were states, mixing up two countries' borders. Manitoba was described as a treeless, icy wasteland, ignoring the 148,000 square kilometres of boreal forests that supported a rich habitat of coniferous and deciduous trees. There was no discussion about the southern Wheat Belt with its beautiful river valleys filled with elm, ash, and maples. The notion that Canada was a frozen hinterland held "in bondage by the iron grip of ice" was a hard one to shake. According to the British press, Canadians went about in sleighs that were drawn by dogs. It would have come as a surprise for Canadians to learn that their milk came in a solid state because of the cold. Any mention of Ottawa, the seat of government, was dispensed with as being insignificant despite the fact that it was a thriving city with a population of over eighty-six thousand people. Canadians took heart from Cameron's "corrections" and whenever such pronouncements came to light, Canadian newspapers would make a plea for Cameron to wield her remedial pen.

After the close of school in July 1904 Cameron, along with a few other teachers, boarded the Canadian Pacific Navigation Company's side-wheeler *Yosemite* for the four-and-a-half-hour trip to Vancouver. They were on their way to catch the Canadian Pacific to Winnipeg to attend the Dominion Teachers Convention. Cameron was to give a talk on the unique and important relationship between parents and teachers. They spent a wonderful three days aboard the train watching the magnificent scenery speed by, and enjoying afternoon cups of tea, sharing confidences, and playing whist. When they stepped off the train in Winnipeg they were met with a loud clapping thunderstorm.

Undaunted by the sheets of rain that poured down upon them, the women were in high spirits and looking forward to the four-day conference. It was the fifth time that teachers, educational administrators, and university educators from across the Dominion had come together to meet and exchange the latest ideas in education. The Dominion Educational Association began in 1891 by teachers eager to advance the status of education. This year's conference offered a wonderful roster of interesting presentations. There were papers on the status of the newly added manual training schools, the influence of kindergarten on children's future learning, music programs, and physical training classes. Participants listened to discussions on the commercial aspects of education, the relationship between education and social progress, and other issues such as home study, teacher training, and the place of school inspection as an agency in public education.

Cameron was to present her paper on Wednesday in Assembly Hall, in the newly built Somerset School on Nena Street (now Sherbrook Street). As most presentations did not start until two o'clock she was able to slip out and visit the Winnipeg Fair. The fair was quite a different experience from the serious academic discussions heard at the conference. There were vendors selling lemonade, Coney Island frankfurters, popcorn, peanuts, and candy. There was a six-legged calf, and pen after pen of baby lambs, fat pigs, plucky chickens, and spirited horses. One of the highlights of the fair was the display of the Ivanhoe electric car belonging to the Canada Cycle and Motor Co. It was a two-passenger open runabout that would look quite nice touring down Fort Street in Victoria. Mademoiselle Adgie, who was locked in an enclosure with snarling lions, held Cameron spellbound; then there was the man who dove from a high platform into a small, shallow pool. "We deprecate the practice of needless life-risking, and cheerfully pay our quarter to perpetuate it," she wrote in an article she published about the fair.[4] She passed by the Turkish dancers that were advertised as "Rich, Rare and Racy: Hot, Juicy and Spicy!" She noted the cleverness with which vendors vied for attention.

The following year, 1905, was set to be an extraordinary one. Captain Amundsen piloted his ship, the *Gjøa*, through the Northwest Passage, and the Ottawa Silver Sevens trounced the Dawson City Nuggets twenty-three to two to win the Stanley Cup, but only because it took the Dawson City Nuggets an exhausting month of travelling by dogsled, ship, and train to get to Ottawa. Farmers were experiencing abundance in their crops, industry was thriving, there was an increase in international trade, and workers were optimistic about the new jobs in mining and fishing. Canada added two new provinces, Alberta and Saskatchewan, increasing its domain to include ten provinces and the Northwest Territories. Technology was increasing its pace with ground-breaking inventions; Albert Einstein introduced his theory of relativity, Orville and Wilbur Wright's Flyer III flew for thirty-eight kilometres, and the first steamer propelled by turbine engines revolutionized marine transportation.

It was also promising to be a good year for Cameron. For any passing her house on Birdcage Walk, the sound of a typewriter clacking away became familiar fare. Paper seemed to fly off the carriage of her typewriter. She published a book review of Vincent Harper's novel, *The Mortgage on the Brain*, a work of science fiction that advanced the view of moral responsibility over religiosity. She wrote about the one hundredth anniversary of the British Naval victory at Trafalgar. And she continued with her many speaking engagements, entertaining her audiences with humorous recitations that often brought forth roars of laughter. In April she had an article, "Humour in School," printed in the *Century Magazine*, a monthly publication known for attracting well-known writers. Her accomplishment was lauded in the paper: "This is perhaps the highest point Miss Cameron has yet touched in placing her stories, the *Century* being considered one of the best, if not the best of all the American magazines."[5] Victoria was now on the map as a literary centre.

Chapter Nine

A LONG ORDEAL

Now, I fight in the open and if, after twenty-five years'
service, I am to be killed, I prefer to be killed in the open.

— AGNES DEANS CAMERON

In November 1905, Cameron was fired from her teaching position.
She was stunned; her faculty as well as her students did not understand—no one did, not even Cameron herself. The path that led to
her dismissal began innocently enough. Near the end of the school
year, in June, those wishing to continue their studies at the high
school level had to sit for their entrance exams. The exams were
difficult. There were eleven subjects to complete and each exam
took between one and two hours. The first subject the students
had to tackle was English literature and last two were drawing and
nature. By the time her students came to the drawing part of their
exam they were exhausted, as they had been writing for several
days. It didn't seem possible for any of them to cram one more

bit of information into their brains. Their neural networks were in need of a rest, but their chance to attend high school depended on their perseverance. They were well aware of the fact that thirty-five percent of those taking the examinations usually failed. They needed to be sharp; the pressure was on. They had only to complete the drawing exercises and the nature exercises and they would be finished. They felt optimistic; they had studied drawing with Miss Fraser, a well-liked and very experienced teacher who had been teaching drawing to the senior grades for the past eight years. She had a bachelor of arts and science degree from Queen's University in Kingston and had taken the drawing examination at the British Royal Academy. She was also present at the examinations as their supervisor.

There were two parts to the drawing exam—a model drawing and a scale drawing. Miss Fraser had drilled into her students the importance of presenting a neat and tidy exam paper. South Park School had received a favourable report the previous year on their drawing results from the examiner, so they felt they were on the right track. When Miss Fraser told them to begin, each student took their newly sharpened pencil and carefully wrote their name and that of their school in the upper right-hand corner of the test paper. They had two hours to complete both parts of the test. According to the instructions the drawings were to be freehand, which meant that ruling was not allowed. Miss Fraser did tell her students that it was permissible to rule the datum line, which they could use as a base or line of reference. The first part of the test was a scale drawing that resembled a freestanding notice board. It included triangles and rectangles in various lengths and proportions. They had to draw a freehand, dimensioned sketch of the diagram according to a specified scale. When they completed their sketch they moved on to the second part of the exam, which dealt with a series of models. The instructions to the candidates required the students make a freehand drawing from a model that was provided by the teachers. The instructions specifically stated that no ruling was allowed. The drawing should be between twelve and fifteen centimetres across the longest side. Miss Fraser placed the objects around the room so students could get different perspectives on the models. They were allowed to use their pencils held at arm's length between the eye and the model to estimate proportion. The bases had to be parallel to each other and the radius and axis in alignment. There was no room for interpretation on the drawings.

Drawing was first introduced into the school curriculum in 1872 but was not a required course until 1894. It was not a particularly popular subject with most schools in the province. Many teachers saw it as a waste, crowding out time and space for the more important academic subjects. But the superintendent of education and some of the school trustees saw it as a natural corollary to the new technologies. If students could be trained in technical drawing and the use of line diagrams for schematics, it was thought that their chances of finding work would be easier.

David Blair, the examiner for the drawing portion of the tests, had a reputation for being uncompromising and exacting in his approach to drawing. He was passionate about art, not as an artistic or aesthetic endeavour, but as a practical and technical course of study. He had personally designed the drawing program for the British Columbia school systems. Blair had an impressive curriculum vita and appeared to be well versed in technical drawing. He was an alumnus of the South Kensington National Art Training School in England, a school whose focus was on mechanical and architectural drawing. Upon graduation, he became an examiner for the school's art department and was the headmaster of the Islington School of Art in London. He then spent eighteen years in New Zealand. He first worked in Christchurch, where he opened the Canterbury College School of Art. His emphasis on the mechanical aspects of drawing over the artistic point of view was not particularly attractive to the artistic liberalism that was in favour in Christchurch, so he left to teach at Wanganui Technical School. He spent the next thirteen years teaching and revising New Zealand's elementary school drawing program and producing drawing books to be used by the schools. He was not well liked in New Zealand. His books were very unpopular with teachers and drew vigorous protests across the country. Teachers and administrators found him difficult to work with. He was considered overbearing and not a person who worked particularly well with others of differing opinions; a personality trait that would eventually set Cameron and Blair in a nasty contest of wills. Teachers felt that drawing was a program that was foisted upon them without sufficient training, and that it did not significantly contribute to a well-rounded education.

New Zealand and Blair parted company. After a concerted effort looking for a job in another country, he received an offer to teach theoretical and practical drawing in Vancouver, British Columbia. He initially began giving talks at Teachers' Institute meetings about the importance of geometrical and freehand drawing. A year after his arrival, in 1902, he published a series of workbooks authorized by the Council of Public Instruction of British Columbia titled *Blair's Canadian Drawing Series*. His books focused solely on training the hand and eye to replicate mechanical drawings. He did not approve of art education for the sake of aesthetics. Many of the teachers did not understand or like the curriculum of drawing that he developed. They found his program confusing and archaic, one geared toward creating copiers and not thinkers. Blair believed that self-expression was not the point of learning to draw so there was to be no room for interpretation in the drawings. It was not long before Blair became as unpopular in British Columbia as he had been in New Zealand. Despite this he eventually became the science art master for the province as well as the examiner for the high school entrance exams in drawing for the province.

Despite Blair's best efforts, the weakest link in the curriculum was the drawing program. Most students across the province seemed to struggle with the precision demanded for technical drawing, which was duly acknowledged in the Public Schools Report for 1903–1904. The results of the drawing books submitted across the province for that year attested not only to the difficulty in understanding the instructions, but also to a lack of skill and commitment in the teachers. The Superintendent of Victoria City Schools, F. H. Eaton, wrote that the teaching of drawing and nature was woefully inadequate and could not meet the requirements posed by the examination. Over seventy-three percent of the work submitted to the examiner was unacceptable. Blair did recognize that only one to five percent of the teachers in British Columbia were qualified to teach drawing. Fortunately for the students of South Park School, Miss Fraser was one of those teachers.

Miss Fraser was a very conscientious teacher and knew of Mr. Blair's penchant for exactness. She had attended his lectures and carefully read the circulars that came from his office instructing teachers on the art of drawing. She even talked to him on several occasions to try to get a better understanding of his methods. However, like the teachers in New Zealand, she too thought that the highly technical aspects associated with Blair's techniques were unnecessarily complicated and a waste of time. To her credit she worked hard at perfecting the Blair system and tried to follow the program as best she could. She did share his opinion that it was important for the students to have their drawings as near perfect as possible. In the main, Blair's drawing program was a system that set students up for failure. The perfection and accuracy demanded by him was not possible to accomplish without ruling. To understand perspective and space is one thing, but to accurately draw it was quite another.

In any case, the exigencies of the drawing curriculum and surrounding politics were of no consequence to the students. What was important to them was passing their exams. They needed to obtain a grade of thirty-four percent to pass each subject, but a mark of fifty percent overall. Simply getting the base amount of points would not be enough for a pass. As time ticked by Fraser and Cameron walked up and down the aisles watching over their charges, making sure no one was cheating. Even with such scrutiny students can be very inventive when it comes to deception. There was a myriad of ways to cheat. One clever lad ran his fingers along the side of his paper using the straight edge as a guide. It gave him the perfect straight line. Neither teacher saw any indication of cheating, for if they had the offending student would not have gone unpunished. At the end of the two hours Miss Fraser instructed the candidates that the exam was over and to immediately put down their pencils and she would come around and collect their papers. Each hoped that they would be going on to high school in September. The drawing exams were certified and signed by both Fraser and Cameron and then sent to the examiner, along with the drawing exercises each student had worked on during the year. Mable Booz was proud of the fact that she could sketch a very straight line. Thomas Briggs ruled the datum line but felt positive about the quality of his drawings, as did Sidney Wilson who was one of the better scholastic students. Anton Henderson was pleased with his performance and felt he did well in the drawing test.

David Blair sat comfortably in his office surrounded by examination papers and drawing books from the aspiring high school entrants. After many lectures and notices sent to the schools throughout the province he felt this year, 1905, would be the one that showed that his drawing program was finally on its way to success. Yes, he was demanding and rigid, but that made for successful students, he reasoned. His position had not come easily for him. After being driven out of the New Zealand school system he had to wait nearly two years before he found a job that accorded him the status that he sought. He was fifty-four years of age and was no longer in a situation to find another posting, but he was confident that the teachers here had finally understood the logic of his methods. He and his wife had made the right choice in coming to British Columbia, he told himself. It was a good fit.

Blair looked at the pile of exams and the accompanying books on his desk and picked the first one up to begin the lengthy process of evaluating the drawings. The more he looked the angrier he got. He was shocked with what he was finding. It was becoming obvious that the students had not grasped the idea of proportion and worse, booklet after booklet showed evidence of ruling. This was shaping up to be another disaster. The models looked as if they had been drawn from a copy on the blackboard, not from a three-dimensional object as required. Sometimes a student would rule a line and then try to disguise it by drawing over it freehand or they would use the rough edge of the paper as their guide. He suspected that teachers were deliberately ignoring his directions. At first he was furious, then he became anxious. What was the problem with the teachers? How many times had he told them that rulers were not to be used? Could they not see the importance of what he was trying to accomplish? It seemed like a repeat of New Zealand all over again. He could not, would not let that happen. The idea that his instructions and exercises might not have been clear or valid would not have occurred to him. His intransigence would not allow him that insight.

When the exams and student workbooks were assessed, he found the worst offending schools were Strathcona and Mount Pleasant in Vancouver, and North Ward and South Park in Victoria. In particular, he said, the students from Strathcona had deliberately attempted to hide their ruling and there was evidence of ruling on every drawing. It was imperative to drive home the necessity of careful supervision over students' work and the importance of seeing that the work was done according to his instructions. He decided that the teachers needed a lesson in following directives. He could not do this alone; he needed backup. He asked for a meeting of the eight members of the examining board. Some had knowledge of drawing and others did not, but after looking over some of the papers they agreed that ruling had taken place. In a unanimous decision, they decreed that no marks should be given for any of the workbooks from the four schools. Alexander Robinson, the superintendent of education, was subsequently informed of the recommendation of the committee and was sent the drawing books for his assessment. The decision to discount the drawing books stood, but to make the situation palatable Robinson decided to allow thirty-four and one-third marks to any student whose aggregate marks totalled five hundred and sixteen, which added seven more students to the register of those who passed.[1] After taking everything into account they agreed it was a fair outcome considering the results.

It was not until late July when Cameron received the list with the marks of those who had taken the exam. The students from South Park School did not do well in the drawing part of their exams. Only three received the minimum thirty-three and one-third percent needed to pass that part of the exam. Their class average for the exam was twenty-six percent, a very poor showing. Cameron was perplexed, as the previous year South Park had been one of the schools singled out as doing an acceptable job of teaching drawing. In fact, in the previous year's annual report on the status of education in the province, South Park School had received satisfactory comments on their drawing program. Feeling as unsettled as the gloomy July weather, she wrote a letter to the superintendent of education. Robinson and Cameron reportedly did not get on well together, but she respected his office. In her letter, she politely asked why the students had received such low marks. "During the term just closed very special attention has been given to this subject, I would ask you to kindly give me some idea of the point in which we have failed."[2]

Robinson responded to her inquiry by return mail explaining that marks had been allowed on the exam portion of drawing, but that the drawing books showed evidence of ruling. Dumbfounded, she went to her typewriter and wrote her response; every keystroke was imbued with emotion. "In addition I would state that instruction in drawing for the school term just ended has been given under my personal direction and of my own knowledge I testify that the work has been honestly and fairly done.

"This information I intended to convey by my endorsation of the individual books submitted. Kindly let me know what steps our department intends to take in the matter."[3]

Cameron also included a letter written by Miss Fraser, who explained that she had diligently overseen the drawing books and had followed Mr. Blair's directions punctiliously. She asserted that no ruling or construction lines or any other lines other than the datum line had been used: "I gave strict supervision to these books and it is my conviction that the work of the class was done honestly and in accordance with the printed directions."[4] Robinson was not convinced by the teachers' arguments. Cameron then went to the minister of education, Mr. Fulton, and protested against the actions of the Department of Education. Was there perhaps any possibility that the students might have used a ruler in drawing their lines without her knowledge? he asked. No, she replied, the work had been done under her supervision. He then offered to look at the examinations himself.

It was to be the beginning of a very long and increasingly heated ordeal for Cameron, Robinson, the school board, and the school trustees. Every teacher in the province would take note of the fracas; their teaching certificates depended upon careful attention to the process and outcome of the ensuing tussle. Also, their students' futures were at stake. No teacher wanted their students held back because they did not agree with the Blair system of drawing. Cameron rolled up her sleeves, dug in her heels, and prepared for battle, the likes of which would merit multicolumn daily newsprint that shared space equally with the country's most pressing national issues. The fact that she was after justice for her students was natural, but were her actions and efforts misplaced? Was she perhaps reacting more to Blair's and Robinson's effrontery? She said that if she had not fought for her students she would have never been able to live with herself, but she also did not like Blair or Robinson.

She wrote another letter to Robinson with what she thought was the perfect solution. She agreed that if some of the children had ruled their drawings they should be punished accordingly. "That is just," she said. "But it is also just that pupils who have conscientiously carried out instructions and put in fair work should be exonerated from the charge of dishonesty, and of these South Park has an overwhelming majority . . . I ask that the last South Park entrance class be gathered together, that new No. 4 drawing books be given them, that the drawings in dispute (seven in number) be drawn again under Miss Fraser's tuition and my supervision: and as my word regarding the honesty of the class is not convincing to the Department of Education, I would ask for a committee of impeccable character to see that no ruling is done. The finished drawings can then be compared with those already handed in and a conclusion arrived at."[5] Her reasoning was that the drawings could be compared with what the children had previously handed in to ascertain validity in the matter. Her appeal was quickly dispensed with. She then met with Robinson to ask that she be allowed to inspect the books herself. The angrier she got the more forceful she became, and the meeting erupted in an argument between the two, with accusations being fired from both parties. In exasperation, she said to Robinson that if the superintendent thought that she and Miss Fraser were knowingly untruthful then she would have more respect for him if he cancelled their teaching certificates. Robinson made it very clear to her that if she persisted in defending the children and asking for new testing then indeed she would lose her job and her certificate. It was obvious that there was to be no negotiations. She left the meeting shaken.

It seemed to her that she was being pilloried with a constant barrage of defamatory statements. She began to question her motives. Am I "a deep-dyed villain and didn't know it," she wondered.[6] It would be easier, she told herself, just to give in and say that Blair was correct; the three other schools involved had done just that and were released from any further investigation. On the other hand, she believed it was no small issue to accuse twenty-nine children of dishonesty and condemn them unheard. She was well aware that this case was being closely watched throughout the country. After much soul searching and conferring with others, she decided that while it would be easier for her to acquiesce to Blair's assessment she would continue her fight for the children. She was deeply concerned about the threatened loss of her job and of her teaching certificate but, as she said, "Had this frightened me, in my own opinion, I would have been unworthy to retain either."[7]

The school trustees and superintendent of education should not have been surprised that Cameron fought back. Human nature dictates that when one party sets an adversarial tone, all future interactions will be difficult and combative. The more they questioned Cameron's integrity and that of her students and her drawing teacher, the less likely there would be a negotiated settlement. Trying to get ahead of Cameron on this issue the trustees approached Miss Fraser, who they surmised was more easily intimidated. They pressured her to drop the issue. She could redeem herself, they told her, if she would get Cameron to abandon her current course of action. Miss Fraser said that she too would be happy to see the matter resolved, and though she thought there was cause from both sides, she explained that she and Cameron were fighting the injustice of charges made against the pupils and the teachers. In her opinion focus should have been on the specific marks the students received, not on fanning the flames of discontent by defaming their integrity and hurling personal attacks on the teachers and the students.

According to Cameron, Robinson then told her to have the children sign an affidavit attesting to their truthfulness, the logic of which does not ring true. In any case, he later denied any such request in court. Cameron said she complied with his directive and wrote out the affidavits for the children to sign. She thought it a good idea to have this information before the children scattered for their summer holidays and while it was fresh in their minds. Most of the children swore that they did not rule except for the lines that divided the printed exercise copy from their drawing, so as to separate one from the other. Sixteen children signed the affidavits and two wrote separate letters attesting to their innocence. She then gave them in trust to Mr. Pierson, a notary in the city.

Once the school trustees learned of the affidavits they demanded that Cameron turn them over to them; she politely declined. She was distrustful of the trustees and concerned that they might destroy the affidavits, which one of the trustees later admitted was their intent. It would certainly help in their case against her if they were destroyed. A tug of war ensued. They belonged to the children and were taken in their interest, she told them. She did win a small victory when legal opinion determined that the trustees had no legal or moral right to the declarations.

Her next move was to approach the minister of education, the Honourable Mr. Fulton, to ask that he look at the workbooks. It was not an unreasonable request, he said, and agreed to examine at least a few of the books personally. He concluded that many of the books showed evidence of ruling. He decided to bring in a group of people who could offer an unbiased and professional opinion, two of whom had extensive experience in detailed technical drawings. One was the surveyor general of British Columbia and the other a bridge draftsman with the Department of Lands and Works. There was no doubt in their minds that rulers had been used in many of the books. This was not the outcome Fulton had hoped for. Looking for an amicable resolution, Fulton asked Cameron if it was possible that the children had used rulers without her knowledge.

On Monday, the thirteenth of November, six men and one woman, Mrs. Margaret Jenkins, gathered for their regular meeting of the Board of School Trustees. Mr. Boggs, the chairman, brought the meeting to order while Miss Macdonald, the assistant secretary,

The view today of the street on Birdcage Walk where Agnes Deans Cameron lived. *Photo by author.*

Top: Cameron family, Michigan Street [187?]. Courtesy of City of Victoria Archives, M07345. Bottom: Angela College as seen today. *Photo by author.*

The young teacher. Maynard, Hannah, photographer. *Courtesy of City of Vancouver Archives, CVA 1477-646.*

Top: First female teacher at Victoria High School, 1891 (Agnes Deans Cameron far left). *Courtesy of Victoria High School Archives.* Bottom: South Park School as seen today. *Photo by author.*

Agnes Deans Cameron portrait. *Courtesy of Victoria High School Archives.*

Top: CPR Depot, Winnipeg, Manitoba. *Courtesy of Winnipeg Public Library, WP0805*. Bottom: Deer Lodge Hotel. *Courtesy Winnipeg Public Library, WP0567*.

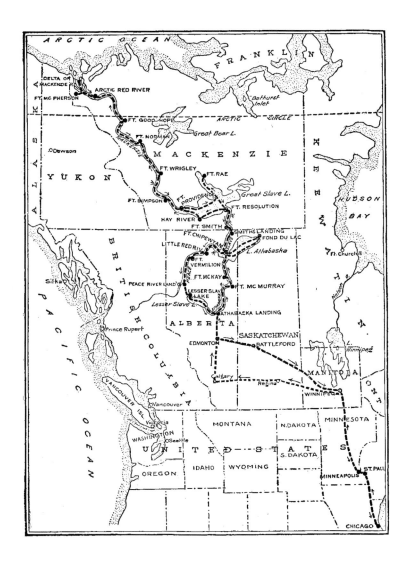

Map of Agnes Deans Cameron's route to the Arctic and back. *Courtesy of the Legislative Library of British Columbia.*

Top: Cameron's family church, St. Andrew's Presbyterian Church, in Victoria, BC. *Photo by author.* Bottom: Steamer *Mackenzie River* and dogs, 1908. *Courtesy of City of Victoria Archives, M07362.*

Top: The day's work. *Courtesy of City of Victoria Archives, M07366.* Bottom: School teachers at South Park School, Agnes Deans Cameron far right. *Courtesy of City of Victoria Archives, M09491.*

Top: Here and there a lusty trout and here and there a grayling. Great Slave Lake. *Courtesy of City of Victoria Archives, M05825.* Bottom: Luncheon on the *Mee-wah-sin. Courtesy of City of Victoria Archives, M07373.*

Agnes Deans Cameron holding an infant during the Mackenzie River
Expedition, 1908. *Courtesy of City of Victoria Archives, M07353.*

Top: Our camp on the Peace (Agnes Deans Cameron and Jessie Brown at camp at Peace River, Alberta), 1908. *Courtesy of City of Victoria Archives, M10136.* Bottom: Our premier moose. *Courtesy of City of Victoria Archives, M06473.*

Agnes Deans Cameron, 1910. *Courtesy of the Royal BC Museum and Archives, G-04056.*

Cartoon on front page of the *Victoria Times*, September 1, 1909. *Courtesy of the* Times Colonist.

Agnes Deans Cameron and Jessie Brown collecting flowers in the ruins of Fort
McLeod. *Courtesy of City of Victoria Archives, M05824.*

Agnes Deans Cameron and Jessie Brown inside Hudson's Bay Company house at Fort Vermilion. *Courtesy of City of Victoria Archives, M07384.*

sat off to the side taking notes. The most important item on their agenda was the question of the drawing books. It was an intense meeting; their remarks about the issue and the unrepentant teacher were pointed. It was clear that they were upset and extremely displeased that Cameron had taken the case to the newspapers. It was fast becoming a scandal and with an election just a few months away, it made them look as if they had lost control. The trustees of course wanted to get re-elected. Each one of them was cognizant of the fact that Cameron was a very popular teacher, reputed to be the best one in the province. They also knew that as a director of the very prestigious Dominion Educational Board, the only woman to hold that position, she was highly regarded and well respected in her profession throughout the country. They had to tread carefully, but their animosity toward her made that difficult. From their point of view they had an unruly teacher who did not bend easily to their will; she always insisted on doing things her way. They were the ones elected, they affirmed, not her. Besides, they reasoned, how can children learn obedience if their teachers are disobedient?

The school trustees had been looking for some time for an excuse to rid themselves of this pesky woman. The drawing books provided them with the perfect opportunity to put their plan into action. They came to the unanimous decision that Cameron had to go. Transcribing the resolution, Miss Macdonald carefully wrote that as of December 15 the services of Miss Agnes Deans Cameron as principal of the South Park School would be dispensed with. They had done it. The ruling in the issue of the drawing books was so blatant, they thought, that there would be no cause for the public to rally to her support. They assured themselves that this time they held the trump card. Cameron was dismissed for insubordination and was given only thirty days' notice to clear her desk. In the whole history of teaching in British Columbia only two teachers had ever been given such a short notice: one was for a charge of indecency and another for insubordination.

In the years to come, long after Cameron's firing, teachers could still be fired with only thirty days' notice, and if they wished to give notice, for whatever reason, they could not leave until the end of the year otherwise their salary would be reduced. It was all part of the McBride Conservative Government's promise to stabilize the economy and cut spending by rationalizing education. Schools were to be organized more like a business enterprise. School boards were given more power and in the process teachers' rights were constrained. Although his policies were in their infancy at the time of her dismissal, Cameron certainly felt the sting and confusion of that early restructuring.

Not only was Cameron summarily dismissed, but her teaching certificate was suspended for a period of three years. That edict, in effect, hobbled her ability to earn a decent living. It not only punished Cameron, but also affected the standard of living for both her mother and her sister Jessie, who depended upon her income for their support. She was distraught and sought council from her many friends.

By Friday, November 17, a petition was already circulating asking for her reinstatement. Many of the notables of the city signed the petition, people whose names today grace many of British Columbia's towns, streets, and landmarks, like the Honourable John Sebastian Helmcken, Charles E. Redfern, F. B. Pemberton, Lindley Crease, the Reverend J. H. Sweet, archbishop of Victoria, and the Right Reverend Bishop Cridge. The petition was sent to the Board of School Trustees along with a letter that read, "We the undersigned, petition your honourable body to reinstate Miss Agnes Deans Cameron as principal of the South Park School forthwith. We refrain from commenting upon the reason you gave for dismissing her, also our reason for wishing her reinstated. Her not only local but national reputation as an educationalist is so well known that we would not insult the lady by offering you an ordinary explanation, but simply ask you to reinstate her."[8]

The shocking story of the firing of the city's most popular teacher was the major topic of conversation around town. In shops and on the street people were saying that "it was unfair," "the school trustees acted in haste," "they had been out to get her for some time." More petitions were to come. Anyone who wanted to protest her firing could go into Hibben's Book and Stationery Store.[9] Hibben's was centrally located in the shopping district and served as a gathering place for the men of the city to meet and discuss politics, sports, business, or other issues of significance in the news. People lined up in a steady stream to sign their name for the reinstatement of their favourite teacher.

Fearful that they were losing public support, the Board of School Trustees called a special meeting for Monday, November 20, 1905, at five in the afternoon. They met in the school board office to discuss ways to garner support for their side of the story. It was a very quick meeting. They drew up a simple statement declaring that Cameron was fired for failing to surrender the students' affidavits. There were other reasons, they said, but they did not consider it necessary to state them at this time. To deflect any negativity away from them they decided to send the matter to a judicial inquiry. They were confident that once the public was apprised of the facts they would agree that the board had no choice but to let her go. Just eight days after that meeting the minister in charge of the Department of Education asked the premier of the province, the Honourable Richard McBride, to request the Lieutenant-Governor of British Columbia establish a commission to enquire into the matter of the drawing books submitted by the pupils of South Park School. It was to be adjudicated by His Honour Peter Secord Lampman, Judge of the County Court of Victoria.

Cameron and her supporters were aghast. "Now, I fight in the open," she said, "and if, after twenty-five years' service, I am to be killed, I prefer to be killed in the open," which was just what the board was afraid of. Alluding to the recent civil unrest in Russia, she went on to say, "If this really is a 'Western outpost of Empire,' and not a little bit of St. Petersburg crept by mistake into the map of Canada, I ask that the trustees call a public meeting and state to the public, whom they and I alike serve, what the other sins are of which I am guilty."[10]

The media went into full gear and began reporting daily on the issue. The school board requested that all newsprint feature their side of the story too, instead of constantly showing favour to Cameron. Readers found the story riveting. People were not only genuinely interested in the facts, but they also served as a relief from the emotionally wrenching headlines about the Russo–Japanese War, the pogroms against the Jews in Odessa, and the beginnings of the Russian Revolution. The story was so popular with readers that it even superseded interest in the Stanley Cup, as well as the saga of the pet boa constrictor that got loose and ate someone's rabbit.

While Cameron was fighting to keep her job and her teaching certificate, she was also working to save her house from the wrecking ball. The City of Victoria had approved an expenditure of 4,865 dollars to extend Birdcage Walk through to Toronto Street. Her house was in the corridor slated to be demolished. The city had been chipping away at the pioneer houses for some time. The Cameron house was now the oldest in the city, having been constructed in 1860 by her late father. Their back garden was well known throughout Victoria for its lush and delicious apples. It was sadly the last remaining orchard in the city. Even their three-and-a-half-metre prickly Oregon grape tree, reputed to be the tallest in British Columbia, failed to daunt the "improvements." Cameron had lived in that house since her birth and her mother, who was eighty-four at the time, did not want to leave the home that she and her husband had built so many years before. Try as Cameron might her pleas went unheard.

Because the house was such a well-known landmark, the media sent a reporter to interview Cameron's mother. Despite the impending loss of her home, the reporter found Jessie sitting in the parlour contently knitting a sock, as if life would continue as before. Never one to let much get her down, she cheerfully relayed the history of the house and the neighbourhood. When they built the house, she said, Birdcage Walk went as far as Superior Street. Behind them, she explained, was a large cluster of Garry oak trees and across the street from their house was a snarl of blackberry bushes that provided them with the sweetest-tasting blackberries every August. In those early days a pine forest surrounded them and was an excellent place for hunting birds and deer. It is where her husband used to go to bring home a bird or two for supper. She told the reporter that she used to watch as Lekwungen hunters cleverly dug deer pits in the forest to capture various animals for food. Despite her calm demeanour, she said it was going to be hard to leave the house that she had spent the better part of her life in along with the memories that she and her family had built up over the years. Cameron began looking for other living arrangements for the family. They could move in with relatives, but for three independent women that was not the most ideal situation.

The case against Cameron continued. The gravity of a public inquiry was very much on her mind. She knew that she could no longer fight this on her own. She reached out to Richard Thomas Elliott, a prominent lawyer in the city with the law firm Higgins and Elliott. She hoped he would represent her. With Elliott at the helm, she thought, she would have a good chance of winning her case. Her first meeting with him was at his office at the Law Chambers in Bastion Square. As she walked through the city to meet with Elliott she was oblivious to her surroundings but she couldn't help notice the Palms, a lovely new tea and coffee house that had recently opened on Fort Street. She remembered reading that it was reported to be the prettiest tearoom in the Pacific Northwest. It was certainly inviting with its ornate wall fresco, luminous veils of soft brown draperies, and small tables set with dainty teacups and fresh flowers. Maybe when this was all over she could sit down and enjoy a cup of deliciously scented tea with friends. Elliott was aware of the matter at hand and listened carefully to Cameron. He would take her case but forewarned her that it was not going to be easy to win. His best defense, he told her, would be to raise the anomalies in the instructions given by Blair, point out the weaknesses and inconsistencies in the Blair method of drawing, and have each of the children present their story to the court.

Chapter Ten

A ROYAL COMMISSION

I was present at the investigation, and I am
absolutely satisfied that this woman was most
grievously and most cruelly wronged.

—MR. HAWTHORNTHWAITE, BC MLA, 1908

The inquiry was set to begin on Friday, December 15, 1905. That day started early for Cameron. It was cloudy but mild and butterflies were flitting about the garden. She thought it an unusual sight, so near to Christmas. The shops in town were gearing up for another holiday season, but twinkling lights, Swiss chocolates, sweet meats, and fat turkeys were far from her mind. She was in a very sombre mood. This was her last day as a teacher and principal at South Park School. A group of the boys from her school wished to show their support for their principal and took a British Blue Ensign, which they had previously won in a drill team competition, reversed the Jack and raised the flag at half-mast. It stayed that way for the remainder of the day.

As Cameron entered Bastion Square, the location of the courthouse, she was enveloped by the scent of the ocean as it wafted through the quadrangle. There was a dampness in the air reminding any who cared to notice that Victoria had a maritime climate. Bastion Square was rich in history. Cameron might not have remembered that this area was once part of Fort Victoria, for it was torn down when she was just four years old. It was on this site that the Hudson's Bay Company had run their Pacific coast empire expeditions. The square had once seen traders bartering for furs and whale oil, all hoping to get the best price before shipping their goods to foreign ports, but there was also a sinister undertone to Bastion Square. The courthouse opened out onto the site of the old jail, where people gathered in the 1860s to watch hangings in the public square. Some of the bodies had remained unclaimed and were buried in the yard, their graves lying underneath the foundation of the courthouse. Rattling chains have been heard and illusory emanations have been seen floating in and among the buildings. It has been said their spirits are troubled and are unable to rest. In 1905, however, Bastion Square had become the economic core of the city. It was where barristers, architects, accountants, and financial moguls had their offices. Just a few steps from the courthouse, Burnes Hotel, a popular Italianate-style luxury inn, pandered to wealthy clientele. With its assortment of late Victorian and early Edwardian architecture, Bastion Square presented a modern progressive look to the city.

When Cameron walked through the dramatic arched entrance and into the notable, castle-like courthouse the ghosts were not active, or if they were no one took any notice. Facing her was an exquisite, ornate gilded birdcage-style elevator that would take her up to the third floor to where her case was being heard. The intricately entwined grillwork was not unlike her case, which was similarly entangled. It was a strange coincidence that her fate would be decided in a building that had been designed by the same architect who built South Park School. When Cameron walked into the courtroom the dark panelled walls smelled faintly of beeswax. The wide planked floors rested heavily with the weighty issues that trod upon its timbers. It was a busy day; barristers were coming and going. William Reid, a former bartender of the old Delmonico Saloon, was charged with stealing ninety-five dollars from an R. Oday, and a young boy, Douglas McGeary, was to answer to the accusation that he illegally shot two hen pheasants. The police court was filled with seven well-known and respected barristers who were in arrears for not paying a ten-dollar city tax that had been recently instituted. They were arguing that the bylaw was *ultra vires*; they would rather go to jail than pay.

The courtroom was packed with teachers, school administrators, newspaper reporters, and a substantial assemblage of students from South Park School. Cameron sat quietly with an air of composed determination. Everything she had worked for, her professionalism, her integrity, and the person she had become, hung in the balance. She would have her say and hoped to be finally vindicated. His Honour Judge Lampman was the adjudicator. Also present were Mr. D. M. Eberts, KC, lawyer for the Council of Public Instruction; Col. F. B. Gregory, representing the Board of School Trustees; and Mr. Elliott, counsel for Cameron. All letters written concerning the case, copies of newsprint, reports of school trustee meetings, fifteen affidavits, twenty-nine drawing books, copies of circulars written by Blair, and Blair's annual report about the status of drawing in the province's schools were surrendered to Lampman.

Peter Secord Lampman was fairly new to his position. He was appointed Judge of the County Court of Victoria as well as Judge of the Supreme Court of British Columbia on June 14, 1905, just six months prior to hearing the South Park Drawing Book case. He was not without experience. He was a partner in George E. Powell and Lampman and was an extremely popular and well-respected barrister. He held the position of Secretary of the Law Society of British Columbia and was judge of the small debts court. He had received accolades for his judicial grasp of the evidence as a commissioner, enquiring into the cause of the devastating explosions that took over one hundred lives in the early evening on May 23, 1901, at the Crowsnest Pass coal mine in Fernie, British Columbia. He was on friendly terms with Cameron's lawyer. In fact, he had invited Elliott to his very elegant society wedding to Miss Cecilia Maud Prior in 1901. It was likely that he knew Cameron as well, as he raced in the Victoria/Sidney bike races at the same time Cameron was racing. He was a fair judge but was very much his own person. He would not be swayed by friendship or feelings of empathy and was not afraid to go against popular opinion. He would get to the heart of the issue and render an impartial verdict.

And so the hearing began. Mr. Eberts spent the first day laying out the facts of the case. On the second day Blair was put on the stand. In his cross-examination Mr. Elliott made the point that Blair's instructions were unclear and the exercises in his drawing book series were confusing in that students were supposed to use a ruler while lining in the first three books. Elliott posed a question to Blair saying, "When the pupils reach the fourth book, do they not recollect the way in which they did the previous examples? . . . Will they not retain the same ideas as to the way in which the copy should be made?"[1] In response Blair said that students are not supposed to think for themselves, why else have teachers, he quipped. "If the teachers have common sense they will show the pupils how the copies are to be made."[2] Throughout the hearings Elliott continued to pick apart the inconsistencies of Blair's instructions as well as the validity and reliability of the drawing book exercises. He also pressed the point that the examiners had not given Cameron a chance to be heard. In questioning the Honourable F. J. Fulton, the minister of education, Elliott asked, "As a barrister is it not your opinion that it is an axiom that no one shall be condemned unheard?" Fulton's response was a clear "yes."

Elliott continued, "Did you not condemn her unheard?" Fulton stated that the books spoke for themselves. Elliott then asked Fulton if Cameron had requested that she be given the opportunity to discuss the matter. "Would it not have been possible to send an inspector to South Park School?" Fulton responded by saying, "It did not occur to me as necessary." Continuing this line of inquiry, Elliott pointed out that the witness heard only one side of the issue and condemned Cameron without a hearing. Fulton agreed saying, "If that is condemning, I did so."[3] A further witness, Allan S. Stewart, inspector of schools and one of the examiners, righteously summed up the feelings of the plaintiffs when he stated that the drawing books were thrown out as a punishment to the teacher. The court adjourned for Christmas.

Despite the current grim reality of her life there were a few highlights that brightened her days. On the eve of Christmas, students across the city made special presentations to favourite teachers, as a gesture of appreciation for their hard work, professionalism, and devotion. Above all the city's teachers, two were of note: Samuel John Willis and Agnes Deans Cameron. Willis had an illustrious and distinguished career in education, first as an educator and then as principal of Victoria High School in 1908, where he raised the profile of the school to become the most highly regarded high school in British Columbia.[4] His students presented Willis with a handsome marble clock and cut-crystal bowl, and Cameron received a handsome gold ring as a reminder of the affection her students had for her and of her positive influence on their education.

The final push for Christmas was on as downtown shoppers were finishing up their last-minute purchases. "The best season ever," stated Angus Campbell of Campbell & Co. Ladies Outfitting Emporium. Business was up forty percent over the previous year—people were spending liberally. The only hitch in an otherwise perfect holiday was Santa's visit. He was due to appear on Christmas Day at Watson's Theatre to hand out presents to the children who were attending the play *Cinderella*. Unfortunately, he had experienced a very severe burn when a candle-lit Christmas tree caught fire at a parish house of a Unitarian church in Leicester, Massachusetts, and was unable to make it.[5]

The hearing resumed on Wednesday, December 27. During the previous night, a southwest gale blew through the city, dampening everyone's mood. By ten-thirty in the morning everyone was seated and in their rightful places. Resuming the case for the Department of Education, the first witness called was Alexander Robinson, superintendent of education. He told the court that only three of the twenty students would have passed if he had not raised their marks. He also stated that the school trustees had come to look at the books, but after three-quarters of an hour they became weary of seeing the amount of ruling and decided they need not look any further. They then threw the books out as an act of discipline to the teachers. Testifying to Cameron's performance as a school principal, Robinson said that, "In many respects Miss Cameron was the best of organizers and had a wonderful control over her school, but she had one objectionable habit, namely, giving notes to the children, especially in arithmetic. In other respects she was one of the best principals in the city."[6]

The case for the trustees was mostly a recounting of the list of events as it unfolded. One trustee, Huggett, under examination by Cameron's lawyer, stated that while he was initially in support of Cameron he changed his opinion upon inspection of the drawing books. He felt that there had been significant ruling. He had been on record as saying the Blair method of drawing was "rotten," an inferior system imposed on teachers and students. When questioned about that statement he backtracked stating that he was in a bad mood when he made that pronouncement.

Finally, on Friday, December 29, Cameron took the stand. Elliott chose not to examine the value of the evidence, but rather the weaknesses inherent in Blair's methodology. He also focused on Cameron's reputation; he was careful to point out that she was meticulous in performing her duties as a school principal. He started by explaining that as far back as 1903 Cameron had requested specific instructions for the drawing program and received in reply only a circular, which was confusing and far from adequate. Elliott told the court that Cameron and Miss Fraser had taken drawing seriously and added extra drawing lessons before and after school, in addition to the regularly scheduled Thursday in-school classes. He said both Cameron and Miss Fraser had gone beyond what was necessary to ensure students' work was as near perfect as possible. Elliott questioned why students were not allowed to use a measuring device when doing technical drawing, particularly when ruling was the norm in the industry primarily because it was the only way to assure the accuracy of minutely detailed technical diagrams.

He brought expert testimony to the stand that pointed out the futility of the Blair system of teaching drawing. According to Mrs. Mary Daniells, the drawings were entirely mechanical and of no use whatsoever; "it was not an exercise to educate the eye . . . If you want children to draw a straight line then have them use a ruler."[7] Daniells had studied at the prestigious Royal Academy of Arts in London for seven years. She had also been tutored by several world-famous artists. In all the different systems of drawing she had studied, she stated, she had never seen the Blair method in England. She further testified to the fact that she thought Blair's workbooks and methodology were so flawed that as a drawing teacher she would certainly not allow any of her students to be taught from such a system.

It was an opinion shared by Miss Fraser, who also considered Blair's system a great waste of time. She did say that she doubted she would ever be able to satisfy Mr. Blair. Even with her expertise in drawing, she did not think she could herself have completed the drawings to his satisfaction. On cross-examination Cameron acknowledged that she too thought the Blair system was dated but, she told the court, her opinion did not in any way affect Miss

Fraser's dedication to teaching drawing nor the school's commitment to the drawing curriculum.

By the time the court recessed for New Year's the hearings had been going on for three weeks. A short break was a welcome reprieve. It was difficult sitting day after day listening to the minutiae of the proceedings. There were so many features to weld together that the case was not always easy to follow. What was clear, however, was that Blair's system of teaching drawing was outdated and that the instructions given to those tasked with teaching drawing were open to interpretation. Also, Blair and the Department of Education had not done their due diligence in introducing the program to the teachers. Teachers were used to hierarchical structures and tried hard to fulfill their duties as required, but when directives do not mesh with reality and administrative inflexibility rules the day, confusion and distrust begin to inch their way into future directives.

The proceedings began again on January 4, 1906. Several of the students who had signed affidavits were in the courtroom to give testimony. They were in unfamiliar territory; none had ever been under examination in a courtroom before. They were extremely nervous and apprehensive. The room itself seemed heavy and dark and there were so many people crowding the courtroom that the timbre of their voices was unsettling. The students found the questioning intimidating, but they were all anxious that their statements be heard. Each student who was questioned confirmed for the judge that their drawings were freehand; none had used a ruler for the exercises themselves. A few students did qualify their testimony saying they used a ruler to separate one drawing from another in their exercise books, and they ruled the datum line as Miss Fraser had told them was acceptable. Miss Fraser had previously told the court that she was under the impression that such ruling was permissible. After taking statements from a few of the pupils and noting their unease with being the centre of attention, Judge Lampman decided that the best tactic for examining the rest of the students was to continue their hearings in private, away from the public spectacle.

After talking to each of the students Lampman asked a few of the pupils to do some drawing for him at the high school with Miss Fraser present to assist them. He was shocked at how much erasing the students had done. In fact, he said, the students seemed to use their eraser far more than their pencils. After they had finished he collected the papers and compared a number of books with the new drawings. He noted a distinct difference between the two samples: the workbooks looked too perfect. He went over to the window in his office and held up one student's earlier worksheets to a lighted window. It was clear that the line had been ruled. The ruled line had not been completely erased after the "freehand" line was drawn over it. The lad whose book it was admitted that he had ruled. Lampman pressed the students harder and, despite their affidavits to the contrary, several admitted to ruling their workbook exercises while others said that they might have used a ruler but couldn't remember. The case began to turn against Cameron.

With the daily reporting of the hearings in the media, readers were growing weary of the story and others were simply confused. Cameron may have been a very popular figure with a great deal of support behind her, but for some enough was enough. One letter-writer who wrote under the name "Citizen" mirrored what many others were thinking: "I . . . believe that too much space has been given in explanation of her [Cameron's] virtues, and too little of her manifest failings, especially that 'of her overbearing qualifications' . . . your description of the whole affair most appropriate when you designated it as 'a storm in a teacup.'"[8] Another anonymously wrote, "Her conduct must be considered in relation to a series of acts and circumstances, all of which point to a flippant disregard for the wishes and opinions of the Board of School Trustees, and other constituted authority as well. We cannot assume that there is any reason why Miss Cameron should be exempt on account of her extreme cleverness, which everybody admits, from the application of disciplinary methods necessary to the proper regulation of our public schools.

"We cannot help but feel that Miss Cameron brought her present trouble upon herself, and, there, does not deserve the sympathy of one who is persecuted or unfairly treated."[9]

Cameron was not single-minded, difficult, self-righteous, or uppity as some have characterized her; she was a woman operating in a position of authority in a predominately male milieu. Despite the fact that she had risen to an esteemed level in her profession, Canada in the early 1900s was not a society receptive to women working in a professional capacity. True, she had opposed cooking classes for girls and manual training for boys in the curriculum, which angered many people, the Local Council of Women included. As for the drawing curriculum, she felt that it was too restrictive and tightly controlled. Drawing programs in Britain had long since changed their curriculum to include the exploration of aesthetics in drawing. They no longer asked that their students spend hours perfecting the drawing of straight lines, or copying diagrams. Technical drawing was still important but so too was learning brushwork, colour, pottery, and self-expression. Theirs was a program aimed toward nurturing creativity in children, a principle very dear to Cameron's heart and a focus of her teaching. Blair had not kept up with the changing nature of his field, although in later years he added colour, design, brush drawing, and lettering to his *Canadian Drawing Series* books. He still remained fairly inflexible when it came to any departure taken by teachers.

All throughout the trial Cameron had been anxious over the state of her mother's health. Jessie had been diagnosed with diabetes and was very ill. There was nothing her doctors could give her to allay her symptoms. While the cause of diabetes was known, there was no effective treatment until 1921. Cameron was torn in several directions. After a long and strenuous day at the hearings, she would come home to tend lovingly to her mother. At the same time, she was still in litigation with the City of Victoria, trying to prevent her home from being demolished. She knew that diabetes was a death sentence and she was desperate to have her mother live out her last days in her own home. Cameron was jumpy and raw. Whenever a messenger entered the courtroom, she tensed up thinking that it might be about her mother. Once again she questioned herself as to whether she should just give up and let the whole school matter drop. "I couldn't do it," she said. "I spent one whole night alone out at the beach trying to find some way in which I could honourably let the school-matter drop . . . The very love I had for my Mother made me unable to dishonour her by cowardly silence."[10] It was heartbreaking for Cameron to watch her mother weaken. Jessie was now a shadow of her former self; it was obvious her body was failing her.

Chapter Eleven

POLITICAL ASPIRATIONS

As citizens we are all parts of a self-governing
whole, and as such have duties which we can
neither ignore nor relegate to others.

—AGNES DEANS CAMERON

In the midst of the seemingly endless chaos in her life came an opportunity for Cameron to defy her detractors. Civic elections for the City of Victoria were due to be held, with several positions for school trustees open. Cameron was strongly encouraged by her supporters to run for election. There were ten candidates for the four vacancies advertised. On the evening of Thursday, January 11, 1906, a meeting was held at the YMCA building on Broad Street. The purpose was to put forward a slate for the forthcoming elections for school trustee. Cameron was in attendance. Her adversaries heard of the meeting and threatened some of the trustees that were planning on attending. Hinkson Siddall was told that if he were to go to this meeting he should not speak up in her favour, otherwise his status in the community would be affected. His response was to stand up in the meeting and say that although he was friendly with the trustees he thought they had made a great mistake in dismissing Cameron. She was one of the best teachers in the country and a great friend to the children. He believed that "if she had given up the affidavits then she would be false to her trust." The trustees "need to go away back and sit down."[1] There were many at the meeting who were of a like mind. They thought Victoria would benefit from having Cameron as a school trustee and spoke in her defense. Alderman Hanna stood up and said that Cameron should not have been dismissed for a trivial offence and that it was a mistake to have thrown out all the books because one or two had used rulers. Another from the audience said that he was strongly opposed to the actions taken by the school trustees. He spoke from personal experience, he said, because all his children had been educated by Miss Cameron. She was a good teacher and highly supportive of the children.

Cameron along with George Snider and John Samuel Matson, both brokers, and William McKay, a stonecutter by trade, were the four people selected that night. In speaking to her nomination Cameron told the group that she felt it an honour to be nominated for the position of school trustee by such an eminent group of citizens. She said that the accusations against her were keenly felt and were a serious repudiation of her character and that of her students. She had not wanted a fight. It would have been much better to sit down and take the consequences, she said, but she felt strongly that she had to do what was right. Four days later she announced her candidacy in the newspapers. The paper listed her as "Agnes Deans Cameron, spinster." Outside of the exciting and hotly contested race for mayor, Cameron was the focus of the voting public's interest and questions.

The next day, along with cold southerly gales and dropping temperatures, a letter to the *Victoria Daily Colonist* by an anonymous "Elector" was a harbinger of the stormy fight that was about to erupt in the coming election. "The old members [school trustees], Mrs. Jenkins, R. Mowat, E. Lewis, Beaumont Boggs, believe that it is impossible to respect discipline in the schools when teachers show a spirit of 'insubordination.' It is their contention that Miss Cameron objects to be disciplined: while she, on the other hand, would force others to be subordinate to her wishes. This position is obviously inconsistent and cannot have the support of those who believe that authority must be recognized, if order is to be maintained."[2] Her supporters came to be negatively referred to as "Cameronians." Another letter referred to the three other nominees as Cameronians, charging that all four were a tight-knit group running together. They "do not recognize authority, do not believe that the board (elected by the people) should condemn the action of those in their employ, do not have faith in those who have been the choice of the people on many occasions . . . but they do believe that teachers should do as they like . . . Will the electors endorse those who aspire to office for one purpose only—that they might show their heroism by fighting for the 'rights' of the lady candidate? Will not the people demand some better reason? Do these gentlemen only aspire to become gladiators? They ought to present something more worthy of the indorsation [sic] of an intelligent electorate."[3] They were accused of trying to split the vote so that Cameron would gain a seat on the board.

An all-candidates meeting was held at City Hall on January 16. It was not a quiet, genteel type of meeting; opinions were issued with verve and energy and much of that centred on the candidates' perceptions of the drawing book scandal. One nominee, Mr. McKay, stated that he had been told that Cameron had been dismissed not only because she had refused to give up the affidavits, but also because she had broken the rules for ten years. "The school trustees had not taken action previously against Miss Cameron," he said, "because they found no fault with her and, moreover, were afraid they would not be re-elected because the people were behind Miss Cameron."[4] Further he had been told that three months prior to the drawing book incident the trustees had planned to replace Cameron along with two other teachers and that they would be hiring Mr. Deans, an outsider, to be school principal. He went on to say that one of the trustees told him that the students at South Park School were liars and cheats. This was the first time Cameron had heard that there had been a previous intent to remove her from her position.

People stirred in their seats. A voice from somewhere in the audience shouted out to Mr. Mowat, one the trustees seeking re-election, "Why did you dismiss Miss Cameron?" Mowat shot back, "She was not doing her duty." McKay stepped in and said, "What were the duties Miss Cameron would not do?" "Miss Cameron was insubordinate," Mowat quipped. Jeering and heckling from the audience ensued. "Take that back!" several cried. "What is the meaning of insubordination?" another asked mockingly. Somewhat unnerved and with a growing sense of irritation in his voice, Mowat tempted fate by saying, "I'm sorry, but you wouldn't be able to grasp the meaning."[5] The audience erupted with booing and hissing. They had not only been insulted but the original question had been sidestepped. They were not going to let that go. Someone else in the assembly repeated the question: "Mr. Mowat has stated Miss Cameron was dismissed for insubordination: we would like to hear what it was."[6] Mowat invited more derision when he exclaimed that he was surprised that anyone would ask such a question in light of what had happened. He had done what was in the best interests of the city, he said, and now none of the previous school trustees could run for re-election without being condemned in some quarters.

Cameron had been working in a politically divisive environment for a very long time and was not daunted in the least. She pointed out that if the current political situation continued, no decent man or woman would willingly choose to teach in Victoria.

To emphasize the point, she said, "There is a danger in having the schools run, as they are, as a political machine by one man."[7] She told the audience that she was not seeking election out of popularity or revenge, and she was not a representative of any group, church, or society. In fact, she would not solicit any vote, but would be happy to have the support of those who would vote for her on merit. As to the drawing book issue, she believed that she had been made an example of. She said that the principal of the North Ward school had not been "put on the rack," even though ruling was found to have been done by many of their students. She did not consider that it was a trivial matter to abandon twenty-nine of her pupils. If she had not taken the course she did, she said, she would have been ashamed to look the children in the face again. As to the seven-thousand-dollar cost of the commission, she asked only that her students be given the opportunity to do their work over again: it was the school trustees who requested a commission. She also took issue with Mowat, who alleged that she had been dismissed for insubordination. She explained that she was dismissed for not giving up something that she did not have and did not legally belong to her, the students' affidavits. She turned toward Mowat and asked him what he had intended to do with the affidavits. A voice from the audience said, "To lose them." Mowat, side-stepping her gaze, said quite perfunctorily that they intended to destroy them. Cameron prided herself on her integrity and honesty and said that if people thought she was dishonest then she did not want them to vote for her out of some misplaced sense of obligation.

There was also some discussion about her legitimacy as a candidate. To stand for election a candidate had to have paid directly into the municipal tax rolls. This was most commonly done through payment of one's property tax or the water rate. There were less important taxes that also qualified, such as a levy the city collected for owning a dog, which facetiously became known as "the dog tax." It came as no surprise that during the campaign

Cameron was publicly accused of qualifying for her candidacy by paying a dog tax, rather than the more significant and onerous burden of a property tax. It was an absurd gibe as she had been a property owner for the past twenty years and paid all the taxes on her house. Responding with her famous sense of humour, she retorted with the comeback, "Dearly as I love dogs, no dog is my sponsor in this election."[8]

Voting was scheduled for Friday, January 19. The day dawned bright and crisp. Frost hung on the rooftops and blanketed the ground, as if covering up the contentious attitudes displayed in the election campaign. A record number of voters were expected to turn out and anyone needing transportation to the polling stations had only to take advantage of one of the dozens of hacks lining the streets. Cameron was in high spirits. She had the support of the Trades and Labour Council, along with that of several other organizations. Her campaign had worked hard canvassing every woman on the voters list. While women could not yet vote federally, they had been allowed to vote in school board elections since 1884, providing they paid city taxes. Canvassers were out making their last pitch for their candidate. Many of Cameron's friends and supporters enthusiastically offered their help. Even school children voluntarily participated, passing out leaflets that read, VOTE FOR MISS CAMERON, THE CHILDREN'S CHAMPION. There was a jovial mood among the voters even though the election, particularly for the seat of mayor, was one of the most contested in the history of the city.

It was a long and weary day for the candidates, but they were sustained by excitement and anticipation. The tallying of the ballots was painstaking; 2,697 votes were cast. Hour by hour ticked by while each vote was counted and recorded. Around two o'clock in the morning, after seventeen hours of waiting, the votes were finalized. As soon as the winning candidates were notified they made their way to the police courtroom. In the case of the aldermen, many of the old guard were re-elected, which was expected. It was the mayoral contest and the slate for the board of school trustees that had the electorate anxiously biding their time. The fight for City Hall between A. J. Morley and the incumbent, Charles Hayward, had been tense. Morley, campaigning on a promise for more openness and transparency in City Hall, and the assurance not to be swayed by corporate influence, won the day by a mere 188 votes. The *Daily Colonist* wrote that, "Outside of the mayoralty contest perhaps the most exciting feature of the campaign was the contest for seats at the school board—the South Park school controversy and Miss Cameron's dismissal being made an issue which engendered the keenest public interest. Miss Cameron was heading the polls when the ballots were counted, though the ticket nominated in her behalf went down to defeat."[9] Cameron topped the list for elected school trustees with 1,291 votes, which was 125 votes more than Mowat, her nemesis. It was a stunning win for Cameron and flew in the face of the actions of the school trustees, who were responsible for the loss of her job. "I had given twenty-five years of my life," she said, "that victory at the polls I considered my vindication."[10]

The irony of her win was not lost on her. "I was half amused, I confess, when the 'congratulations' were offered." Turning to Margaret Jenkins, who had voted to have her removed from South Park School, she said, "Well, I can scarcely understand your position, Mrs. Jenkins: I can't see how you can consider me worthy to fill the one position and unfit to hold the other." She had received 204 votes more than Jenkins. To the media she said, "I have been consistently fighting for six months for the sacred rights of truth and justice. I cherish no personal animus toward Mrs. Jenkins, or any other member of the board, and trust that I can work with them all for the general good. There is much to do. May I take this opportunity of thanking the many citizens who have reposed their trust in me?"[11]

The confidence voters felt about their future quickly dissipated when they read the morning paper and learned there was a strong movement afoot for separation of British Columbia from the Dominion. Secessionist movements were not new to the province; there had been many such debates over the years. Filial loyalty to the Dominion of Canada had not endeared itself to most British Columbians, who historically had a prickly relationship with Ottawa. Ottawa was somewhat despondent over its petulant province, whose raucous politics had seen thirteen different premiers in thirty-two years. British Columbians' discontent over the refusal of the Dominion government to abide by the tenets of confederation periodically boiled over. They had been pressing British Columbia to renegotiate the terms of the province's entrance into the union. Ottawa considered the promises made in 1871 excessive and unrealistic. British Columbia did not care much for a faraway and seemingly unresponsive overlord. Financially they were attached more to California than to Ottawa, and socially they looked to Britain for their bearing. The threat of separation was always one slight away. Debating this issue once again in 1906, the member for Vancouver City, H. B. Macgowan, postulated that, "The time has come for this province to act for itself in this matter and to demand better financial terms from Canada not as a favour, but as a matter of business justice—and failing this, to go direct to King Edward by petition praying for a dissolution of the unfair terms that bind us to the Dominion."[12] Not much came of British Columbia's posturing and over time the cry for separation faded into the background, although British Columbia has never lost its vituperative edge in its dealings with Ottawa.

Before the newly appointed officials could take up their posts the province was faced with an unfolding disaster. On Monday, January 22, gale force winds battered the coast of Vancouver Island. Heavy seas and southeast gales beset the ss *Valencia*, which was en route to Victoria from San Francisco. The *Valencia* was not an appropriate ship for the rugged west coast. She was mainly a backup ship and spent most of the winter tied up alongside the docks in San Francisco. That morning visibility was poor and

Captain Johnson had to navigate by dead reckoning, a method subject to errors, particularly in the kind of conditions in which they found themselves. Around midnight the *Valencia* was approaching the area on the west coast of Vancouver Island known at the "Graveyard of the Pacific." It is a foul stretch of water where strong currents drive weather-tossed ships toward hidden reefs and the craggy shoreline. Captain Johnson ordered the leadsman to the chains to check the depth.[13] Minutes later the *Valencia* shuddered violently as it struck heavily against a reef. The jolt was so strong that it woke both passengers and crew and sent them running from their bunks. It struck a second time and water quickly filled the hull causing the boat to list. Heavy seas swept through the main deck.

The news coverage was grim in detail. Would-be rescuers watched helplessly from shore as wave after wave smashed the ship. There was a small child seen on deck crying for his mother and father who had been swept overboard. A baby fell into the sea and was crushed between the hull and a lifeboat as he was being lowered down to his mother. Eyewitness accounts told of the horrific incident of two lifeboats filled with women and children, feeling grateful to have escaped a watery death, being overcome by the frothy turbulent water; the passengers drowned as their boat was smashed against the hull of the ship. The *Valencia* went down at Seabird Rocks near the entrance to Pachena Bay, joining the *Michigan*, another vessel that had sunk during the same month thirteen years earlier at Pachena Point. Just five weeks earlier a British ship, the *King David*, was grounded a little farther up the coast. The night the *Valencia* sank, all the women and children perished, bringing the total dead to 117 people. The wreck of the *Valencia* was to haunt the news for weeks and people's hearts for a lifetime.[14]

With the addition of her tenure as a school trustee, Cameron's schedule was extremely full, and yet she managed to continue writing and publishing. "The Most Western Outpost," an article she wrote about the early history of Victoria, was published in *Britannia* and the *Daily Colonist*. Toward the end of January, she was a featured speaker at a very well-attended meeting on women's suffrage. As the fight for the franchise was gaining ground, women's suffrage was a popular topic among the women in the community. Cameron, who was a firm believer in legal equality for women, had always been a strong supporter of women's enfranchisement. She was active not only in the Women's Christian Temperance Movement, a big proponent of suffrage, but also in the Dominion Enfranchisement Association. They had a champion in the British Columbia legislature, Mr. James Hawthornthwaite, member for Nanaimo, who introduced a private members bill supporting provincial voting rights for women. While his bill did not make it beyond the second reading, there was a small short-term victory when a loophole in the Municipal Elections Act extended the franchise to any woman unless otherwise exempt to vote in municipal elections. One hundred and fifty women immediately registered for the voters list in 1906. Discovering their mistake, the legislature quickly amended the clause to exclude women. Among the reasons given was that women who owned bawdy houses would be allowed to vote, an abhorrent thought at the time. However, having had the franchise for even a small amount of time, women fought even harder for their right to vote.

Less than a week after the election, the school trustees had their first meeting. Even though the old guard had publicly stated they were willing to put the past behind them, it is doubtful that in private they were so accepting of Cameron. They often ignored her suggestions and tried to block her motions. In any case, Cameron did not let that affect her. The first thing on the agenda was organizing the second annual convention of province-wide school trustees. With her characteristic enthusiasm, she set immediately to work arranging the program and speakers. The conference was to be held in the middle of February, just a few weeks away. She presented a talk on the important relationship between the school and the home. She also led a discussion on the topic of establishing a university for British Columbia. There was a bill before the BC legislature for the province to hand over control of post-secondary education to McGill University. Proponents of the bill argued that it was still a long way off before BC would be in the position to provide a university, and it would take years beyond that for any new post-secondary institution to develop a reputation similar to that of McGill. Since 1896 high schools in British Columbia were free to affiliate with any Canadian university of their choice, but by handing control to McGill the school trustees would no longer have any influence over post-secondary education in the province. Opponents to the bill contended that by eliminating the chance of other universities to compete for individual high schools, all high schools would become a nursery for McGill. After a prolonged and testy fight the bill in favour of McGill passed, which meant that McGill could now set up first and second year arts and applied science programs in the high schools. They were also free to design the curriculum and write the examinations as well as choose the instructors. After successfully completing the first two years, students would then continue their third and fourth year studies at McGill University in Montreal. Students would not be able to attend a homegrown university until 1915, when BC finally opened the doors to the University of British Columbia.

On Friday, February 23, 1906, His Honour Judge Lampman handed his findings in the drawing book case to the provincial secretary, F. J. Fulton. Cameron's lawyer had always been forthright about her chances of success, but she was not prepared for Lampman's summation. His report was well thought out and exhaustively detailed all aspects of the case in a thirty-three-page document. He found that there was a great deal of ruling and that the examiners' decision to toss out the students' workbooks was completely justified. He did not believe that so doing would create additional hardship for any of the candidates hoping to enter high school. He also said that the clarity of the instructions, which were the subject of debate among the teachers, were unambiguous; no ruling was allowed. He chastised Cameron for failing to ensure the students' work was done fairly and according to the rules and regulations: "If Miss Cameron, when she certified to the books, did not know of the ruling she should have known it. She admits she may have been careless in certifying Muirhead's book, but I think she was careless in certifying too many others besides."[15] As to the assertion by Cameron that South Park School was discriminated against by the Department of Education when the Boy's School was allowed to take Euclid and Latin as optional subjects for their high school entrance exams, rather than English and Canadian history as required by South Park School, it was, he said, an empty claim. He pointed out that it was merely an experiment by the Department of Education.

The ruling was a crushing blow for her, although she must have suspected at various points throughout the hearings that the case was not going in her favour. It was also a difficult decision for her supporters to hear. Cameron felt that she had let everyone down. It is impossible to dissect the rationale for her actions; that lay deep within her psyche. On the surface, she said she believed that she had to protect the integrity of her students. It is possible that she may also have been weary of the constant haranguing she received from the school trustees and hoped to teach them a lesson. She brought professionalism to the job of teaching and was possibly impatient with those who were not as conversant as she was in educational methodology. She was not inflexible and unbendable as her opponents claimed. She was present at the beginning of the development of the public school system in British Columbia, which was still struggling to find its way. In every sense, she helped to shape that system. At times, she was at loggerheads over the purpose of education. She was uncomfortable with the direction away from a classical and liberal arts curriculum toward a more practical job-oriented approach. Although she was aware of the important interplay between education and the economy, apprenticing for occupations, she often said, was best learned on the job, but should be augmented by a classical education. She believed that logic, debate, writing, and mathematics were critical to any job and should not be crowded out by vocational courses.

The trustees too were caught in the shifting sands of power. As duly elected officials they were responsible to their voting public who were concerned about the rising cost of education and the continual controversies besetting education. As the arbiters for curriculum they often came head-to-head with teachers when they unilaterally tried to affect the actual process of learning—a realm that teachers felt was best decided by themselves and their professional teacher associations. The teachers found decisions about the course of education were often politically motivated and frequently based on conjecture and supposition about the state of the economy and the current direction of society. One of the problems with the drawing book exercises, which were at the root of the case, was the amount of subjectivity, both in the design of the questions and in the marking. Lack of objectivity necessarily leads to bias and prejudice. It was impossible to test the strengths and weaknesses of Blair's system as he had not developed any criteria to analyze the reliability and the validity of his drawing program. It is likely that Blair's system would fail both measures today. Many of the teachers decried the lack of such measures for assessing their students' work. In 1905, teacher training had not been significantly addressed nor had learning goals been clearly established. There was no way to ensure the existing teaching methods were appropriate. In the absence of such self-examination, Lampman's only option was to find fault with the actions of Cameron. This was a tiff that had spiraled out of the control of all the parties in question; a Royal Commission should never have happened.

Lampman's decision pained her deeply because it questioned not only her integrity but also her professionalism. The trial had lasted for sixteen weeks. She was exhausted in body and soul and was deeply in debt over the cost of the case and the fight to retain her house. Try as she might she could not summon up her mother's adage of never letting sorrows or hardship take the joy out of life. Some years later she wrote, "When I think how I suffered those days in that iniquitous Royal Commission watching the door for a messenger from home where the dear Mother was slipping away from me hour by hour, I have murder in my heart."[16]

The teachers in the province took note of the decision. The Thirty-Sixth Annual Report of the Public Schools of British Columbia, 1906–1907 stated that the biggest improvement in individual subjects that year was in drawing and art. Many of the schools increased their time spent teaching freehand drawing from objects and incorporated art with the other subjects of the curriculum. Blair had won the day, but he was a deeply unpopular man and his drawing program was not well liked by the teachers.

A day after Judge Lampman's findings were announced, Jessie Cameron's final chapter on this earth came to a close; she was eighty-four years of age. She was a well-known and respected person in the city and was greatly admired for her cheery attitude, which she displayed even during the last days of her life. With her passing, Victoria lost one of the oldest residents in the city and the last of the early pioneers. Jessie was survived by her five children and thirteen grandchildren. She left behind a strong and successful family who made their mark on British Columbia's history. Her eldest son, William George Cameron, owned a successful clothing and mechanics business located in the W. G. Cameron building on Johnson Street.[17] He was a popular city councillor for seven years and a member of the Legislative Assembly at the time of his mother's death.[18] Her eldest daughter, Barbara, had been the matron of the BC Protestant Orphans' Home for four years prior to her marriage to Robert Austin Brown. Barbara's husband was a successful hardware and china merchant on Douglas Street. Charles Napier Cameron was a salesman. He married twice, and lived with his mother for a time after the death of his first wife. Jessie Clara lived at home with her mother and sister, Agnes Deans.

In the familiar surroundings of Jessie's home, her family gathered to say their final goodbyes to an indomitable spirit. Reverend Dr. Leslie Clay of St. Andrew's Presbyterian Church was at the house for a private ceremony. He had been their minister for the past twelve years. He was an exceedingly bright, kind, and thoughtful man. When it was time to leave, six friends carried Jessie's casket to the horse-drawn hearse waiting for them by the front gate. A large funeral cortège had gathered to accompany the family on their silent walk to the church. As the procession made their way over the James Bay Bridge and into town, there were many on the side of the road paying their respects to the entourage. When they arrived, the pallbearers carried their light charge through the nave and into the transept where they set the casket down among a voluminous display of flowers and floral emblems. Reverend Clay, assisted by Reverend Dr. Reid, gave a heartfelt eulogy to the packed church. He concluded the ceremony with a reading from Alfred, Lord Tennyson's "Crossing the Bar," fitting for a woman who left her home in Scotland and travelled to a faraway land across the sea—the flood did bear her far.

Fate was not finished with Cameron yet. In April, a few months after the ruling of the Royal Commission, the Department of Education formally suspended her First Class teaching certificate for three years, beginning June 1, 1906. She would not be allowed back in the classroom as a teacher until 1909. She had not only suffered a very public humiliation, but now her ability to earn a living had been taken from her. Cameron did not walk quietly away. She fought hard to have her teaching certification reinstated. She was supported by her many friends who presented a petition to the Department of Education. However, all pleas were ignored. Despite all that had happened to Cameron, her ambition, curiosity, zestful energy, love of life, and sense of humour were not so easily repressed.

Chapter Twelve

A CHANGE IN DIRECTION

*The Sea has revived you and set throbbing old life-currents
that the strenuous years had almost strangled at their source.*

—AGNES DEANS CAMERON

In early June 1906 Cameron left Victoria to attend the first annual
meeting of the Canadian Women's Press Club, which was being
held in Winnipeg, a city that she had visited on several previous
occasions. It would prove to be a valuable trip for her and one
that would change the direction of her life. When she boarded
the train in Vancouver, she was ready for a new experience. As the
clickety-clack of the train's wheels grew into a predictable hum,
Cameron moved farther away from the tangled mass of pit vipers
that had destroyed her career. She would be joining a cadre of
intelligent, ambitious, and dedicated women, who like her were
refugees from the teaching profession. She loved taking the train
and always marvelled at the country unfolding before her. It was

not long before they began the long climb up and over the Rocky Mountains—the cordilleran backbone of the West, she used to tell her students. It was magnificent with its spectacular spires and verdant alpine meadows. Then, dropping down into the flatlands of the Prairies, they sped across the expansive grasslands of the newly created provinces of Alberta, Saskatchewan, and Manitoba. As they reached the northern edge of Winnipeg the train began to slow in preparation for its arrival at the Canadian Pacific Railway station. There was a loud screeching of the brakes, which set everyone's teeth on edge, and was followed by a long hiss as if it was relieved to finally stop. Cameron gathered her things, packaged her troubles into a temporary "do not disturb" portion of her heart, and stepped out onto the landing of one of the most impressive railway stations in the country. Making her way along the platform she went through two sets of doors that opened out into the interior of the station. As she walked over the white marble terrazzo floors, the sound of her steps reverberated in the grand hall. She stopped for a moment to take it all in. Imposing marble columns, softened by green walls decorated with bronze ornamental plasterwork framed the lobby. The arched barrel-vault ceiling of the rotunda bore a backlit panel of amber glass, highlighting the sumptuous interior. Cameron was well travelled and had seen many grand buildings, but the Winnipeg station was extravagant in its design. Built in the grand Beaux-Arts style popular in Europe, the building towered over nearby sites, announcing to all visitors that Winnipeg was a robust city of sophistication. The station, located at 181 Higgins Avenue, stood as a monument to the railway's part in nation building. As the entry point to Western Canada for hundreds of thousands of immigrants, it was a hive of activity. Seventeen trains a day transited through Winnipeg's grand central station. As Cameron pushed through the massive front doors, the feeling of chic urbanity instantly evaporated in the deluge of rain that soaked everything and everyone who left the station's confines. Fortunately, the organizers of the meeting met the delegates at the front door with opened umbrellas to keep the women dry.

The meeting was an important one for Winnipeg. It was a great opportunity to showcase the city and indeed the province to journalists from all over North America. Winnipeg had recently experienced some negative press. Despite the push for immigrants the city itself had grown too rapidly and outstripped the capacity of the public services, such as water and sewage. Two months earlier the city had been at the centre of a major strike by the employees of the Electric Railcar Company. The mayor, Thomas Sharp, had called in the militia, who came ready with bayonets and machine guns to clear Main Street. It was not a popular move. Winnipeg needed the journalists to help boost the city's image as well as attract business to the area. The city's officials hoped that the women journalists would write about the exuberant growth of the province, its potential, and the benefits that would accrue for those who wished to settle in the West. As recent entrants to the Dominion, Alberta, Saskatchewan, and Manitoba needed a larger population base to expand their economies. The West was the new land of opportunity and had vast tracts of land available for homesteading and farming. They wanted people who were willing to work hard and had generations of farming experience behind them. As part of their marketing plan, they wined and dined the journalists in the hope of fostering a long-term working relationship with the media.

Despite the rain the women were very impressed by the newness of everything and marvelled over the wide, well-lit streets, paved boulevards, and tall buildings. One of the American delegates was pleasantly surprised and commented that she expected to see a "bunch of shacks" and a rough and tumble Wild West. They thought the city was very progressive. As soon as the women were picked up they were whisked away to Elks Hall. One of the goals of the Canadian Women's Press Club (CWPC) was to professionalize journalism, which was part of Cameron's message too.

It came as no surprise to anyone when she was elected vice president representing British Columbia. Among some of the issues addressed that day was the imbalance of pay between female and male journalists. In all but a few cases it was impossible for women to earn a living wage from writing. At the turn of the century there were about sixty female journalists, writing mostly for the society columns or "women's" pages, but journalism was on the rise as an occupation of choice for women. In subsequent meetings, they created a beneficiary for members who faced financial difficulties and included mentorship programs as an important adjunct to their association.

After the business section of the meeting was concluded, the journalists boarded a chartered streetcar that took them to a fashionable lunch at Deer Lodge Hotel, a lovely modified Tudor-style inn located west of the city that overlooked the Assiniboine River. Business leaders understood that these women journalists were making history and thought it important for the town officials and their wives to greet the delegates. After lunch the mayor took the podium and told the gathering that the women before him were leaders of the "best in public thought" and should be treated accordingly. Cameron was tasked with giving a speech. As she stood she said she was humbled by the honour conferred upon her. She started her speech with a humorous quip about the sumptuous dessert before her: "in the west they attempt everything, and since I came from the west, I ought to be able to attempt this trifle." She then went on to present a well-received talk on the importance of business to a growing country. She ended her presentation by reminding the participants that it was important not to waste time jockeying for position in the world of journalism, but rather to write articles that worked for the benefit of the country and the unity of the Empire.

Their schedule was packed. The organizers wanted to make sure they saw the best Winnipeg had to offer. Still satiated from the lavish luncheon, they made their way to Government House for a tea, hosted by His Honour Sir Daniel McMillan and his wife, Lady McMillan. The evening entertainment was pure fun, a trip to Happyland Park, the new amusement park on the outskirts of town. Even though it had been open for only a week it was proving to be a very popular attraction; the first two days alone saw forty-four thousand visitors pass through its gates. Despite the fact the journalists had just spent the last few days on a train, they leapt at the chance to tour around the park on the miniature train. They revelled in the bright lights and the carnival-like atmosphere, tried their hand at the rifle range, and dared each other to ride on the Ferris wheel, banishing any thoughts of bilious heights to their inner psyche.

Herbert Vanderhoof, the secretary of the Western Canadian Immigration Association, saw an opportunity to capitalize on the meeting of the Canadian Women's Press Club, and arranged for his organization to fund part of the conference. The Western Canadian Immigration Association was organized by a group of sixty-four Canadian and American businessmen. They had met in St. Paul, Minnesota, just two years before the conference, in 1904. The organizers, who represented the affairs of the Board of Trade, the Grain Exchange, and the Real Estate Exchange, came together through mutual interests for the promotion of immigration into Western Canada. While it may seem strange that Americans were keen on helping Canada populate its west, the financial destiny of the two countries was tightly bound. Canada was America's best trading customer. Canadian purchases of American goods for 1904 amounted to twenty-four dollars per person, significantly more than they spent on English goods. Anything that benefited Canada helped the United States. Canada had over eighty-one million hectares of land, ripe for growing wheat. That would average out to five times more wheat than was cultivated in the United States. There were also large tracts of land available for ranching and mixed farming for crops like sugar beets, alfalfa, hay, and fruit. Vast resources of timber were to be had merely for the asking.

Not everyone was eager about the proposed plan to bring Americans to Western Canada. Most of the opposition came from the western states, which saw a prosperous Canada more as a threat than as an adjunct to their businesses. To counter the Western Canadian Immigration Association, millions of dollars were spent in a vigorous advertising campaign extolling the benefits for Americans to stay at home. The very powerful American railroad companies also waged a malicious crusade against emigration to the Canadian West. They argued that they would lose customers, and without a robust supply of goods being transported across the country their profits would decline, which would have a negative impact on growth and prosperity in America. The United States government was not particularly pleased either with an upstart country luring their citizens away, particularly as they had spent over one hundred million dollars on irrigation systems to open land west of the Mississippi Valley to agriculture and farming. In truth, the American West had been overdeveloped and there was little land available for homesteading and farming. Most of it was beyond the price of what the average farmer could afford. Western Canada offered homesteaders a chance to obtain land relatively cheaply. The Western Canadian Immigration Association would have to work hard to show the benefits that would accrue to the United States from their plan.

Their first order of business was to correct the proliferation of erroneous information on the state of Canada's west, which in most cases occurred because of lack of knowledge about the country. They needed journalists working on their behalf to get publicity into the appropriate newspapers and magazines. They appointed Herbert Vanderhoof as their general manager. Vanderhoof was a widely respected and well-known advertising executive who had represented several railroad companies, the Canadian government, and the Hudson's Bay Company.[1]

To attract homesteaders, they had to do more than buy advertising space in the press. They needed to excite readers while providing an accurate and truthful portrayal of the climate, soil, and resources of the west. The meeting of the Canadian Women's Press Club offered the opportunity they were looking for. Now the association had an opportunity to engage the best and most famous women writers from both the United States and Canada. Vanderhoof wined and dined the journalists and took them on a guided train tour across the west culminating in a stay in Banff. Along the way the group made scheduled stops at Brandon, Manitoba, and Indian Head, Saskatchewan, to visit two farms that were part of the Dominion experimental farm system. Each of the farms had just under a hundred hectares in use for testing crop rotation and at least eight hectares for soil experiments. They were also studying animal husbandry, finding which animals could be successfully adapted to the Canadian prairies. Cameron was drawn to the hectares of golden wheat that lay before her and was fascinated with the entire process of getting wheat from the fields to the table. Later she would revisit the area to learn as much about wheat growing as she could. She would go on to write many articles about the potential for farming and the place of wheat in the development of the economy of the west as part of her campaign to bring more people to the Prairies.

As guests of the Western Canadian Immigration Association it was expected that the journalists would write about their venture, re-mythologizing the west by creating a narrative showcasing the opportunities and availability of land on offer. It was a move they hoped would attract immigrants to Western Canada as well as beckoning commercial interests to invest in the growth of cities and communities. It proved to be a tour de force of publicity for Vanderhoof. In return for their trip, the journalists provided millions of dollars' worth of advertising through the publication of their stories and articles in popular magazines and newspapers throughout Canada and the United States.

Two days into their trip one of the journalists suggested that for fun they produce a newspaper. Groans could be heard throughout the car. It was too much like shop they said, but it wasn't long before the typewriters were out and the *Sunset News Bulletin*, named after the railcar they were riding in, began to take shape. Mrs. Cynthia Westover Alden, who was the international president of the Sunshine Society, the *Ladies' Home Journal*, and the *Brooklyn Daily Eagle*, said of the enterprise, "Our staff will look like the roster of a South American army. Everybody wants to be a general and nobody wants to be the private."[2] Cameron was chosen as the editorial writer for the paper as well as the reporter for the Children's Corner. She peppered her articles with wit and humour, as only she could. Most wrote about their impressions of the trip. They had an advertising section and photos of the Banff Hotel, and they even cajoled the hunters on the trip to supply the larder for the newspaper car. The resulting paper was heralded as a great piece of journalism and was in demand from readers in both Canada and the United States.

The trip to Banff was a highlight of the conference for the women. Known for its magnificent hotels, hot sulphur baths, and stunning scenery, Banff was heralded as one of the finest tourist destinations anywhere. The women wholeheartedly agreed with the promotional literature, which advertised Banff as being like fifty Switzerlands in one. The soaring mountains with their emerald-coloured lakes presented some of the most exquisite scenery in the world. As guests of the Canadian Pacific and the Western Canadian Immigration Association, the journalists most likely stayed in the elegant Banff Springs Hotel, a chateau-style beauty nestled between Tunnel Mountain and Mount Rundle. Once they were settled in their rooms, the women readied themselves for a carriage and pony ride to the top of Sulphur Mountain to bathe in the healing waters of the hot springs. The trip up the mountain was steep and laden with switchbacks; the bravest among them rode side-saddle on rented ponies. The clear, sharp mountain air shook them out of the staleness of their long journey. None were shy when they waded into the baths. The water was hot and inviting and the view was simply stunning. They congratulated themselves that not one photo plate documenting their bathing escapades would make it into print. The time slipped by too quickly and before they knew it they were on their way back.

On the return trip, they enjoyed a picnic hosted by Charles Peterson, a prominent businessman and Deputy Commissioner of Agriculture for the Northwest Territories, as well as CPR's General Manager of Irrigation and Colonization. He was very interested in presenting his plans for immigration to the journalists. After a delightful lunch they continued to Cardston, a highly successful farming community located in the foothills of southwest Alberta. Cardston was the largest settlement in the Dominion of adherents of the Church of Jesus Christ of Latter-day Saints. It was a relatively new community, established in 1887 by those seeking relief from persecution in the United States for their practice of polygamous marriage. They enjoyed the relative sense of freedom their new country offered and put all their energies toward working the land. It was not long before the community became a showcase for co-operative farming. Along with growing wheat, they built a flourmill, a cheese factory, a sawmill, and a state-of-the-art steam-threshing unit. They were particularly adept at designing both large and small-scale irrigation projects to cope with the unique climate of the area. When the train pulled into the station, the entire town of one thousand people turned up to welcome the journalists. By now their celebrity preceded them and everyone wanted a chance to see these women. After their visit they made a running stop at Magrath, about forty-three kilometres northeast from Cardston. It too was a Mormon settlement, slightly smaller, with a population of 884 residents. Again, the entire town was there to greet their distinguished visitors. The school children presented the women with bouquets of flowers, silk flags, and ribbons that bore the town's sentiment: "Awful sorry you cannot stay, but mighty glad you came our way." Cameron gave a heartfelt speech thanking the children for their kindness. As their train pulled away, a group of women and men crowded together on the platform and bid them adieu with a lovely melodious song. The journalists' general impression of the west was very positive and created much discussion among them. They were particularly impressed with the fact that the farmers appeared to be healthier and had a better life than many who lived in cities.

Upon their return in Winnipeg, the women had so many invitations to tea that it was impossible to accept them all. It had been a remarkable trip for them and one that would provide many columns of publicity. The journalists left feeling that the west was progressive and boundless, and that opportunities were stemmed only by one's imagination. Those from eastern Canada continued to Ontario and Quebec in a special train. Cameron accompanied them as far as Montreal. Their American counterparts carried on south in the "Sunset Car." The women went back to their newspapers and magazines and started writing their impressions. The trip and advertising campaign had been a great success for Canada's west. Advertising dollars could not have bought the high quality of publicity that the journalists produced. Previously, most advertising appeared in the back pages of newspapers sandwiched in between the latest remedy for grippe or Meerschaum cut plug smoking tobacco. It was not long before articles began appearing in *Collier's Weekly*, which had a circulation of six hundred thousand, as well as *American Monthly Review of Reviews*, *Scribner's*, *Metropolitan*, and many others, all with similar rates of readership. Cameron wrote articles for *Vancouver World*, *Atlantic Monthly*, and *Century* magazine.

Not surprisingly, interest in Canada's west was piqued, so much so that the railways could not cope with the numbers of people who were moving to Canada. Sixty thousand immigrants, eager to get to the front of Western Canada to claim homesteads for themselves and their families, moved from the United States in 1906, a thirty percent increase over the previous year. Some came by train and others by wagons. Trains coming from the United States often left hundreds of disappointed immigrants stranded on the platforms. In Minneapolis for example, on one day alone, thirteen coaches left full of settlers to Western Canada with twenty-two booked for the following week. Cameron personally witnessed the success of the marketing campaign when she had a chance to visit Alberta again in August. She said she saw two covered wagons and a buggy approaching the outskirts of Calgary. On the side of one of the wagons was a sign that read, WE DROVE FROM INDIANA. She also saw a dusty caravan that was being driven by an all-female team. Similarly, the next day she passed a plough led by six horses operated by a woman who jubilantly shouted out to her, "It's easy, real easy and such fun!" For an article she wrote on Canada's wonderland of wheat for the *Vancouver Daily World*, Cameron observed, "Surely Western Canada is the country for brave workers and neither nationality, age, sex nor previous condition imposes a limitation."[3]

Canada stood on the brink of becoming the breadbasket for the world. It was estimated that two hundred million bushels of wheat could be wrested annually from western soil. Cameron was passionate about immigration and felt that the mix of so many different people would give strength and character to Canada. "Greater Canada must have an analysis of destiny," she wrote, "for a country depends not upon its material resources, but upon the character of its people."[4]

Cameron's life took on a whirlwind of travelling, writing, and giving speeches. Returning from Montreal she stopped in Kenora, Ontario, and by July 19 was in Minneapolis, Minnesota, the headquarters of the Western Canadian Immigration Association. She had always been adept at maintaining her contacts and taking advantage of an opportunity when it presented itself. Vanderhoof offered her a job working for the Western Canadian Immigration Association. It was the right opportunity at a time in her life when she needed one, and Vanderhoof was delighted to have such an august writer on his payroll. Minneapolis was equally honoured to have such a well-known person staying in their city for the month. The *Minneapolis Journal* wrote glowingly of her life, pointing out that she was the first woman pedagogue in British Columbia who as a child experienced the financial hardship of a western mining life. Americans liked stories of an underdog triumphing against all odds. Rather than condemn her for losing her position as a school principal, they loved the fact that she proved to be such an agile fighter against Victoria's Board of School Trustees.

In the meantime, the Western Canadian Immigration Association decided to transfer their headquarters to Chicago. The board felt that Chicago was a major national centre and the hub of the press corps. The move was slated to take place in early September. It was time for Cameron to let go of one life and embrace another; there was no future for her in Victoria. Her home on Birdcage Walk had been demolished for the Government Street expansion and she did not have the luxury of waiting for three years to regain her teaching certificate. On September 12, 1906, she resigned from her position as a school trustee. Cameron had been absent for two of the board meetings and, according to the election bylaws, if she missed a third meeting her seat would become available. It was a logical step to take. Without any hesitation, she left the place of her birth behind and moved to Chicago.

Chicago was an exciting and vibrant city, full of opportunity, much suited to her own vitality and energy. Without much trouble, she found a place to live in the Woodlawn area on the south side of the city. She moved into the Colonial, located at 6325 Monroe Avenue, near 63rd Street. It had charm, she thought. It was a moderate sized, four-story building that had 150 rooms. She was comfortable knowing that the Colonial was one of the most popular family hotels in Woodlawn. She overlooked a beautifully manicured lawn that supported several large trees. It would provide her with privacy from the busy comings and goings along the wide avenue that abutted the property. Her new residence, while different from her home in Victoria, contained many elements that were familiar to her. She lived near a park, the area was treed, and Monroe Harbor was nearby. It was a nice middle-class community, populated by many of the professors that taught at the University of Chicago. It was the perfect place for her. The only disadvantage was that she was close enough to Lake Michigan to feel the biting chill that whips off the lake in winter, threatening to turn unprepared visitors into ice sculptures. She made a note to herself to invest in a heavy woolen coat, warm scarf, hat, and gloves. She was used to a more temperate climate. Every morning Cameron walked the block from her residence to the South Side Rapid Transit System, which took her into the downtown core in just under fifteen minutes. From there it was only a short distance to her office in the Marquette Building, one of the most sought-after addresses in the city.[5]

Pleased with the success of the publicity the Western Canadian Immigration Association was garnering from the journalists, Vanderhoof wanted to capture a regular readership, so began a monthly publication, the *Canada West* magazine. He appointed Cameron assistant editor. Before the first issue rolled off the press in October, there were already fourteen hundred subscribers. It quickly became a very popular magazine, particularly among American farmers and American investors who had an interest in Canada.

Cameron worked hard and rarely took a break from writing. The star attraction in her room at her boarding house was her typewriter. She had positioned it on the desk to face the view, although she seldom took the time to notice the scenery. Most of the residents knew when Cameron was writing. The constant tap-tapping of the keys, broken only by the ding of the carriage bell, told them another story was in progress. Cameron turned out article after article, writing of "Western's Canada's Wonderland of Wheat," "What Men Have Said About Women," "The Last West," "Alberta Red," "Succulent Dinners That Swim in the Sea,"

"On the Flowing Silver Saskatchewan," "The Empire of Larger Hope, "Wheat, the Wizard of the North," "Whale Hunting in the Pacific," and "Pathfinders of Silence, the Indian Trappers of Fort Edmonton." As soon as one article rolled off her typewriter, she barely took a breath before she slipped a new fresh page onto the carriage and began anew. She typed with energy and passion and always with her mind on paying back her outstanding debt. Her diligence paid off. "I have lived mean and cheap," she wrote, "and I have paid off the lawyers' bills for both the Royal Commission and the City of Victoria litigation about the old home . . . I did the meanest kind of office work; I worked at anything and everything I could get and I worked often 18 and 19 hours a day . . . I have managed to keep my head above water."[6]

The life of a journalist, especially for women, was not an easy one, nor was it financially rewarding or secure. For most female journalists there was often a struggle over money. It was particularly difficult for those women, like Cameron, who were dependent on their pen as their sole support. It meant constant scrambling for articles and writing until they were ready to drop. The newsprint business was notorious for paying women a poor salary and working them as lackeys. Women who wrote literature, poetry, or novels had to be supported by their husbands or families or would end up destitute. The more ambitious had to leave Canada and move to England or to the United States to earn a better wage. To garner a better wage and have more articles accepted, many wrote under masculine names; Cameron did not. She was well known and respected and was one of the fortunate women who could write under her own name. It is hard to imagine Cameron having a conversation with respect to salary in which she might say, "If you think the salary I am asking for is too much, then I will take less," as did some journalists. She knew her worth and would not sell herself short. The Canadian Women's Press Club was vitally responsible for helping women establish themselves as journalists and paved the way for helping women set professional standards as well as learn how to work in the business of journalism.

As more women became consumers, magazines and newspapers began to hire women to write women's columns. The popular ones quickly developed a cult of personality among their readers. People were just as fascinated with the lives of the authors as they were with the content of the articles. Readers wanted to know who the writers were, what they did, how they lived. Not so different from the current paparazzi press. As women tried to build an archetypal female to follow, by default many of these working women acted as role models. This often presented a conundrum for the journalists, particularly in the manner of their dress and behaviour. They had to be exemplary in their manners and dress, but to what standards? Here they were charting new territory. As they were working in a man's world they had to adapt their clothing styles to suit. They tended to be more subdued in their choice of clothing. Cameron always chose smart suits that were tailored, but she sported a large brimmed hat, as was the fashion. Her clothing was sometimes commented upon when she was giving a presentation at a meeting, tea, or luncheon— she was known for wearing a "smart-looking silk lavender."

Cameron was at the high point of her career as a writer. The top literary magazines at the time welcomed any article written by her. Many of her articles went to syndication and appeared regularly in Rhode Island's *Newport Daily News*, Texas's *Houston Post*, Kansas's *Lawrence Daily Journal*, the *Chicago Daily Tribune*, and Virginia's *Daily Press*, as well as newspapers in California, Massachusetts, North Carolina, Pennsylvania, Oregon, North Dakota, New York, Minnesota, Oklahoma, Indiana, Utah, Wisconsin, Georgia, Michigan, Ohio, and in papers throughout Canada and London, England. She became one of the most well-known and respected writers in all three countries and was touted as Canada's darling. The *Daily Colonist* was very proud of their daughter and never failed to mention when she had written an article and where it appeared, in many cases reproducing the article itself.

She was a natural fit with literary groups in Chicago and quickly became in demand as a speaker and a mentor for several clubs. For example, as vice president of the Canadian Women's Press Club she spoke to the Commonwealth Club of Chicago on the Doukhobor commune as a Canadian utopia, addressed the Authors and Literary Students' Club of Chicago several times, and helped guide the Women's Press Club of Illinois through their beginnings. Her writings were popular and acted as great advertisements for Western Canada. Victoria's *Daily Colonist* wrote a piece on her in May 1908 stating that, "Victoria is getting a lot of excellent advertising in one way or another, but in none more effectively than through the persistence with which Miss Agnes Deans Cameron keeps contributing manuscript to the popular magazines of the continent. One can hardly pick up a monthly nowadays without running across something from the pen of the industrious principal of the South Park School."[7]

Meanwhile, debate continued over her dismissal and the loss of her teaching certificate. Much to the despair of the Department of Education and school trustees this issue would not go away quietly. The very public and vocal debate, which reached into the legislature, continued for the entire three years of her suspension. On March 2, 1908, Cameron received an unexpected letter from the Honourable J. S. Helmcken on the topic of the restoration of her teaching certificate. At first she was taken aback. His letter brought back to the surface that terrible time in her life as well as the anguish and anger she still felt. From her expatriated residence in Chicago she wrote:

> *My dear Dr. Helmcken,*
>
> *Your letter surprises me not a little. Do I want my certificate back again? Of course I do. If you found yourself in the position of an unfrocked priest, would you not wish to be restored to your lost dignity? Your notice from the minutes of the house is the first intimation I have*

received of an effort being put forth toward this act of tardy justice. I have not the slightest idea of the personality of the people who are moving in this matter; it is with them clearly a question of right and principle and decency. It cannot be a personal matter, for I don't even know who they are.

The status of the affair is briefly this; the Education Department of the Province of BC punished a whole class of children for alleged dishonesty and refused them a hearing in their own defence. As the guardian of the honour of those children, I demanded that they be heard, contending that if but one was innocent, it was a gross act of cowardice and injustice to punish him for the sins of the others.

Even in that travesty of Justice, the farcical "Royal Commission" (so-called), the Government-appointed sole arbiter, Justice Lampman declared that one lad (Anton Henderson) was wholly guiltless of all the false charges of the government.

My certificate was rescinded for three years on the ground that I had made charges against the Education Department that I had failed to prove. I made no charges. My crime was that I insisted that defenceless children were entitled to the British fair-play of an opportunity of speaking in their own defence against a wholesale charge of dishonour.

For this crime, I was subjected to the indignity of a reversal of my certificate, branded as one unworthy to hold the position of teacher, and turned out in the world with that slur upon me to make a living after a quarter of a century spent in the service of the young people of British Columbia.

The Royal Commission had run me into debt, debt
incurred on behalf of those children to whom I held the
place of guardian; the fight was never a personal one
with me. It would have been infinitely easier to have
followed the line of least resistance, shut my eyes to all
the heinous rottenness of that Education department,
and continued to draw my salary.[8]

A few days later in the British Columbia legislature, the
Honourable J. H. Hawthornthwaite introduced a heartfelt motion.
"I do not wish to see this lady's name dragged in the mire . . . I
was present at the investigation, and I am absolutely satisfied that
this woman was most grievously and most cruelly wronged."[9] He
pointed out that the commission's actions had deprived the province of one of its finest teachers and professional educators. Several
positive comments on the motion were voiced. The provincial secretary, the Honourable Dr. Young, mentioned that a number of
conditions were imposed on her from an impartial tribunal, but
added that the Department of Education was willing, upon application by Cameron, to favourably consider her reinstatement. A
sigh of relief was audible in the legislature and the decision was met
with deafening applause.

As relieved as Cameron must have been to receive such news,
it was a gesture much too late. By then she was working with
the Western Canadian Immigration Association. She had left
Victoria behind and her old life along with it. In the interim she
had fashioned a new direction. She was most likely not willing
to come back to a situation in which she would have to watch
every step and be completely under the authority of those who
had initially caused her so much grief. Her love for Victoria and
British Columbia never wavered and she wrote robust articles
about the province, extolling the beauty, the economy, and the
advantages of her homeland, that appeared in major international
magazines and newspapers. She was on a new journey discovering

new realms and, most importantly, in command of her own life. A speech she presented at a meeting of the Canadian Women's Press Club provides insight into her ability to quickly regain perspective. Her talk titled "Now Is the Accepted Time" focused on enjoying life now. She told her audience that simple acts of kindness like offering a smile, bringing joy to someone, or doing a kindly deed for them should not be put off for some time in the future or in the hereafter. "Eternity in the Bible is not, I think, hereafter and yonder, but rather here and now, and joy is our eternal portion," she told them. "Some men walking in eternal sackcloth have been noble—few have been great. Christ was acquainted with grief, but he could not say with Petrarch, 'I am one of those who delight in grieving.'

"Old Watts, the hymn maker, was a libeler, in my opinion, worse that Jeroboam the son of Nebat.

> *How vain are all things here below,*
> *How false, and yet how fair:*
> *Each pleasure has its poison too,*
> *And every grief a snare.*

"If this be true, life would not be worth living. But it is not true. Life is real. You know not just who needs the smile, the kindly work, the moral uplift that you alone can give. Remember, it is the feet of him who bringeth glad tidings that are beautiful. And now is the accepted time."[10]

Chapter Thirteen

TO THE ARCTIC AND BACK

The greatness of a country, does not depend upon its material resources, it depends upon the character of its people.

—AGNES DEANS CAMERON

Cameron lived frugally, and after she had paid her debts she began saving for an adventure that would not only prove to be an experience of a lifetime, but also cement her reputation in the international annals of writing and celebrity in the process. She had written for years about the west and the more settled parts of Canada and the great bounty on offer, but to the north and farther west lay a great stretch of land that few had read much about. Canada was stretching its horizons; sovereignty, land development, population growth, and settlement were part of the founding thoughts that formed the creation of the Dominion. Progress was seen as essential to the human condition as was breathing. Agriculture, mining, and natural resource extraction was thriving in areas previously believed to be unproductive or uninhabitable. Settlement along the great waterways of the west was growing. But for the writings of a few explorers and trappers, however, there was little accurate information in the popular press for readers who were curious to know more about that area of the country.

Cameron was a traveller at heart and as a successful and popular writer she reasoned that she could use her talents to offer her perspective to readers on the geography of the northwest. A book was on her agenda and she needed raw material that only a first-hand account could provide. She wanted her niece, Jessie Cameron Brown, to accompany her as her companion and secretary. It would be an arduous journey deep into the north and into the western Arctic to write about a land that, until the arrival of Alexander Mackenzie in 1789, had been the home and the sole domain of Indigenous people for over fourteen thousand years.[1] Her plan was to travel along the great river systems of the country—the Peace, Athabasca, and Mackenzie Rivers. It was a long way to travel in one summer, but as she put it, "Shakespeare makes his man say, 'I will run as far as God has any ground,' and that is our ambition. We are to travel north and keep on going till we strike the Arctic—straight up through Canada . . . To what end? . . . We want to come near to the people . . . We want to see what they are doing, these Trail Blazers of Commerce . . . There has always been a West . . . But the West that we are entering upon is the Last West, the last unoccupied frontier under a white man's sky.[2] When this is staked out, pioneering shall be no more, or Amundsen must find for us a dream-continent in Beaufort Sea."[3]

Other women writers had struck out to explore and write about the Mackenzie region. In 1892 Elizabeth R. Taylor, the daughter of the American consul in Winnipeg, ventured up to Fort McPherson on her own and then published a four-part series titled "A Woman in the Mackenzie Delta" for *Outing*, an illustrated monthly sport, travel, and recreation magazine. In 1899

Taylor wrote "Up the Mackenzie River to the Polar Sea" for *Travel*, also a popular illustrated monthly. Two years later another journalist, Emma Shaw Colcleugh, made the same trip, returning to write and present lectures on and photographs of her journey to the Arctic. As a prolific reader Cameron most likely knew about both women, although she was travelling farther and would be making her own observations.

The first order of business was to find a travel company that would help her put together such a trip. The dominant travel company that specialized in exotic and unusual trips was Thomas Cook & Son. They planned trips, organized bookings, and provided the essentials including travel books, clothing, maps, and luggage. Their services covered Europe, the Middle East, India, China, Africa, Canada, the United States; almost anyplace one could think of going. As it happened, a friend of Cameron's who was seeking information on a Mediterranean tour was going to Cook's office in Chicago. While there Cameron took the opportunity to talk to an agent about her proposed trip. She approached a young man at the desk and asked, "I wonder if you can give me information about a trip I am anxious to take? I want to go from Chicago to the Arctic by the Mackenzie River and return home by the Peace and the Lesser Slave. Can you tell me how long it will take, what it will cost, and how I make my connections?" Somewhat haughtily he said he was sure they could, but he would check with his boss. Cameron wrote, "He didn't move an eyebrow, but went off to the secret recesses in the back office to consult 'the main guy,' 'the chief squeeze,' 'the head push,' 'the big noise.' When he came back he laughingly said, 'Well, Miss Cameron, I guess you've got us.'"[4] He told her they did have very useful information about travelling up to Hudson's Bay in the northeastern part of the continent, but nothing for her itinerary. Luxury caravan trips to Egypt were quite popular, he said, but nothing to the Western Arctic. It was not the kind of trip that would entice the average traveller, he explained. Their customers looked for

colourful and glamorous trips in comfortable and luxurious surroundings. Somehow jostling along in a wagon train, walking,
portaging, travelling in dugouts, small tugs, scows, and paddle
wheelers, battling bugs and eating muskrat did not have the cachet
offered by shopping trips to Peking or camel rides in Egypt.

For her purpose, there was only one organization with sufficient knowledge that could provide the information and support
she needed, and that was the Hudson's Bay Company. The HBC
was well versed in outpost travel and living. They had been tramping all over the north, surveying, exploring, and trading since
the 1670s. They knew the routes, had the connections, could
supply transportation, and would put together the necessary kit
needed for travel. Cameron and her niece left Chicago and took
the train to Winnipeg to meet with agents of the Hudson's Bay
Company who would plan their trip for them. She was suitably
impressed and wrote, "The Hudson's Bay Company is to-day the
Cook's Tourist Company of the North . . . No man or woman
can travel with any degree of comfort throughout Northwest
America except under the kindly aegis of the Old Company. They
plan your journey for you, give you introductions to their factors
at the different posts, and sell you an outfit guiltless of the ear-
marks of the tenderfoot. Moreover, they will furnish you with a
letter of credit which can be transmuted into bacon and beans
and blankets, sturgeon-head boats, guides' services, and succulent
sowbelly, at any point between Fort Chimo on Ungava Bay and
Hudson's Hope-on-the-Peace, between Winnipeg-on-the-Red and
that point in the Arctic where the seagull whistles over the whal-
ing-ships at Herschel."[5]

Their itinerary would be full. Over a period of six months they
planned to make stops at Athabasca Landing, Fort McMurray, Fort
Chipewyan, Smith's Landing, Fort Smith, Fort Resolution, Hay
River, Fort Rae, Fort Providence, Fort Simpson, Fort Wrigley, Fort
Norman, Fort Good Hope, Arctic Red River, Fort Macpherson,
and Herschel Island in the Beaufort Sea. On their return journey,

they would visit Vermilion, Peace River Crossing, and Lesser Slave Lake, before heading back to Athabasca Landing for their final trip out to Edmonton. Although those names tripped off their tongues easily enough, there were so many places that at the time seemed like mere dots and squiggly lines on a map. To experience them would take months traversing rapids, manoeuvring around shifting sand bars, sleeping in the open, cooking on driftwood campfires, and sharing space with the intrepid northern horsefly and biting mosquito. To acquire a sense of place Cameron would have to spend time in a region where ego loses meaning, and meet those whose narrative of the land was deeply etched into the furrows of their being. Only then would the land upon which they were to travel gain any verifiable meaning.

Lists, lists, and more lists. This was not an off-the-cuff sort of trip. It would require a dedication to lists: making them, following them, checking them, and then rechecking them. Everything, including clothing and gear had to fit into two small steamer trunks. It seemed that for the umpteenth time they had laid out their clothes only to put them away again. They had no precedent, no guides, no one to advise them. The choices were many—women's shoes or men's boots; hats—feminine or practical; dresses or breeches; hairstyle—the rounded pompadour or short cut? Was this a time for dropping all conventions around dress and femininity or not? In the end Cameron made compromises. She visited a hair salon and had her hair cut short, quite stylish and yet daring. It would be easier to manage than packing the hair frames necessary for the fashionable upswept Edwardian style. For hats she decided on the more practical wide-brimmed campaign hat like those worn by the North-West Mounted Police. She added a straw boater and a felt hat that could easily be rolled up and tucked into a small space. Oxfords, popular with outdoor travel suits, were out as were men's boots. She stayed with a pair of lace-up, mid-heeled shoes, the type that she usually wore. She thought they would be more suitable for tramping through the bush. She chose a tailored travel suit with an A-line floor length skirt, typical for the time. She added a few short jackets and several high-necked blouses. While she did not deviate too far from women's fashion, the overall effect was slightly masculine in appearance. The most important thing was comfort and practicality. Her only toiletries would be a brush, a comb, and a small bar of soap. Baths would be few and far between, a luxury at best.

Their gear had to be carefully considered. The Hudson's Bay Company was a big help here and supplied most of the necessities. The most important items were her Underwood typewriter and her two cameras, which she took great care to ensure would be protected from damage. She carefully wrapped her film in oilcloth and packed it in a biscuit tin. Added to the list was a tent, tent poles, and the "Hudson's Bay suit-case," which included the tent pegs and a tin washbasin. They had to take their own bedding, which consisted of a thin mattress with a waterproof bottom and waterproof extension-flaps and two blankets. The raincoats, while bulky and heavy, would be worth their weight. At the last minute Cameron sent her niece in search of a hatchet and a copper kettle to add to their growing provisions. "The bits of impedimenta look unfamiliar as we take our first inventory," she wrote, "but we are to come to know them soon by their feel in the dark, to estimate to an ounce the weight of each on many a lonely portage."[6]

Their plan was to leave during the first week of June. In the interim, Cameron had interviews with the media and several speaking engagements, some off the cuff. One such incident took her by complete surprise. She had been busy with her packing and took a short time off to drop into a meeting of the Canadian Women's Press Club. "I snatch half an hour to look in at the Royal Alexandra upon the reception which the Canadian Women's Press Club is tending to Mrs. Humphry Ward . . . Rain-bespattered, short skirted, and anchored with disreputable rubbers gluey with Winnipeg mud, I sit on the fringe of things, fairly intoxicated with the idea that we are off and this North trip no dream . . . Like a bolt from the blue came the summons from the president, and I, all muddy, am called to the seats of the mighty. I have never seen a more splendid aggregation of women . . . To face them is a mental and moral challenge. I try to hide those muddy shoes of mine. The Winnipeg women are indulgent, they make allowance for my unpresentable attire, and shower upon me cheery wishes for the success of my journey."[7]

Finally, everything was packed and tags with the name of each stop appended to their gear. As they boarded the train that would take them from Winnipeg to Edmonton, they waved goodbye to their friends and shouted, "All aboard for the Arctic Ocean and way ports!"[8] They spent ten days in Edmonton waiting to catch a ride with Kennedy's horse-drawn mail stage to Athabasca Landing. The only route to Athabasca Landing was from Fort Edmonton by way of the Athabasca Landing Trail, a road that would have sent most urban sophisticates on a hasty retreat to the security of the city. In the 1840s miners and fur traders hacked a rough path through forest and swampland to connect the North Saskatchewan and Mackenzie Rivers. Nicknamed the 100-mile portage, the trail became the major route into the north, opening access to trade goods along the Peace and Mackenzie Rivers. During the 1898 Klondike Gold Rush, it became a popular route for six hundred prospectors looking to fulfill their dreams of striking it rich.[9] Even though the Hudson's Bay Company refined the trail in 1876, it was still muddy and difficult when Cameron and her niece followed it.

Their departure from Fort Edmonton threw them immediately into the adversities experienced by travellers into the north. It was like boot camp for the uninitiated. "At seven in the morning," Cameron wrote, "the stage pulls up for us, and it rains—no gentle sizzle-sozzle, but a sod-soaker, yea a gully-washer! The accusing newness of those raincoats is to come off at once. Expansive Kennedy looks askance at the tenderfoots who climb over his wheel. His Majesty's Royal Mail Stage sifts through the town picking up the other victims."[10] They quickly came to understand why the road they were about to embark upon was commonly referred to as "the bugs, mud, and moonshine trail." It was a quagmire of one mud hole after another. Periodically, the passengers had to get off the wagon to lighten the load on the horses. They walked up steep hills and clomped through boot-sucking mud that seemed to go on forever. Despite Cameron's ankle-length skirt and heeled shoes, she matched her stride with that of Sergeant Anderson. She was keen to get to know more about Anderson and talk to him about his experiences in the north. Sergeant Anderson was one of the most respected and experienced NWMP officers in the Peace River Country and was intimately acquainted with the most famous murder trial in Saskatchewan's history. In 1904 Edward Hayward, a professional hunter and trapper, was killed by his partner Charles King at Lesser Slave Lake. Anderson tracked King down and gathered the evidence that led to King's execution in the following year. "It is hard to induce a Mounted Police man to talk," she wrote. "However, to be striding Athabasca Trail with the hero of the Hayward-King murder-trial is too good an opportunity to lose, and, reluctantly rendered, bit by bit, the story comes out."[11]

Fortunately for the weary travellers there were a series of rest houses, which Cameron referred to as the "Waldorf-Astorias of the wilderness." The most popular was Newton Egge's Half-way House, where the smell of fresh pies, along with a bath and clean sheets greeted the two women. The coach ride hardened them up and served as a good introduction for the next leg of their trip, which would include sluicing down ninety miles of rapids in an open flat-bottomed scow.[12] "We acknowledge with inward shame," she wrote, "that two years of city life have given us the soft muscles of the chee-chaco[13]; we'll have to harden up a bit if we are to reach that faraway ocean."[14]

When they finally disembarked at Athabasca Landing they stepped into a hub of activity. On May 12, the ice had broken on the river, so the Landing had suddenly become a busy place with Cree and Métis trackers, boat builders, and trappers intent on getting their furs to southern and European markets. Athabasca Landing was in the first stages of a building boom. There were two hotels, a post office, a school, about a dozen stores, a blacksmith shop, a parsonage, a Catholic church, and a reading-room. Boat building was a flourishing business that brought in loggers, carpenters, and sawmill operators. What started out as a free-for-all, where anyone who had ever thought of being a boat builder could try their hand, ended up as a highly efficient industry producing river-worthy steamboats, scows, and York boats.

Kennedy's coach dropped them off in front of the Grand Union Hotel where they had arranged to stay. They were muddy and tired from their trip and were eager to soak off their travels in a nice hot bath, but that was not to be. The Grand Hotel was not as distinguished as its name suggested; it had a leak problem. "If local colour and local smell is what we have come north for, we find it here," Cameron said.[15] They were destined to have an uncomfortable night, for shortly after their arrival it started raining. "The room assigned us becomes a living illustration of the new word we have just learned—'muskeg,' a swamp. Putting the precious cameras on top of the bureau, we let the rest of the things swim at their pleasure . . . For thirty-six hours on end it rains. That roof was full of surprises; you never knew where it would spring a fresh leak."[16]

The next morning, they set out to explore their surroundings, eager to learn about the history of the area and talk to as many people as they could about life at the Landing. Cameron was surprised to hear that the Hudson's Bay Company was held in high regard. "It has been fashionable to paint the H. B. Co. as an agrarian oligarchy," she wrote. "Organized for the purpose of 'making fur'. . . it is true that The Company, throughout the years, devoted itself to peltries and not to plotting town sites. This was its business." The company had consistently kept faith with its traders, she said. "The word of The Company has . . . ever been worth its full face value . . . in the past, as in the present, they were large men; they honoured their word, and you couldn't buy them . . . because the North still breeds men of the H. B. type, the eye of The Great Company is not dimmed, its force not abated."[17] She did acknowledge that the HBC also made many mistakes that it needed to account for—"we couldn't picture one of them with a saintly aureole," she said.[18]

During the early part of Canada's European history, the land outside of the urban boundary was considered a storehouse of resources, but was untouchable due to the harshness of the environment. Despite the known hardships the Dominion government had an almost missionary zeal in wanting to settle the land. Most immigrants to the area were not prepared for the sub-arctic temperatures, the short growing season, devastating summer storms, and poor soil, so left their promised land almost as quickly as they arrived. It was only when farmers became more familiar with working within the confines of the environment, and improvements in agricultural methods increased their yields, that the northwest began to be known as a potential breadbasket. From 1909 to 1914 fifteen hundred settlers arrived to homestead, and while some left for the more favourable climate of the Peace, others stayed. Today, Athabasca remains the entry point to the north and the town itself has around thirty-five hundred inhabitants.

Cameron believed that although Athabasca Landing did not have the best farmland, the surrounding area had good farming prospects and should be advertised as such. In a talk she later gave in Chicago about her trip she said that, "Everyone who had thought of the North knows that the country of the Peace is rich in agricultural possibilities, but it is remarkable how many think the whole North to be the Peace River Country. It is no more than half of it."[19] As for its future, she pointed out that although the resources of the Athabasca were known, until a road went through the area there would be no development. "Gold may be packed out in buckskin bags," she said, "but it takes trains to carry out petroleum, asphalt, lumber, salt, and the like." One day, she said, there will be great cities: "The country will doubtless develop great mineral wealth, and its timber and fisheries are very rich."[20] In the meantime, fur was the dominant reason for its existence and would be for some time. In her writings Cameron referred the north as the region of "the Fur Belt." "One illusion vanishes here," she said. "We had expected to find the people of the North intensely interested in the affairs of the world outside, but as a rule they are not . . . The one conjecture round the bar and in the home is, 'When will the rabbits run this year?' The rabbits in the North are the food of the lynx; cheap little bunny keeps the vital spark aglow in the bodies of those animals with richer fur who feed upon him . . . As surely as wheat stands for bullion in the grain-belt, little Molly cottontail is the currency of the North."[21]

Before they could get to the Mackenzie River they had to find their way down the Athabasca River, starting at Athabasca Landing. Entering the traditional territory of the Dene, Cree, Gwich'in, and Inuvialuit peoples of the Western Arctic, they would be travelling through a harsh and unbroken wilderness known only to a scattering of trappers, miners, RCMP officers, and missionaries. Once on the river, all trappings of urban life would be left behind as they journeyed into lands where wits, strength, and intimate knowledge of the wilderness were essential for survival. Bravado, courage, and eagerness would not be enough to support them in their venture; their lives would be completely dependent upon their various guides. Even today, particularly in the Mackenzie River Delta with its hundreds of snaking tributaries, a knowledgeable guide is essential.

Their itinerary included stops at the Hudson's Bay posts along the river. Fort McMurray was first on their agenda, but to get there they had to take a boat down the Athabasca River for over two hundred miles and transit through a series of daunting rapids. When they left the evening of June 6 the entire population of Athabasca Landing was on the riverbank to see them off. They were travelling with a flotilla of seven boats filled to the gunwales with goods and people destined for various communities in the north. Some were coming this way for the first time, while others were returning home. Cameron and Jessie were on a trip few non-Indigenous women had undertaken. The other white women who had travelled the liquid highway to communities north were mostly wives of missionaries and trappers. In Fort McMurray they would meet Christina Gordon, a gritty, self-sufficient woman who came with her brother from Scotland in 1897 to open a trading post. She not only built her own cabin and ran the business but made herbal medicine to administer to those in need. About their meeting Cameron wrote, "We call upon Miss Christine Gordon,[22] a young Scottish woman and a free-trader, if you please, in her own right, operating in opposition to the great and only Hudson's Bay Company. The only white woman on a five hundred mile stretch of the Athabasca, she has lived here for years with the Indians for companions, her days being marked out by their migrations and tribal feasts. We question, 'Are you not lonely, especially in the winter?' But she smiles and refuses to be regarded as heroic."[23] At Fort Chipewyan they spent time talking with Sister Burnelle, one of the Grey Nuns of Montreal, who told Cameron that she had been teaching in the north since 1866. Cameron never claimed that she and her niece were the first white women to travel up into the Arctic Circle; it was the media that made such assertions, writing that Cameron travelled farther into the Northland than any other woman. Some articles even drew pictures of her paddling her own canoe, which she did not do. Readers loved stories of bold and fearless adventurers, conquering high mountains and struggling against harsh environments. Cameron and Jessie would not endure the hardships and privations that early explorers had, nor were they discovering new land, but she knew that the image of the intrepid traveller, writing about the far reaches of the world, sold more copy. Cameron did point out, however, that they were the first white women to make such a trip in one summer and claimed to be the first to visit Fort Rae, a small Dogrib community on the north arm of the Great Slave Lake, as well as the territory of the Dënesuliné (Dene-su-lee-neh) First Nations, at the eastern end of the Great Slave Lake. "No white woman has yet traversed it to its eastern extremity," she wrote, "and we would go if we had to work our passage at the sweeps of the scow."[24]

As they pulled away from the bank and headed into the mainstream, Cameron waved goodbye and shouted, "Farewell, Nistow! We are off."[25] Their flotilla of scows, commonly referred to as the Athabasca Brigade, were large flat-bottomed bulk carriers fortified to handle between nine and eleven metric tons of freight. Each scow was equipped with a long sweep, four oars, and a crew of five men. "The steersman is our admiration, as with that clumsy stern-sweep he dodges rocks, runs riffles, and makes bends," she wrote. "The scow is made of green wood, and its resilience stands it in good stead as, like a snake, it writhes through tight channels or over ugly bits of water. Everybody is in good humour; we are dreamers dreaming greatly. Why should we not be happy?"[26] They would not make it far this first night, but it was no matter. In the north one obeys the dictates of the elements, not an arbitrary timetable. Toward suppertime they could hear the cook several boats over, whistling a merry tune, a signal that he was beginning to prepare their evening repast. It was not long before a scrumptious odour wafted over the boats, readying their appetites. By the time they came ashore their meal was steaming hot. Bannock and sowbelly were on the menu, a staple on the river. The hungry travellers devoured their supper leaving nothing for begging scavengers. Cameron remarked that they had left their dainty cloth napkins and finger bowls behind them, "From here to the Arctic are no domestic animals, the taste of beef or mutton or pork or chicken is unknown, bread gives place to bannock (with its consequent indigestion 'bannockburn'), and coffee is a beverage discredited. Tobacco to smoke, strong, black, sweetened tea to drink from a copper kettle—this is luxury's lap."[27]

They left very early the next morning, although not soon enough, some thought. A pall had descended upon the group; no one felt like talking and any sort of undertaking exacerbated their itching. Everyone had spent an uncomfortable night sleeping in the rain and fighting off capricious mosquitoes. Farther along the river one of the passengers picked up his fiddle and livened the group with his cheery tunes, and soon all was forgotten. They travelled all day and through the night, passing Lac La Biche, Calling River, and Swift Current. It was that magical time of the year when night was beginning to edge into day, with barely a flicker. With less than four hours of darkness the days seemed to linger, outpacing their energy. That first Sunday night on the river was clear and beautiful, pushing any thoughts of sleeping aside lest a twinkling star or a commanding constellation be missed. A sense of agelessness and wonderment crept into Cameron's thoughts. Wanting to capture the moment, she took out her notebook and wrote, "Making a pillow of a squat packing-case consigned to the missionary at Hay River, and idly wondering what it might contain, I draw up a canvas sheet. But it is too wonderful a night to sleep. Lying flat upon our backs and looking upward, we gaze at the low heaven full of stars, big, lustrous, hanging down so low that we can almost reach up and pluck them. Two feet away, holding in both hands the stern sweep, is the form of the Cree steersman, his thoughtful face a cameo against the shadow of the cut-banks."[28]

Around five o'clock in the morning the stern sweeps began to bring the scows closer together in preparation for Pelican Portage. It was hot, nearly forty degrees Celsius, and there was no shade to escape the glare from the sun. The lassitude that gripped them was suddenly broken by a loud hissing noise. As they neared the source of the disturbance they saw a large gushing fire spout that looked and sounded like a fire-breathing dragon. "We are not a hundred miles from Athabasca Landing," Cameron noted. "On the left bank we come across a magnificent gas-well with a gush of flame twenty or thirty feet in height . . . the sound of the escape ricochets up and down the palisaded channel so that we cannot hear each other speak . . . There is gas enough here, if we could pipe it and bring it under control, to supply with free illumination every city of prairie Canada." The well, which had become a landmark for all who passed by, burned steadily throughout summer storms and winter snowdrifts until it was finally capped in 1918. "It has destroyed all vegetation for a radius of twenty yards," Cameron wrote, "but, oddly enough, outside this range of demarcation the growth is more luxuriant and comes earlier and stays later than that of the surrounding country."[29] Farther down river, between Grand Rapids and Brule, they saw more gas reserves. "Another manifestation of gas is here," she wrote. "It bubbles up on the shore and through the water at the boat's bow, and as we strike a match the whole surface flames like the brandy on a Christmas plum-pudding."[30] The Dominion government was aware of these gas reserves, but not of their size. It was something they intended to examine later, but for the time being they were more interested in putting their efforts and money toward the exploration of oil. As early as 1894 a team was sent to Athabasca Landing to drill for oil. They found a large field of natural gas, but no oil reserves. Presuming they had drilled in the wrong place, three years later they bored a second well at Pelican Rapids. Again, they found a huge field of natural gas, but no oil. Further surveys were seen as unproductive, so the exercise was abandoned.

Those first few days on the river were easy and relaxing. The water was pliant and surrendered readily to the oarsmen; the sound of the riffling water was calming, creating a momentary sense of serenity. By now they were a hundred miles downriver from Athabasca Landing. Around each bend in the river was a new adventure, Cameron exclaimed, "The old heart-hunger for new places and untrod ways—who would exchange all of this for the easy ways of fatted civilization!"[31] They passed House River, marked by several graves whose stories were too gruesome to recount. As the surrounding valley began to give way to steeper banks, the current became more demanding. They were entering the first of fifteen rapids that would challenge them over the next 124 miles. Tension mounted as they moved into the entrance of a lazy S-bend in the river. The water was choppy and the oarsmen had to man-oeuvre around rocks and standing waves. The first three rapids were a disappointment for Cameron. "The Pelican Rapid and the Stony we shoot without turning a hair; the Joli Fou is a bit more insistent, but, as the cook says, 'nothing to write home about.'"[32] Twenty-one miles farther on they meet the hoped-for challenge at Grand Rapids. About a mile upstream, the roar of the rapids blocked all other sound. It was not long before they saw spinets of frothing water, signalling what was to come. From afar it looked as if the river dropped off into an abyss. Cameron wrote, "We drift in a drowsy dream of delight, and in the evening arrive at the head of Grand Rapids. If we had looked slightingly on the rough water passed, what we now see would satisfy the greediest. We tie up and get a good view of what lies ahead."[33] The rapids stretch for a mile and are a boiling, frothy cauldron of white water, standing waves, large boulders, and sandstone outcrops, surrounded by vortices and swirling eddies. Grand Rapids has some of the largest concretions in the world that create a natural dam; there are no clear channels marking the way, and it is an extremely dangerous stretch of water. In today's standards, Grand Rapids are marked as a class VI+ dif-ficulty, which means they cannot be navigated. Everyone was on edge. As the excitement built a surge of adrenaline steadied them for the impending event. The old timers told the group about the many lives claimed by Grand Rapids, adding to their anxiety.

Although they would not transit these rapids, they did need to get the scows safely to their portage point at Grand Island in the middle of the river. After they shoved their boats out from the shore they had to manoeuvre across the upper reach of the channel. As they came closer to the rapids, they felt the urgency of the river pushing their boats ever faster toward the great maw of destruction. After many tense minutes and with great relief, they reached the safety of their destination. As they unloaded their gear, the voyagers were calmed by the familiarity of setting up camp. "Inside our tents we arrange the mosquito-bar (a tent within a tent looking something like a good-sized dog-kennel), and here we lie in our blankets," Cameron wrote. "The hum of the foiled mosquito is unction to our souls. It is a relief too, to remove the day's clothing, the first time in ninety-six hours."[34]

Once the boats were empty, a group of sixty Métis from Lac La Biche transported their supplies to the north end of the island where the boats were reloaded in calmer waters. While they waited, Cameron and Jessie spent four days logging information on the plant life and writing about their travels. In describing their surroundings Cameron made mention of more evidence of lignite: "The river has weathered the banks into vertical cliffs four or five hundred feet high, imbedded in which are wonderful cheese-shaped nodules, some the size of baseballs, some as big as mill-stones . . . The sandstone banks opposite the island are overlain with a stratum of lignite three or four feet thick, which burns freely and makes acceptable fuel. Sections of fossil trees are also seen, and the whole thing is fascinating, one's great wish being for a larger knowledge of geology so as to read aright this strange page of history in stone."[35] Back on the river, the group pressed on. Just as they were beginning to relax, an unmanned scow filled with cargo sluiced past them. Two quick-thinking guides grabbed the RCMP canoes they were carrying and paddled out into the rapids to try to rescue the boat, but to no avail. Was this an ominous sign of what was to come? they wondered.

As they navigated through Brule, Boiler, Middle, Long, Crooked, Rock, and Little Cascade Rapids, once again their Cree guides deftly avoided the standing waves, ledges, boulders, shallow bits, sharp bends, and cataracts. These rapids, referred to as class III and IV, are not advisable for open canoes and must be paddled with great care. They had been running rapids continuously for nineteen miles and were exhausted, but before they could rest they had one more hurdle to overcome. By late afternoon the current had picked up speed, and the group could feel the powerful force of the river egging them on. It was not long before they heard the ominous roar of the Big Cascade. They entered the rapids on a sharp right bend and were immediately caught up in the river's exuberance. The sight was intimidating; the rapids looked ugly, Cameron said. They were met by a blockage of angry water that stretched across the breadth of the channel. It was here that the entire river spilled its ferocity over a long line of backbreaking limestone ledges. To the travellers it looked impenetrable. Everyone was alert; muscles tensed, hearts beat wildly, and breathing quickened. Their lives depended on the skill of their oarsmen and their ability to read the river. The crews doubled up and aligned the boats in a single file. The first hurdle was a six-foot drop, at the bottom of which was a confusion of swirling water, large standing waves, and mean-looking whirlpools, just waiting for another victim to add to its score. The guides looked for a V in the river indicating the location of a chute. The oarsmen had the job of ensuring that the fifteen-metre scow, carrying nine metric tons of goods, lined up at just the right angle. If the stern and the bow were improperly aligned, they would be in serious trouble. Once they entered the rapids there was no stopping. Cameron and her fellow passengers readied themselves; they moved to the middle of the boat for stability. The lumbering vessel felt like an elephant to her, but as she said, "For all we own in the world we wouldn't be anywhere but just where we sit. If it is going to be our last minute, well, Kismet! let it come. At least it will be not be a tame way of going out." They felt a jolt as their vessel struck something but they kept on going, and then almost as soon as it began it was over. Everyone breathed a huge sigh of relief. "For the life of me I cannot forbear a cry of exultation," she said.[36]

When they reached the shore Cameron hurriedly unpacked her camera to photograph the next scow shooting the falls, which as it happened was just in time to capture one of the boats filling with water and breaking apart. Almost immediately a rush of scows and canoes pushed through the swirling cauldron of frothy water to rescue the passengers. They were told to jump into one of the rescue boats. They were terrified. To leap from one boat to another when both were being pushed and pulled in a violent manner was asking the impossible, but their lives depended upon doing so. Fortunately, everyone was rescued and all were safe, but valuable cargo was lost. The river had claimed life-saving medicine that had been sent from England, bolts of fabric for making clothes, packets of Hudson's Bay blankets used in the trade of furs, religious relics, bear traps, a missionary's box of toys for children, and astronomical instruments critical for scientific exploration. Over five thousand dollars' worth of goods were destroyed in just three minutes. Although it is a point of honour in the north not to complain, Cameron said that the scow and its cargo looked like an "abomination of desolation." Despite the day's disaster, when evening twilight unfolded and revealed the beauty of the night, all was forgiven. Describing the scene Cameron wrote, "The sun sank in a crimson splendor . . . A low-hung moon comes out and is visible . . . With a blanket thrown over me, as the others sleep, I lie along the gunwale, and the beauty of it sinks into my very soul."[37] The date was June 13 and it was their last night sleeping among the tangle of lines and ropes that had served as their bed since leaving Athabasca Landing. They had been on the water for eight days and would not return this way until early October, when the evening frost signalled an end to the warm balmy days of summer.

The next morning the remaining six scows limped into Fort McMurray. They were a sorry-looking lot. They had quite an ordeal going through the rapids, and losing one of their vessels to the rocks at Cascade Rapids was disheartening. Fort McMurray was a welcome sight. The crew set about unloading and drying out the cargo they had rescued from the river. Cameron described a scene that looked like the aftermath of a great flood. "Bales of goods are unwound and stretched out for hundreds of yards in the sun. Bandanna handkerchiefs flutter on bushes, toilet soap, boots, and bear-traps are at our feet . . . Mathematical and astronomical instruments consigned to a scientist on the Arctic edge are shaken off centre and already have begun to rust, and there are miles and miles of cordage and nets, with braids and sewing silks and Hudson's Bay blankets!"[38] Fortunately their cameras, film, and typewriter were dry and safe. An event such as theirs was not unusual, which was one of the reasons that items shipped north were so expensive.

As Cameron and Jessie looked out over the broad flat plain of Fort McMurray they saw a small gritty hamlet that was scraped out of the boreal forest. There were a few dozen people living there at the time, some log cabins, and a couple of stores that catered primarily to the traders. The first post office had opened just twelve days before their arrival. Fort McMurray had been one of the Hudson's Bay Company's major fur trading posts, but as the wildlife population became depleted from over-hunting, fur traders no longer frequented the post as they once had. Fort Chipewyan, on the western point of Lake Athabasca, became the major trading centre, while Fort McMurray developed into a transportation post focused on moving goods from the south into the north. Despite its humble appearance, Cameron saw a great future for Fort McMurray. She had heard that the Alberta and Great Waterways Railway planned to build a line that would link Edmonton with Fort McMurray, opening access to the rest of the country.[39] She also knew that the area harboured oil reserves, the size of which was still unknown. Today Fort McMurray has a population of around seventy-four thousand people and, despite the periodic collapse in oil prices, remains the oil centre of Canada.

Leaving behind them, for the moment anyway, sowbelly, bannock, and bug infested campsites, Cameron and Jessie entered the comfort of the Hudson's Bay Company's twenty-four-year-old stern-wheeled steamer, the ss *Grahame*. They planned go as far as Smith's Landing at which point they would change vessels and carry on to the Arctic. "Fort McMurray is the parting of the ways where the Hudson's Bay Company's steamer *Grahame* meets us bringing her tale of outward-going passengers from the North . . . We shake hands with those going out to civilization and take our dunnage aboard the steamer."⁴⁰ As supplies were being loaded on the bottom deck, Cameron and Jessie settled into their cabin on the upper deck. The steamer seemed beyond luxury. Here they had a bathroom, blankets, and a bed with sheets. There was a formal salon where delicious meals were served for fifty cents. Like the bigger ocean liners there was an evening dress code, although somewhat tuned to the lifestyle of the north. Entering the salon in shirtsleeves was strictly forbidden; men had to wear a suitable jacket for meals. "The *Grahame* has its advantages," Cameron wrote. "Clean beds, white men's meals served in real dishes, and best of all, a bath!"⁴¹ Their next stop was Fort Chipewyan across Lake Athabasca.

Not long after they pulled out from shore they noticed an acrid odour in the air. Thinking at first it was the exhaust from the engine they soon realized they were entering the tar sands area. For the next eighty miles, they saw patches of a bituminous outpouring trickling down from high cut banks, oozing its way into the river below. What would eventually become known around the world as the Alberta tar sands began millions of years ago when oceans first rose and then retreated, trapping marine organisms under layers of sand and clay where compression, heat, and bacteria slowly transformed the decaying plants and animals into fossil fuels. The Hudson's Bay Company had been made aware of the oil in the early 1700s by a Cree trader, but at that point in time it was of little interest to them. Alexander Mackenzie also made mention of it when he saw the Chipewyan using the black gooey substance to waterproof their canoes. In 1875 the Dominion government sent in geological surveyors to drill test holes hoping to find free-flowing oil. By the end of the century it was estimated that the Athabasca deposit covered over 146,000 square kilometres and would potentially produce close to two trillion barrels of oil, making it the largest deposit of crude bitumen in the world. Extracting oil from sand was a labour-intensive process and despite the surge in population, success was limited, although there were many who made their fortunes to the contrary. It was not until Great Canadian Oil Sands constructed an efficient extraction plant in 1967 that oil and profits started flowing. In the meantime, the world would have to wait, for the process of extracting the oil from the sands was not yet born, though that did not dissuade prospectors from trying.

Count Alfred von Hammerstein was the first of the prospectors to attempt to turn the tarry substance into a profitable enterprise. Between 1903 and 1909 von Hammerstein sunk eighty-five thousand dollars into ninety metric tons of drilling equipment, achieving some success and proving that it could be done. When Cameron cruised by she noticed a line of nine drill rigs dotting the banks of the river. Her commentary provides an interesting description of the operation. "In all Canada," she wrote, "there is no more interesting stretch of waterway than that upon which we are entering. An earth-movement here has created a line of fault clearly visible for seventy or eighty miles along the river-bank out of which oil oozed at frequent intervals. Count von Hammerstein, building derricks from point to point along the stream, has put in much time, toil, and money in oil development here . . . The Count tells us of striking one hundred and fifty feet of rock salt while 'punching' one of his oil-shafts through the ground . . . Out of the over-hanging banks it oozes at every fissure, and into some of the bituminous tar-wells we can poke a twenty foot pole and find no resistance . . . We speak only of what we observe from the deck of a boat as we pass down this wonderful river. What is hidden is a richer story which only the coming of the railroad can bring to light."[42]

After days of following the winding twists and turns of the river delta, they entered Lake Athabasca on the morning of June 2. Not wanting to miss the opportunity to see the transition between the river and the lake, Cameron and Jessie stationed themselves on the top deck. Their only company was the sound of the swooshing of the water slipping over the paddle wheel as it pushed them ever closer to their destination. The other passengers were still asleep, having expended themselves with a night of exuberant, fast-paced, foot-stomping Red River jigs. Suddenly the river stopped and the horizon opened in front of them; the lake seemed to go on forever. At 2,140 kilometres Lake Athabasca is the eighth largest lake in the country. Looking out over the lake it was not hard to imagine that only a few weeks before freezing temperatures had locked its vast reserves in a sea of ice. For the moment, however, the sun danced across the lake showcasing the natural beauty of the area. Cameron wrote, "The great lake-scape is blue and green and grey and opaline as the sun strikes it and the surface breaks to a south wind. Ours is the one craft on this inland sea, but overhead a whole navy of clouds manoeuvres, the ships of the ghostly argosy doubling themselves in the lake."[43]

As they made their way across the western portion of the lake, Fort Chipewyan gradually came into view. Cameron had read that it was the oldest post in the north, established in 1788, and had been the site of fierce struggles between the rival North West Company, New North West Company, and Hudson's Bay Company, with the latter gaining control in 1821. Once they entered the lake the sternwheeler increased its speed, as if it was anxious to return to its homeport. Fort Chipewyan had a thriving boat-building industry, which serviced the river. They built the first York boats for the region and the ss *Grahame*, completed in 1882, was the first steamship launched from its shores. Cameron was excited to see the place from which so many noted explorers had started their journeys. In 1789, at twenty-five years of age, Alexander Mackenzie set out from Fort Chipewyan on his first voyage of discovery to find a route to the Pacific Ocean, but missing the route travelled the Mackenzie River and out into the

Beaufort Sea instead. He also used Fort Chipewyan as a staging spot for his second and successful attempt in 1792. In 1820 Sir John Franklin used Fort Chipewyan as his base for his overland Arctic explorations, and seven years later spent the winter and spring at Fort Chipewyan. Other famous explorers like Peter Pond, David Thompson, and Simon Fraser passed through on the way to their discoveries. When the *Grahame* pulled up to the landing, Cameron and Jessie were struck by the wide-ranging diversity of people. There were Métis, Cree, Chipewyan, English, French, Scots, and Orkney Islanders, many of whom were brought together to satisfy the global market's desire for fur. The community was a thriving hub of activity. Cameron wrote, "At one end of the village are the little smithy of the Hudson's Bay Company and the pretentious buildings of their establishment. At the other . . . rise the steeples and convent-school of the Roman Church, with the free-trading-post of Colin Fraser. Midway between is the little Church of England, and higher up and farther back the Barracks of the Royal Northwest Mounted Police. The white-washed homes of the employés [*sic*] of The Company, little match-boxes dazzling in the sun, stretch from one end of the beach to the other."[44] Eager to learn more about the ss *Grahame*, Cameron and Jessie met with Wyllie, who had forged the steel and ironwork for the vessel. He told them that he had come to Chipewyan from the Orkneys in 1863 and had been living there ever since. He had travelled to Hudson Bay and then across the country. He proudly told Cameron that he had never set foot in a city. "Mr. Wyllie has never seen an electric light nor a railway train nor a two-story building nor a telegraph wire nor a telephone," she wrote.[45] Wyllie was typical of many who had made the north their home. In his forty-five years of living in Fort Chipewyan he never ventured farther north than Fort Smith or farther south than Fort McMurray, a distance of about five hundred kilometres. He forged his tools himself and wielded them with the hand of an artist. He was not much for modern ways or modern luxuries. He lamented that life was becoming too easy—he preferred it when times were tougher, he said. "It was much better in the old days when we had only dried meat and fish-oil . . . Nowadays, when we have flour and tinned meats and preserved fruits, all my teeth are coming out!"[46]

Cameron and Jessie received a welcome invitation to stay with Mr. and Mrs. William Johnson, who provided them with fulsome meals and lavender-scented sheets. Mr. Johnson was known throughout the region as an expert at repairing time-pieces and the genius who set up the electric light plant at Fort Simpson. The Johnsons' cozy, well-lit home was a delight for the two women, although after several days of unaccustomed luxury Cameron was anxious to leave the confines of such gentility to explore the area. She particularly wanted to read through the journals of the Hudson's Bay Company factors and spent every spare minute making notes from the entries for her book. Sitting on a dusty floor among old flintlocks and discarded ox-yokes, she riffled through some of the old journals feeling somewhat guilty for poking into people's secrets from the past. From one entry she noted, "On this page the ink is thin and one can see the old writer thawing out his frozen ink-pot of stone at the end of a tired day and sitting down to write his simple tale . . . He is far from those who direct his fate, and recognition and reward are slow in coming. Companionship and the gentle arts of 'outside' are denied him."[47] Reading another more cheerful entry she wrote, "We get a delightful picture in an entry under the date of Wednesday, 23 May, 1827, when Sir John Franklin was on his way back to England at the end of his second journey. 'To-day William McGillivary and Katherine Stewart, daughter of Alexander Stewart, Chief Factor, were joined in holy wedlock by Captain John Franklin, R.N., Commander of the Land Arctic Expedition.'"[48]

While there they had the good fortune to accompany the annual government treaty party to Fond du Lac. Under Treaty 8 the Dominion government promised, among other things, to provide education, medicine, and annuities in exchange for rights to the land.[49] Cameron learned that Fond du Lac was one of several locations for the signing of the treaty. Thrilled to have the opportunity to go to "the far end of the lake" they left on June 29 for a four-day trip aboard the HBC's tug, the SS *Primrose*. Other than canoes, the *Primrose* was the main mode of transportation that carried passengers and cargo between Fort Chipewyan, Fond du Lac, and Fort Smith. It was not the most glamorous of vessels, but it served its purpose well. Cameron described it as a small tug with a wobbly gunwale. It had just enough room on deck to set up her typewriter. Astern, on a long tow, a scow carried the wood needed to stoke the firebox, necessary supplies, trade goods, and six husky dogs who passed their time curled up in balls sleeping.

As they neared the eastern end of the lake the little tug slowed against the current where the Fond Du Lac River rushes out of its narrow confines to meet the lake. From the deck, Cameron saw a community of teepees set up along the sandy beach waiting for the treaty party to arrive. Farther up the banks she could see a long makeshift trestle table, where those who were registered with the Dominion agents would receive their annual allotment of fishing line, ammunition, five dollars, along with an assortment of other items. "It is a beautiful shore," she said, "but lonely even now in the effulgence of the midsummer sun; what it is like in winter we scarcely care to conjecture."[50] She is told a story by one of the passengers who said that the past winter was hard on everyone. There was a little boy who came out on the ice to play with his sled and he slipped and fell, and to the hungry dogs on the shore the small fur-clad figure looked like prey. They set upon him before anyone noticed what had happened. It was a tragic event that affected everyone nearby and a reminder that the north can be unforgiving.

Once they disembarked, the two women created quite a stir among the crowd that had gathered to welcome the treaty party. As the first European women to visit Fond du Lac, they were quite an anomaly. Having no business with the treaty party they decided to explore their surroundings. They walked past the sleek-lined birchbark canoes, admiring the skill of those who made them, and entered a stand of birch trees, which she said were somewhat dwarfed but beautiful. Around them were wild roses and dense clusters of heavily scented ground pine, giant willow herb, and mint. The multitude of mosquitoes flitting around seemed interested in these new morsels of flesh upon which to feast and had Cameron and Jessie wondering if they should return to the safety of the shoreline. They pressed on until they came upon a prolific garden bursting with tall potato plants. Next to the garden was a lonely cemetery tended by Father Beihler, who told them that he had been in Fond du Lac for the last eight years. Originally from Alsace-Lorraine, Father Beihler had been sent to Fond du Lac as part of the Missionary Oblates of Mary Immaculate to minister to the needs of the inhabitants of the Mackenzie region. He had been in the priesthood for only three months when he received his posting and knowing its isolation and the hardships that he would endure, he wept. In looking back over the history of the Oblate missions, Pope Pius XI described the mission in Fond du Lac as a vast solitude of great white silence and one of the most difficult assignments of the church. From Father Beihler they learned that the Mission of Our Lady of Seven Sorrows had been in operation since 1853 and that he was the fifth missionary to take up the post.

Father Beihler was intrigued by the women's presence. He was most insistent on knowing their ages, how much money they made, and whether they were Catholic. They took it in stride and answered all his questions, admiring his direct manner. Their last vision of Father Beihler was watching him carry a cup of water into a teepee to comfort an old man who lay dying. Describing the scene, Cameron wrote, "The slanting sun strikes the tin cup and the big crucifix of the good Father, and so we leave Fond du Lac." Of the people of Fond du Lac she wrote, "They are perhaps the least unspoiled of 'civilization,' as their range is removed from the north-south route afforded by the Mackenzie . . . Their hearts have not learned to hunger for those soggy bannocks, unventilated shacks, and sheet-iron stoves which are luring their tribal cousins on the germ-strewn way to higher culture with convenient stopping places in graves by the wayside."[51, 52] When the vessel was loaded with furs and trappers the group said their goodbyes and left Fond du Lac. They arrived back at Fort Chipewyan on Dominion Day; a day Cameron lamented held little significance to those of the north. "There is no soul who cares a whitefish for the fact that this is Dominion Day, Canada's national holiday."[53] Early the next morning they boarded their trusty little tug once again, swung past English Island and entered the Slave River with its array of snaking tributaries. They were excited to be back on the river and enjoyed an easy ride, covering a hundred miles in twelve hours. Their next stop was Fort Smith. Before they could comfortably disembark at their destination they had one more hurdle to surmount. They had just come around Ryan Island, which seemed to take over the entire river, and were greeted with the now familiar grumble of roiling water. There were a series of four sets of rapids that blocked off river access to Fort Smith. Their only approach was by way of a long twenty-five-kilometre portage starting at Smith's Landing.[54] Cameron had read of the feats and exploits of those who had run this section of the Slave River but did not know what to expect. Alexander Mackenzie met these rapids and noted in his journals the best places for portages, which still hold to this day. The aptly named "Rapids of the Drowned" occur at the point where the Slave River meets the Precambrian Shield. With a drop of one hundred feet over fourteen miles, they are regarded as the most dangerous rapids in North America. Cameron and Jessie had weathered the other rapids, but this powerful display of hydraulics was unnerving. They learned that a few days prior their arrival two priests had capsized and drowned. The only eyewitness told Cameron she saw the boat flip and then an arm lift a paddle into the air, which was followed by a loud anguished cry; and then nothing, they were gone. It was a chilling story; the river had lived up to its moniker. Over the years the rapids have been so analyzed that individual rocks, riffles, chutes, swirling eddies, standing waves, and vortexes have acquired telling names like Hangover Cure, Top Gun, the Hole that Ate Chicago, and the Tube. What once sent fear into the stalwart hearts of voyagers has today become a mecca for high performance paddlers from around the world who guide their small snub nose kayaks through an impossible obstacle course matching their wit and skill to that of the river.

The original plan was to go directly to Fort Smith as soon as they landed, but there seemed to be a problem with some of the oxen so they had to bide their time waiting for replacements. They had long ago left needless timetables behind them and the break would give them an opportunity to collect more plant specimens, but they were in muskeg country, which was made up of decaying plants and stagnant pools of water. It was not long before their conversation turned from the flora of Smith's Landing to the fauna. Now slightly north of 60° they had crossed an invisible barrier that brought them into the territorial realm of a new breed of insects. Mosquitoes and other biting insects had been fairly steady on the journey, but nothing like the ones they met at Smith's Landing: "We thought we had met mosquitoes on the Athabasca. The Athabasca mosquito is gentle, ineffective, compared with his cousin of Smith's Portage," she wrote.[55] Their new companions were avaricious meat-eating deer flies, appropriately referred to as bull-dogs. Travel diaries are filled with references and stories of the Mackenzie region insects. In 1892 Isaac Stringer, a missionary, wrote about his journey to the Mackenzie Delta and said that the mosquitoes at Smith's Landing swarmed round by the thousands and were so loud they sounded like a band playing in discordant harmony. Cameron facetiously renamed the area "Mosquito Portage." She and Jessie realized they would have to come to some accommodation with these new pests, as they would be in each other's company until they reached the Beaufort

Sea. With a new team of oxen in place they set off in a long line, looking like the prairie-bound wagon trains filled with hopeful settlers. Along the way they came upon a sad contingent of five teams of oxen so badly bitten that several had succumbed to their wounds and died while in their harnesses. They would be happy to be gone from this forlorn place.

Fort Smith sits on a level plateau thirty metres above the river. It was originally named *Thebacha* by the Dene, meaning "beside the rapids." The Hudson's Bay Company built an outpost there in 1874 and two years later the Roman Catholics established a mission. When Cameron and Jessie arrived at Fort Smith they were confronted with a large mass of dirt and rubble caused by a series of devastating landslides that occurred a few months before their arrival. The slide levelled many of the Hudson's Bay buildings as well as the docking area. Cameron and Jessie stepped carefully over pieces of scaffolding and logs that had once been part of the HBC, alert to anything that might trip them up. Above the slide and along the ridge Cameron mentioned seeing a series of teepees belonging to the Chipewyan, the Slavi, and the Dogrib who had come from their hunting grounds for their treaty payment. There were also canoes and small boats of various sorts that were starting to arrive for the launching of the HBC's newest paddle wheeler, the SS *Mackenzie River*, the boat Cameron and Jessie were scheduled to take for the next portion of their trip. Farther up the hill they visited the boat yard where their vessel was receiving its final touches. Out of the water it gave the impression of being a lumbering leviathan; it was thirty-eight metres in length and was built to carry thirteen metric tons of cargo and forty passengers. The reinforced bow was strong enough to push its way through ice, which was the intent.

Except for a bit of luck, their trip could have ended here. "The builders of the big boat have had disasters which would have daunted any but the dogged Company of Fur Traders," Cameron wrote. "Two land-slides threatened to slice off and carry into the river the partially-made boat, a fire burned up the blacksmith shop and with it all the imported doors, window-sashes and interior finishings, so that she sails tomorrow with carpenters still at work."[56] The SS *Mackenzie River* was scheduled to run from Fort Smith down the Slave River and into the western portion of Great Slave Lake and across to Fort Providence, the entry point to the Mackenzie River, and onto Fort MacPherson on the Peel River.

While waiting for the launching, the two travellers decided to walk down the bank near the Rapids of the Drowned to watch the famed white pelicans nesting on the rocky outcroppings in the middle of the rapids. For hours they stood and watched as the pelicans picked off unsuspecting lampreys as they made their way through the chutes. Cameron thought they looked prehistoric with the snake-like fish hanging out of their bright orange beaks:

> And now candour compels me to report that the Slave
> River pelican feeds her nestlings on prosaic fish without
> the slightest attempt to "open to young her tender
> breast." It is rank libel for Byron to state
>
> > "Her beak unlocks her bosom's stream
> > To still her famished nestling's scream."
>
> And, when Keats states so sententiously in Endymion,
> "We are nurtured like a pelican brood," he merely calls
> the world at large, fish-eaters.[57]

On the way back to town they found the area to be a veritable "treasure-trove" of pink anemones, delicately coloured harebells, coreopsis, shinleafs, painted cups, yarrow, and goldenrod beautiful in their diaphanous display.

Cameron was intensely interested in the bison. Fort Smith abuts a sizeable boreal wilderness that once supported one of the largest and last remaining free-roaming bison herds in the world. Where once the bison had been a life-sustaining force for the people of the north, the herd was in danger of extinction due to over-hunting both by humans and timber wolves as well as to harsh winters. There were reported to be between three to five hundred animals when she visited. The government recognized there was a problem and by 1894 stepped in to protect the buffalo. In 1922 the government created a park, which encompassed over four million hectares of land, making it the largest contiguous tract of Great Plains boreal grasslands in the world.

It was while she was at Fort Smith that Cameron began pondering the future of the fur industry. While the HBC posts she had visited appeared to have a thriving business, she was not so sure. In her conversations with trappers she seemed to get mixed messages. Those in the field often slanted information to suit their purpose and records on raw skins were spotty. The United States, for instance, did not levy import duties on pelts, so there was no way to trace the number of shipments going south. She did learn that six million dollars' worth of furs were sold annually by auction in London, with Canada being the major supplier. While she recognized the market value of furs and the needs of the industry, she was also concerned with the over-hunting of animals. The fashion industry was fickle, but there was an increasingly strong market for rare pelts. A dealer in Calgary told her that during the past winter he'd had a silver fox that was sold for 1,950 dollars in the London market.

Although she thought Fort Smith the most lifeless and unprogressive of any of the HBC posts they had visited, she did feel it was on the threshold of great things. One can only wonder what she would have thought if she could walk the streets of Fort Smith today, with its many eateries, retail outlets, and businesses. With a population of around twenty-five hundred, it has become a tourist destination for wilderness recreation and the headquarters of Wood Buffalo National Park.

On the seventh of July, the SS *Mackenzie River* was ready to embark on its maiden voyage. Now moored at the river's edge, the sternwheeler gleamed in its newness. The Hudson's Bay Company flag was gallantly flying aft, as if in a salute to its homeport. Big plumes of steam billowed out of the smokestack, sending a signal to prospective passengers to get aboard. Cameron and Jessie walked up the wooden plank that served as the boarding ramp and set about looking for their stateroom. They were surprised to find their quarters so much larger than they had expected. They had been living compactly, as scripted by their mode of travel, but they now had the luxury of space. Getting dressed would become so much easier, they would not have to worry about their possessions getting wet, and rather than spending precious time looking for items sequestered in some hidden spot at the bottom of their trunk, they could concentrate on writing and photography. Cameron gleefully noted, "A double cabin is assigned us on the ss *Mackenzie River* and the nightmare that haunted us on the scows of wet negatives and spoiled film vanishes."[58] Still twelve hundred miles from their destination, they had a very long way to go. The remainder of their itinerary included stops at Fort Resolution, Hay River, Fort Rae, Fort Providence, Fort Simpson, Fort Wrigley, Fort Norman, Fort Good Hope, Arctic Red River, and Fort Macpherson before an open boat would take them into the Beaufort Sea and west to Herschel Island. They made a short stop in Hay River, just long enough for Cameron to call on the school. She was particularly interested in visiting the schools along the way. The educational philosophy of total cultural assimilation had not quite reached the heartland of the Mackenzie and Western Arctic. While the missionaries were subject to proclamations from their home base they were far from overarching eyes, so they had more leeway in developing their own educational programs. The missionary societies in England and France thought that it was important to wean Indigenous people away from their hunting and trapping economies and encourage them toward an economy based on farming, something the religious orders were more familiar with and had been successful for them. The missionaries in the north, particularly the Grey Nuns, were not as naïve and knew that such a platform would be harmful to the people's way of life. Much of the territory upon which they depended for their survival was not conducive to domestic farming. Initially the Grey Nuns thought that too much education would isolate those they taught from their societies and would make re-integration difficult. They believed that the children were happiest when outdoors and so spent a great deal of their time exploring the flora and fauna of the area. Cameron enjoyed interacting with the children she met along the way, but her descriptions show that she approached the schools in the north with a colonialist bias. She referred to the students at Hay River as waifs of the wilderness, while at the Catholic mission at Fort Smith she wrote that she was impressed with how well the nuns were trying to make "reputable citizens" of the "young scions of the Dog-Rib and Yellow-Knife nations."

Six days after leaving Fort Smith the ss *Mackenzie River* pulled in at Fort Providence on the Mackenzie River. It was an exceptionally hot day. "Our coming is a gala day," Cameron wrote. "The hamlet flies three flags, the free trader sports his own initials 'H. N.,' the Hudson's Bay Company loyally runs the Union Jack to the masthead, over the convent floats the tri-colour of France."[59] Fort Providence had a distinctly French flair, she said. They visited the convent to meet the children who showed them the beautiful handiwork of silk embroidery on white deerskin they had been working on. The Grey Nuns who ran the school had a long history in Fort Providence. They arrived in 1867 to help the Oblates establish Sacred Hearts School and later a hospital. The early conditions were harsh and the constant poverty of the nuns affected their ability to properly care for the children. Provisions were meagre and all were frequently on the verge of starvation. It was difficult to obtain meat as it was often in scarce supply and if the river froze early before enough fish could be caught, they would not have enough to see out the winter. Attempts to grow their own vegetables were fraught with difficulty, as locusts and caterpillars would eat through a garden in a matter of hours. The children slept in berths, like the shelves of a bookcase. If there weren't enough beds for the sisters they would sleep on the floor or on the dining table. The children were vulnerable to diseases to which they had no immunity. Just four years before Cameron's visit, Sister Beaudin wrote that on November 21, 1903, "An epidemic, coming from the Good Hope district . . . was raging here. Not one of our fifty-four children escaped it. At first we did not think it dangerous, but we soon saw our mistake. After measles, came scarlet fever, diphtheria, and dysentery. It was heartbreaking to see so many children all at the same time bound on a bed of suffering. We watched over them by day and by night. It pleased God to afflict us by ten deaths. Three of the boys and seven of the girls were carried off . . . We are very sad.[60]

A day after leaving Great Slave Lake, Cameron and Jessie were enjoying a quiet evening reading on the upper deck. Suddenly there was a flurry of activity and they quickly learned that there was a man overboard. It was De-deed, a young deckhand they had befriended. One of the crew threw a life buoy overboard as Captain Tenny Gouley reversed the engines. Cameron could see the lad struggling in the water and shouted out, "Swim, De-deed, the boat is coming! They are almost up to you!"[61] By then everyone was out on deck, and tension mounted as they realized he was not going to make it. A deep, eerie silence fell over the boat as they watched him go under one last time. It had been less than twenty-four hours since De-deed had kissed his mother on both cheeks, grabbed his camera, and cheerfully helped Cameron and Jessie down the bank to the boat. The river had claimed yet one more victim.

On July 10, they arrived at Fort Simpson. Cameron was decidedly unimpressed. Simpson was past its prime, she said. "We look upon the warehouses of its quadrangle with their slanting walls and dipping moss-covered roofs and try to conjure up the time long past when all was smart and imposing. In those days when the Indians brought in their precious peltries they were received and sent out again with military precision and all that goes with red tape and gold braid."[62] She came across an old library that was in a state of disarray. Scattered all around were once venerable books that took readers beyond the Fur Belt, now broken-backed and disemboweled. "Everything is so old in the North," she said, "that there is no veneration for old things."[63] They left that evening and as Cameron turned back for one last look she saw the small settlement bathed in the aurora of the northern lights. Perhaps she had been mistaken, she thought. After stopping at Fort Wrigley to pick up passengers the voyage continued to Fort Norman. Shortly below Wrigley the "boucans," beds of brown coal or lignite, came into view. When Alexander Mackenzie passed by in 1789 he initially thought that the bank was on fire, but later learned that the beds had been spewing fire for well over a hundred years. Always on the lookout for worthwhile resources, Cameron thought the lignite could one day be used as a source of electricity. She recognized, however, that due to its volatile nature, the difficulty of transport, and low energy density, the lignite would remain in its raw state for the foreseeable future. In the meantime the Dene would continue use the site to smoke meat and fish to preserve for the winter.

Sometime in the early evening the wind whipped up and by midnight the ss *Mackenzie River* found itself in the middle of a howling gale. The boat struggled against wind and waves as white water spilled over its gunwales. After a tense ride, they took refuge under a large cliff opposite Fort Norman. The two women burrowed deep into their beds trying to shut out the shrill sound of the wind, hoping they would be alive in the morning. "It is not an easy thing to handle the big steamer in a swift current and in the teeth of a storm like this," Cameron wrote, "and we have been in more comfortable places at midnight. However, after running with the current, backing water, and clever finesse, we come safely to anchor against the shore opposite the Fort, under the lee of Bear rock. This is a fourteen-hundred-foot peak which starts up from the angle formed by the junction of the Bear River with the Mackenzie."[64]

When they arose from their cabin the next morning and saw the sun's rays claiming dominance over the land, the evening's gale seemed all but forgotten. It was July 12, Sunday morning, when the ss *Mackenzie River* docked at Fort Norman. The peal of the church bells ringing in a kind of competitive dissonance signalled the beginning of services for members of both the Anglican and Catholic Church. The Church Missionary Society was the dominant religious force in Fort Norman as it had been the first to establish a presence in 1858, but only by one year.

Beginning in the early 1850s both Christian groups rushed to mark out their territory of this northern region, each trying to best the other. The first Catholic mission, St. Joseph's Mission, was established at Moose Deer Island close to Fort Resolution. Father Pierre-Henri Grollier, a twenty-six-year-old missionary from the Oblate of Mary Immaculate in France, came to the north in 1852. That same year Archdeacon James Hunter from the Church Missionary Society of the Church of England entered the territory and began St. David's Mission at Fort Simpson. Not to be outdone, Father Grollier built a mission at Fort Simpson and Fort Providence in 1858; Fort Rae, Fort Norman, and Fort Good Hope in 1859; and Fort McPherson on the Peel River in 1862. Despite their vigorous building plan, the missionary's initial efforts were largely unsuccessful. The minute differences between the two churches over issues such as life, death, and afterlife were not only strange, but also created confusion and disinterest among the population. Many of the first missionaries were unprepared for the harsh conditions. Loneliness and ill health plagued the missionaries and many returned home to France or England. For those who stayed, the road to success, they believed, lay in learning the languages of the area. To do that they thought it imperative to leave the familiarity of their stationary posts and follow the people as they travelled between their various seasonal camps.

While some friendships and conversions were made, it was only when Indigenous cultures were shattered by disease and starvation that the missionaries begin to gain a foothold into the lives of the people of the north.

As they trekked across the land some missionaries felt impelled to act as surveyors and geographers; mapping the terrain, writing about the geography, people, and natural history of the Mackenzie region. Cameron gave great credit to the efforts of the missionaries, writing, "Are we not as a people too prone to minimize the great nation-building work performed by the scattered missionaries in the long lands beyond the railway? Ostensibly engaged in the work of saving souls, Canadian missionaries, both Roman and English, have opened the gates of commerce, prosecuted geographical discovery, tried to correct social evils, and added materially to our store of exact science. Through their influence, orphanages have been founded, schools established, and hospitals opened."[65] The missionaries, she felt, were among those who were bringing development to the north. Cameron believed that progress in all things would lead to what she considered a "better future," a concept that was left largely undefined, but probably referred to helping people gain more control over their destiny. Although not completely free of her own cultural biases, she was not completely blind as to the negative impact that thinking had wrought. She firmly believed that the south must tread carefully and be cognizant of alternate realities. On many occasions, she reminded people not to judge others based on their own cultural viewpoint. "Along these banks, forgotten tepee-poles, deserted fish-stage, and lonely grave remain, a crumbling commentary of yesterday, a hint of recurring to-morrows . . . Lessons these are for us, too, if we bring the keen eye and listening ear. Among Mackenzie tribes no Yellow-knife, Dog-Rib, or Slavi starved while another had meat, no thievish hand despoiled the cache of another . . . Not all the real things of life are taught to the Cree by the Christian . . . Creeds take a secondary place to deeds in this land, and when you discuss a man, be he cleric or layman, the last thing you ask is, 'To what church does he belong?'"[66] As soon as cargo and people were unloaded the ss *Mackenzie River* left for Fort Good Hope. Around midnight they entered a narrow gorge known as the Ramparts, a spectacular seven-mile-long limestone canyon cut during the late-glacial period. Impressed, Cameron said it was one of the most magnificent views of their journey. "As we pass in silence we can but look and feel. One day a Canadian artist will travel north and paint the Ramparts, some poet, gifted with the inevitable word, here write the Canadian epic. Awed and uplifted, our one wish is to be alone; the vision that is ours for one hour of this Arctic night repays the whole summer's travel. We could not have chosen a more impressive hour in which to pass the portal into the Arctic World."[67] Upon leaving the Ramparts the Mackenzie widens and then spills around Manitou Island, the original location of the HBC post.[68] As the vessel approached the island a volley of rifle shots echoed off the banks, bringing everyone to instant attention. Across the river the entire community was lined up along the edge of the bluff; the shots were a salute to the new boat. Captain Tenny had dressed for the occasion. Fort Good Hope was his homeport and he was proud to be bringing the ss *Mackenzie River* back to "God's Country," he said. As soon as the crew secured their lines ashore, Charles Philip Gaudet, chief trader and veteran of the Hudson's Bay Company, carefully negotiated the rickety steps down the cliff to the shoreline to meet the newest vessel for the fleet. Cameron noted the greeting saying, "Down the steps comes a stately figure, Mr. Gaudet, the head and brains of Fort Good Hope. Of the two thousand servants of the Hudson's Bay Company this is the man who has the greatest number of years of active service to his credit."[69] Gaudet, who had served the Hudson's Bay Company for fifty-seven years, was eighty when Cameron met him. Despite his declining health and asthmatic lungs, he assured her that it was his intention to remain in the employ of the HBC until he reached his sixtieth year of service, which he did.

When Cameron and Jessie reached the top of the staircase, they found themselves surrounded by people wanting to shake their hands. A little overwhelmed, they were thankfully rescued by Mrs. Gaudet, "a dear old lady with a black cap, the pinkest of pink cheeks," who whisked them off to her welcoming home. Cameron found the Gaudets' home to be one of the "sweetest homes" she had ever seen. She described the chief factor's wife as having "the kind of smile that brings a choky feeling into your throat and makes you think of your mother."[70] Sitting around the hearth that evening Mrs. Gaudet told her guests that it had been over fifty years since she'd visited the "outside." In 1867–68, she said, she took her five children to a family reunion in Montreal. Just getting there was a long and arduous trip, fraught with danger, she said. With her voice quavering she said that while there, three of her daughters, Elizabeth age eight, Sarah age three, and baby Marie, all contracted measles and died within a week. She had not been back since. On a brighter note, she also told Cameron that like everyone else in the community she was excited to see the boat come in, as it was often the only time they received mail. If lucky they would sometimes get another delivery in the winter. She thought the new HBC mail delivery system was very modern. She explained that receiving a letter in the winter was not so straightforward. Whenever a family member sent her a letter from eastern Canada it would first travel by rail to Vancouver, then be transferred to a steamer bound for the Yukon. For the next portion of the journey the letter was given to a member of the NWMP who was on patrol. He would tuck the letter into his mail packet and carry the mail, via dog team, to Fort Macpherson, way up in the Mackenzie Delta. From there a runner would deliver the mail across the northern communities by snowshoe.

While at Fort Good Hope, Cameron and Jessie were very excited to visit the much talked about Catholic church Our Lady of Good Hope. The church had a reputation for being the most beautiful in the north. The outside was typical of the churches for the area. It was long and narrow, framed with whitewashed wooden planks and fronted by a pointed arched doorway. The bell tower atop the roof supported a simple cross, rendering it visible from afar. The simple exterior provided no hint as to its interior. Stepping across the threshold was akin to walking into an alien world. The inside of the church glittered with gold paint and delicately carved woodwork, the ceiling was brushed a palatinate blue and embellished with gold stars, creating a heavenly scene. The altar was opulent and adorned by a statue of the Virgin Mary that had been donated by the Gaudets. It was overseen by a fresco of two guardian angels. Construction on the new church began in 1865, but work proceeded slowly. Without the necessary tools and building supplies the Dene and Métis builders found it a challenging task. They had to improvise, making their own tools from what was at hand. For the paint they collected plants from their surroundings, which they rendered into a delightful palette of colours. They decorated frescoes, murals, carvings, and walls in reds, rusts, greens, golds, and blues. One of the Gaudets' daughters, Bella, a gifted artist in her own right, helped Father Émile Petitot with the artwork. It took a long twenty years to complete their task. Their skill and careful attention to detail is a legacy that is forever etched into the fabric of the entire church. Once outside, the sweet scent of roses from the surrounding bushes permeated the air. Cameron wrote, "Our thoughts will often drift back to this restful little sanctuary."[71] Back aboard the *Mackenzie River* they had another 219 miles to travel before reaching Arctic Red River. Just before midnight they came upon the Lower Ramparts, a section on the river where black shale cliffs stood tall at an intimidating ninety metres. At the entrance to the canyon the river narrowed but the current remained moderate. Cameron noticed strange scars on the trunks of the trees and saw deep gouges cut into the side of the banks. The shoreline was littered with splintered and bark stripped logs. Cameron was told that during spring breakup the ice and water from the tributaries could increase the depth of the Mackenzie by as much as ten metres, creating a forceful power that cut down everything in its path.

As they neared the mouth of the Arctic Red River, the Hudson's Bay post of Arctic Red River came into view.[72] For Cameron this symbolized a unique point in their journey, for they were entering the spectral envelope of the Arctic Circle. There is something inexplicable about traversing 66.5°N. For some it is simply a parallel of latitude, a line drawn across a map or chart. However, for many who cross its path for the first time there is an inexplicable sense of wonderment, as if one were part of a grand exploration. The logs and diaries of early explorers are full of writings about the feeling of awe and excitement that awaits visitors to the northern lands. North of the Arctic Circle is a harsh land where months of darkness and bitterly cold temperatures stress life to the limits. It is ancient in spirit and connects us to our ancestors. It is the place where the first Paleo-Arctic people trod across Beringia into a land never before seen by humankind. The vastness, stillness, and isolation of the region invite a sense of solitude that shifts human perspective. Some have said of the Arctic Circle that only God has been there before. It was a sensation that Cameron felt to her very core.

The confluence of the Mackenzie and Arctic Red Rivers had long served as a summer campsite for the Gwichya Gwich'in. After a long, hard winter of hunting, families would come together to set up camp. For days, even weeks, large boats filled with men, women, and children would paddle up the river; the old men often in the bow hunting ducks along the way. The summers at Arctic Red River were for resting and mingling. Stick-ball, football, and tea dancing were the favoured forms of recreation. In their rush to beat the Anglicans the Oblates established a presence along the banks of Arctic Red River in 1869, a year before the Hudson's Bay Company arrived. Cameron only briefly mentions the Gwich'in, which is puzzling given their importance in the history of the area and their relationship with the Hudson's Bay Company. They were particularly significant as intermediaries between the fur traders and the Mackenzie Inuit. In fact, the HBC could not have survived without their help or their furs.

It was while visiting Arctic Red River that Cameron first met what she referred to as the "Eskimo of the Arctic foreshore" or the "Mackenzie River Eskimo." Identification of groups by category names is complicated. Many names used to designate the people of the Mackenzie Delta were names of convenience used by missionaries, explorers, and southerners, but such European categorizations were not a defining feature for many groups. Cameron refers to the group she met at Arctic Red River and at Fort McPherson as the Kogmollyes. She may have been referring to one of the subgroups of the Inuinnait (Copper Inuit)—the Kogluktogmiut, Kogluktualugmiut, or Kogluktuaryumiut—from the central western Arctic. The second group she met were the Nunatalmute or "dwellers of the hills," originally from farther inland, but who, like the Inuinnait, came to trade at Herschel Island and Fort McPherson. Cameron was quite impressed by the people she met in the Arctic, referring to them as, "this Farthest North family of Fellow-Canadians." She wrote, "It was at Arctic Red River, one hundred and ninety miles of river-travel since we cut the Polar circle, that we came upon our first Eskimo . . . A little band of Kogmollyes they were, men, women, and kiddies, who had come in to trade silver-fox skins for tobacco and tea at the Post of the Hudson's Bay Company . . . On the rocks they sat, waiting for the new steamer to make her landing, and much excited were they over the iron bowels of this puffing kayak of the white men . . . The Mackenzie River Eskimo is a man who commands your respect the moment you look at him, and yet he is withal the frankest of mortals, affable, joyous, fairly effervescing with good-humour."[73]

Cameron was at her best when she was in the mode of correcting erroneous assumptions about Canada, its land and people. For years, she had been taking England to task for not only making gross errors in geography but also mythologizing about the land

and people of Canada. It was with great relish that in her writings she instructed her audience that the people of the Arctic were industrious, clever, unsullied in integrity, and that they exuded a quiet dignity. "By natural gifts and temperament the Eskimo is probably the most admirable, certainly the most interesting, and by circumstances the most misunderstood and misrepresented of all the native races of America."[74] She was particularly supportive of their child-rearing practices. She described the family unit as a caring and nurturing unit that fostered independence and strength of character, both qualities necessary for survival in a nomadic hunting society. It would be easy to suppose that Cameron would eschew the lack of formal education, but she thought families were the better experts at teaching their children the necessary skills for life in the north. "Certainly, without churches or teachers or schools, with no educational journals, and no Conventions of Teachers, with their wise papers on the training of 'the child,' the Eskimo children we saw were better behaved, more independent, gentler, and in the literal sense of the word, more truly 'educated' than many of our children are. Instinctively you feel that here are boys and girls being trained admirably for the duties of life, a life that must be lived out in stern conditions."[75]

While at Arctic Red River, Cameron spent ten days sitting around the fire getting to know Mr. Oo-vai-oo-ak, the "headman" of the Kogmollyes as she called him, and his wife. He was a tall, dignified, and quiet man, she relayed. Cameron and Jessie were invited to attend the wedding of Mr. Oo-vai-oo-ak to his second wife, a match instigated by his first wife who wanted a younger, more energetic woman to help run the family. Cameron said she had never seen such a harmonious family; he lived quite happily with his children and two wives. She was emphatic that one's presumptions and judgments not be inflicted on people living in a region so very different from the drawing rooms of southern etiquette: "Before we piously condemn either the lord or the lady in the case, it is well that we adjust our judgment to the latitude of 68° North."[76]

Cameron tended to rhapsodize about the people of the Western Arctic. Her time in the north was too short to gain all but a cursory look into a complex culture that had survived many changes over the centuries. Most of her interactions with people were through the Hudson's Bay Company, which narrowed the range to those fur traders who were connected to a particular post. While she was open to learning other perspectives, the real lives of the people she met were inaccessible to her in part because of the cursory nature of her visit. As well, Europeans were just beginning to learn about differing cultural realities and the vast range of social patterns displayed by people in other parts of the world. At this point they had not gone beyond viewing civilizations that were so different from their own as more than mere curiosity. Cameron tried to break out of her cultural interpretations of "reality," and change such views, but her impressions and those of most others who took up a pen to write about the north were filtered through their perceptions of the world. The very title of her book, *The New North*, indicates that she felt that growth and development were beckoning at the doorstep of the north.

Although Cameron travelled before government policy, treaties, and residential schools disenfranchised northerners, she often talked of the harm that southerners had wrought on the north. She wrote of how disease, against which the people had no immunity, devastated communities. A measles outbreak in the Western Arctic reduced the Inuvialuit population from 2,500 to 250 people by 1905. She informed her readers that two years before her visit eighty people had died of measles in Arctic Red River. They have little to thank the white man for, she chided; these people have "grasped a great truth that his Christian brother often misses, the truth that happiness is not a luxury, but the highest of all virtues, a virtue filling the life where it originates and spreading over every life it touches."[77] She believed that adopting southern values and way of life would be of no benefit: "Civilisation has nothing to teach this man concerning clothing, house-building, or Arctic travel. Indeed, one may hazard the opinion that the ambitious explorer from the outside, if he reach the Pole at all, will reach it along Eskimo avenues with this man as active ally and by adopting his methods of coping with Northern conditions."[78]

They left Arctic Red River around July 14. Around the fifteen-mile mark they reached a spit of land, which in 1826 Sir John Franklin named Point Separation. It signalled the entrance to a vast maze of channels that make up the Mackenzie Delta.

A leftover from the retreat of the last continental glaciation, the Mackenzie Delta is a region of low-lying alluvial islands composed of thousands of interconnected lakes, rivers, and ponds. Fifty percent of the entire area is wetland habitat and home to a rich but delicate ecosystem consisting of shrub, black spruce trees, and countless bird and mammal species. In winter the delta is a land of ice where the permafrost digs into the tundra at depths of up to 120 metres. The mass of fresh water that filters through the undulating surface to enter the Arctic Ocean plays a critical part in regulating the region's climate system. It is here that the land reigns supreme, shaping all life that exists within its folds. The Mackenzie Delta offers up its own determined narrative that cannot be understood nor shaped by those living afar.

Arriving at Point Separation she noted the two lob-sticks, which were a reminder that on the evening of July 3, 1826, Sir John Franklin and Dr. Richardson parted in their exploration of the Arctic coast; Franklin went west and Richardson east. Twenty-two years later Richardson visited Separation Point again with the Relief Expedition searching for the lost Franklin. It was at this point that Cameron's group left the Mackenzie River and entered the Peel River channel for the thirty-three-mile trip south to Fort Macpherson. The Middle Channel at Point Separation carries on to Tuktoyaktuk and the Beaufort Sea, while the East Channel flows past Inuvik. Tuktoyaktuk and Inuvik were mere dots of shrub and lichen when Cameron passed by. Tuktoyaktuk, which today is the northernmost community in Canada, was uninhabited until the

Hudson's Bay Company built a post there in 1912. As for Inuvik, only the occasional trapper visited. It operated as a sort of no-man's land that served as a barrier between the Inuit and the Dene who were traditionally hostile to each other. Since that time Inuvik has become the principal transportation and administrative centre for the Western Arctic.

Once they turned into the Peel River they were in range of the farthest outpost of the Hudson's Bay Company. The sights from the deck of the ss *Mackenzie River* offered the passengers a vista of rolling wooded plains. To the west was a valley of stunted spruce, birch, and pine framed by the eastern extension of the Alaskan Brooks Range—the Richardson Mountains.[79] As they drew near Fort McPherson everyone aboard could hear shouts from the shore, welcoming the new boat. Such vessels were the mainstay of Northerners' contact with the outside world. The revellers had come from all over to pick up mail and needed supplies that would see them through the next few years.

When Cameron and Jessie disembarked, they met a disparate group of people whose only commonality was their loose dependency on the HBC. There were the missionaries from the Church of England, along with traders, trappers, a few Inuvialuit and Inuit, as well as a contingent of Teetl'it Gwich'in, whom Cameron referred to as Louchrux, a name adopted by early French missionaries. Dissimilar though they may be, these people represented the strength and polyglot that typified the north. The lives and stories of the people on the beach that day were far removed from anything Cameron could have imagined. There was John Firth, the Hudson's Bay Company chief factor for Fort McPherson, a solid-looking man who sported a large bushy beard and mustache. He was known for his physical strength, an important quality in the north. His ability to speak to the Gwich'in in their own language, a skill that he learned from his wife, put him in good stead, and his talent at negotiating peaceable outcomes in fractious situations helped keep the peace. His no-nonsense attitude earned him the name of "the Emperor." Cameron learned that Firth joined up with the Hudson's Bay Company in 1867. He was eighteen when he left his home in Scotland's Orkney Islands to take up his first post in the north of Canada. By the time Firth became the chief factor in 1893, he had served in the north for twenty-two years. By then the Arctic had seeped into his bones, claiming his presence, until his death at eighty-four years of age.

While talking to Inspector Francis Joseph Fitzgerald, the first commander of the Royal North-West Mounted Police at Herschel Island, Cameron learned that he had been dispatched to the remote island in the Beaufort Sea in response to repeated requests to quell unrest. Criminal activity and the illegal sale of American contraband was an ongoing problem that threatened the stability of the region. Since 1889 Herschel Island had been the main base in the Western Arctic for American whalers hunting bowhead whales. Even though the island was at the far reaches of humanity, it was a hive of activity. Eight years before Fitzgerald's posting, twelve hundred crew overwintered waiting for spring breakup. With so many people crowded into a small space and nothing to do, it became difficult for the whaling captains to maintain control over their men. Along with illegally selling goods like tea, coffee, clothing, and tents, the whalers sold alcohol, an item purposefully not stocked by the Hudson's Bay Company. Herschel Island developed the reputation of being a "hive of debauchery." The Anglican bishop for the Arctic, W. C. Bompas, had written repeatedly to the Minister of the Interior about the rampant alcoholism and exploitation that was taking place.

In the main the Inuvialuit ignored the whalers and remained aloof from the Hudson's Bay Company. They were not dependent upon anyone or any company other than themselves for their survival. They did enjoy the treats they could get from these interlopers, but they had no need of most goods. They preferred their food and their nomadic way of life to anything on offer by the whalers or the HBC. They had nothing to learn from the whalers and found them to be useless and naive in their approach to the land. Unfortunately, contact with outsiders never arrives without a sting. For ten years, the whalers were relentless in their pursuit of the bowhead, hunting them nearly to extinction. The whales were an important part of the diet of the Inuvialuit; one whale provided a camp with enough food and oil for a year. Along with the decrease in bowhead, the caribou herds were also in serious decline. This was a situation that could have led to starvation for the Inuvialuit, but beluga whales, not favoured by the whalers, were still plentiful and provided an adequate supply of food. The whalers also brought diseases to which the Inuvialuit had no immunity. It was not long after contact that populations dropped dramatically and with them thousands of years of knowledge, threatening their very survival.[80]

With the increase of American presence in the Arctic, the Dominion government became very concerned about its sovereignty. Although the border was firmly established by this time, it was new and still open to dispute. The government wanted an official presence at Herschel Island. They needed to find the right man for the job; someone who could withstand long periods of isolation and had the necessary skills and experience to survive in a harsh environment. They also wanted someone who would dispense Canadian law with diplomacy and a firm hand. Fitzgerald had more than proved himself in extreme conditions, having served throughout the Yukon during the gold rush in the late 1800s. He had the reputation as being one of the most experienced North-West Mounted Police officers patrolling in the north. In 1903, at thirty-four years of age, Fitzgerald found himself in an open whaler heading to the farthest outreach of civilization to establish a post. A small wood shack became the most northern NWMP base in the Dominion. The irony was that the whalers, from whom he was tasked with collecting customs duties, owned four of the six buildings on the island, along with fifteen sod houses. Fitzgerald and his corporal spent their first year in one of those sod huts paying rent to the very people he was meant to regulate. Their living quarters were primitive in the extreme. Their view to the outside world was a small hole built into the roof that acted as both window and ventilation. The inspector quickly developed a reputation for his outstanding service in the Western Arctic, becoming a minor legend in the south.

Cameron liked this straight-edged man with the penetrating eyes and was particularly eager to hear that his opinions of the Kogmollyes and Nunatalmute were similar to hers. "I have found these natives honest all the time I have been at Herschel Island," he told her. "I have never heard of a case of stealing among them."[81] What neither could have known at the time was that the Richardson Mountains that overlooked the party that day would, in three years' time, claim the lives of Fitzgerald and two other constables while they were attempting to cross the mountains on their annual winter patrol. The weather was minus fifty-three degrees Celsius. They were lost and had run short of food so turned around for home, a decision that came too late. In the spring Inspector Jack Dempster, for whom the Dempster highway is named, would head a search party to look for the missing Mounties. Their bodies would be found four kilometres from Fort McPherson. It is said that they died of exposure sometime between February 12 and 18, 1911. In 1915, Smith's Landing was renamed Fort Fitzgerald after Francis Joseph Fitzgerald.

Always ready to take advantage of an opportunity, Cameron and her niece were able to get a ride in the police whaler to Herschel Island. Their vessel, a simple but seaworthy long, narrow open boat, used primarily in the hunting of whales, was loaded up with the supplies brought in by the ss *Mackenzie River*. Bearing favourable winds, the small crew could raise the sails, making their trip smoother and faster. The group most likely went by way of the Peel Channel to the Beaufort Sea. As they neared the entrance to the Beaufort they noticed the deep blue of the ocean contrasted wildly with the muddy silt of the delta. They were immediately met with a strong nor'easter, which slowed their progress considerably. Once they reached Kay Point, a hook-shaped spit of land, they had thirty nautical miles left to go until they reached their destination. Eventually Collinson Head came into view, announcing the entrance to Pauline Cove. A welcoming party of gawking seagulls came looking for proffered morsels. But even they would not lay siege to the year's supply of concentrated eggs and desiccated vegetables, something Cameron agreed with wholeheartedly. "Whale-meat is better than concentrated cooking-egg," she said, "seal-blood piping hot more to be desired than that vile mess of desiccated vegetables."[82] They were now at 69°58'N. They had entered a place where islands of translucent ice hold life in their thrall for all but two months of the year. She wrote, "Little windswept island of Herschel! We reach you to-day not by deep-sea vessel from the westward but up through the continent by its biggest northward-trending stream. Eighty miles through the Northern Ocean itself from the Mackenzie mouth brings our whale-boat grating upon the shingle. As far as we go!"[83]

Herschel Island looked like a postscript created out of sediment from the Laurentide Ice Sheet. The ground was covered with cotton grass, small shrubs, vetches, arctic lupines, and forget-me-nots. They were in the Arctic tundra region and there was not a tree to be seen. The beaches were a jumbled mix of driftwood, carried down from the boreal and taiga forests of the Mackenzie. Sitting at the very edge of the northern continent it was not a peacefully composed place. Cameron felt the remoteness and alienation: "North America here, in profound and lasting loneliness, dips its shaggy arms and ice-bound capes into an ocean illuminated now by the brief smile of a summer but, for ten months out of the twelve, drear and utterly desolate. The most striking features of the off-shore islands is that they are islands of ice rather than of earth."[84]

Pauline Cove appeared to be busy, although greatly pared down from previous years. Cameron was surprised to see such a mix of people. There were whalers from Sweden as well as America, Inuvialuit who were making use of their territorial hunting grounds, NWMP officers, and missionaries. There were only a few of the large whaling ships anchored in the cove. They served as an echo of times past when the bowhead population was plentiful and whale product was in demand. Crews could be seen cleaning the ships' guns, sharpening harpoons, and caulking the whaleboats, waiting for the ice to open for the season. These were the last years that Herschel Island played host to the crews of the whalers. By the following year most of the whalers were gone and by 1914 all whaling operations in the Beaufort ceased.

Cameron was fascinated with the business of whaling and went to great lengths to describe how whales were caught as well as the economic benefit to the whalers. She was blunt in her criticism of Canadians for not recognizing the economic advantages of such an industry. Her comment about this was telling for it represented a pattern of behaviour that was to follow Canadians into the twenty-first century. She said that not only are Americans both more aggressive and progressive than Canadians, but Canadians seem to be content to see "their more enterprising cousins" take whatever they wanted out of their northern waters. One bowhead whale would produce a hundred barrels of oil and seven hundred kilograms of baleen. Cameron estimated that since 1889 thirteen and a half million dollars had gone to American whalers and another one and a half million dollars taken in furs. She felt very strongly that the Canadian government should take steps to preserve the whales and the north for Canadians. "Unless the Circumpolar Bowhead is to become extinct within a decade, the thinking world should strengthen the hands of the Canadian authorities in an effort to put a close season for four or five years on the great Artic Baleen Whale . . . Cutting down a whale which has taken ten centuries to grow is like cutting down an oak-tree with a thousand concentric rings. You cannot in one or two or twenty scant generations of man grow another one to take its place."[85]

Though it would be comforting to think that the Dominion government was sensitive to the hunting occurring in the Western Arctic, that was not the case. Knowledge of or sentimentality about whales was simply not written into the time period. That did not happen until scientific research in the 1960s began informing people that cetaceans are intelligent animals, deserving of our protection. It took until 1972 before a moratorium ended commercial hunting in Canadian waters. Since that time the bowhead in the Beaufort Sea have increased their numbers to around eight thousand animals.

While the island no longer plays host to multitudes of whalers, the Inuvialuit still come to reconnect and to show their children their history. Once, for a few years in the late 1970s and early 1980s, the island became a centre for the offshore oil boom, but in 1987 the island, now known as Herschel Island-Qikiqtaruk (kee keek ya rak), was designated as a territorial park. Today it serves as an archaeological and heritage site as well as an important wildlife habitat. In the summer the island plays host to over a hundred different bird species that come to breed among the rocks and vegetation. Caribou and muskox can be seen grazing along the slopes, while both grizzly and black bears pad around the island looking for roots and berries. But Herschel Island is in trouble. Rising sea levels and increasing virulent storms are threatening the shoreline causing erosion of the permafrost, in some areas up to three metres a year. It is feared that most of the artifacts of the island will be washed away within the next fifty years. In 2007 the UNESCO World Heritage Centre listed Herschel Island as an endangered site and the following year the World Monuments Fund listed the island as one of the top one hundred most endangered sites in the world and in need of immediate protection and funding to preserve it.

Cameron and Jessie were reluctant to leave the north. As they turned their backs on the small windswept island, memories of their time there were duly logged in Cameron's notes, resurfacing in subsequent writings and speeches. "We had gone North with the birds in spring and now as we turn our faces homeward, the first migrants with strong wing are beginning their southward flight. Our travel is against current now, for we make slower time than we did coming . . . We find it a relief to have once more a twilight and a succeeding period of dusk. Yet are we loath to leave this fascinating North with its sure future, its quaint to-days, and all the glamour of its rich past."[86]

They returned the same way they came travelling as far as Fort Chipewyan, where they backtracked on the Slave River before turning west and into the Peace River. Their trip thus far had cost Cameron 291 dollars. To save on their passage they decided to forgo the comfortable sternwheeler with its electric lights, bathroom, and warm meals and instead arranged to spend two days on the *Primrose*, the little tug that took them to Fond du Lac. They then transferred to the *Mee-wah-sin*, a small open craft whose fitness for the three hundred miles to Fort Vermilion was questionable. Before they left, however, they learned that the ss *Grahame* was making a cargo drop to Fort McMurray. They hoped that mail might be waiting for them there. It was a long diversion, but they were a little homesick and had not heard from anybody since May.

They arrived at Fort McMurray during the annual treaty payments. "Tethered horses at the teepee-poles, store-dolls for the babies, and unmistakable 'Outside' millinery prove the prosperity of these Crees," Cameron wrote. "Our little group looks tattered, out-at-heel, and hungry."[87] While walking through the treaty tent she noticed one of the women was having difficulty obtaining payment for one of her children. She had received her annual annuity of five dollars for each of three of her four children. The treaty officials deemed her baby to be illegitimate because the father was nowhere to be found. Lacking a name, the mother was told she could not register the baby. Without her treaty payment, she knew that there would not be sufficient funds to feed her daughter, the result being that the little girl would most likely starve to death. Without a moment's hesitation Cameron stepped up to the commissioners and said she would speak for the baby and offered her name for the registration. "I conclude to father the child . . . My offer to give my name to the girlie, after due deliberation of Church and State, is accepted. Under the name of Agnes Deans Cameron, the Cree kiddie is received into the Mother Church and finds her place on the list of treaty-receiving Indians—No. 53 in the McMurray Band. May she follow pleasant trails!"[88] August 17, the day they left Chipewyan, was marked by the beginning of hunting season. One of the young boys informed Cameron that he had already salted sixteen hundred birds for winter rations.

Cameron and Jessie had been looking forward to travelling upon the Peace River. She relished the peacefulness and the quiet of the river. By the middle of August, the mosquitoes were less vigorous, allowing her to explore the forests without thought of running for cover. On one of her short forays through the forest Cameron came face to face with a grey wolf as it loped along the water's edge. "To make the story worth telling, one should have something to say of 'yawning jaws' and 'bloodshot eyes' and 'haunches trembling for a spring.' But this grey wolf simply refused to play that part. He took one look at us, evidently didn't approve, and turned up from his tracks quietly into the cotton-woods above."[89] There were few people living along the river at the time, but with the coming of the railway it was only a matter of time before large numbers of settlers would arrive to farm the verdant lands of the Peace. "The feeling is insistent here which has been ever-present since we entered this valley of the Peace—here is the home prepared and held in waiting for the people who are to follow."[90]

Ten days later they arrived at Fort Vermilion, a farming community on the edge of civilization. The railroad was still over six hundred kilometres away, which meant that the only way into this northern outpost town was by the river, or an eleven-hundred-kilometre trek across the land. Despite that, people came to settle. Five hundred people supported a mill, an electric plant, two churches, and two schools. Cameron and Jessie were invited to stay at Mr. and Mrs. Wilson's, a generous offer as their next boat was not due to arrive for three weeks. They had been on the river for five months, sleeping in tents and on hard packed ground. They revelled in the chance to soak their now hardened bodies in a hot bath, sleep in a warm bed, and eat a meal other than muskrat and dried crackers. "Can we ever forget the generous kindness extended to us within these walls? Months of travel in open scows, sleeping on the ground, and stretching out in blankets on the decks of little tugs have prepared us to enjoy to the full the comforts of a cultured home."[91]

They left Fort Vermilion in a very tiny steam tug that was only used on the Upper Peace in late summer and early fall, when the river was at its lowest. With no room for berths, the passengers spent their nights camping along the banks of the river. The crowded conditions and the drilling sound of the engine had everyone on edge. Cameron found it impossible to write. Luckily the *Messenger* towed a scow behind it, which provided extra space and gave passengers a chance to escape. Cameron and her niece took advantage of this by moving themselves and their typewriter to the tethered vessel where they could work in peace. The trip to Peace River Crossing took them eight days.

On their second day out they spotted a moose high up on the banks, munching away on some tasty willows. "What an ungainly creature he looks," Cameron wrote. "All legs and clumsy head—a regular grasshopper on stilts! He reminds me of nothing so much as those animals we make for the baby by sticking four matches into a sweet biscuit."[92] Cameron had earlier asked that if the situation arose she would like the chance to bring the moose down. Without a word a rifle was handed to her. As the boat slowed she raised her rifle. The banks were high, making a direct line of shot difficult. She was out of practice and did not want to wound the animal. She took aim but only grazed him; she fired again. "One more shot is effective," she said, "I have killed my premier moose."[93] She was delighted and had her photo taken holding the head of the dead moose. Cameron understood urbanites might be offended at what they perceived to be a senseless killing, but hunting for food was critical for survival in the north.

The previous evening, she had tea with a family of Cree who told her that during the fall season they bagged eighty moose for their winter food. To her detractors she said, "'Cruel!' you say. Well, just you live from mid-May to mid-September without fresh meat, as, with the exception of Vermilion's flesh-pots, we have done, and then find out if you would fly in the face of Providence when the Red Gods send you a young moose!"[94] The meat and hide were divided up. She wrote, "We are to learn that there are many viewpoints from which to approach a moose. The Kid wants its photograph, Chiboo and Mrs. Gaudet each eloquently argue for the skin, the rest of us are gross enough to want to eat it, and Se-li-nah, looking demurely off into the pines, murmurs gently in Cree, 'Marrow is nice.' Poor young stripling of the Royal House of Moose you could not have fallen into more appreciative hands!"[95]

At Peace River Crossing they left the *Messenger* and hired a wagon to carry their gear, while they walked the next 160 kilometres to the small community of Lesser Slave Lake. "This stands out in our memory as one of the most beautiful bits of the whole ten thousand miles that we travelled. With the cool mornings and evenings and the suggestion of frost in the air it is ideal walking and we tramp almost all of the hundred miles, letting the wagons overtake us at meal-times and waiting for them again when it is time to camp . . . The trail is a painter's palette splotched with vivid golds, greens, crimsons, and tawny russets. Robins, little moose-birds, and saucy whiskey-jacks are fairly reveling in the berries, crowding close to us, disputing the very berry we are popping into our mouths."[96] As they got closer to home and the cities they left behind, they had a strong desire to turn around and head back to the world that had been so much a part of them for the past six months. Before they reached Winnipeg and the busyness and anonymity of the city they took another steamer, the ss *Northern Light*, paddled in a "cranky dugout," and hiked through more mud than they ever wished to see again.

When they arrived in Winnipeg, they were invited to a social and reception hosted by Mrs. Bulyea, the wife of Alberta's Governor General. It felt strange to exchange her hiking garb for a black and white silk suit and sit at a formal and elegant mahogany table. She mused to herself that no longer would she need to balance her meal on her knees or partake of salt horse and macaroni, or sowbelly and bannock. The evening décor was not one of logs, shrubs, and tussocks of grasses, but of elegant pots of ferns, artfully positioned around the room. A long lake-like mirror sat on the table and was adorned with glass candlesticks and long streamers of yellow satin ribbon. The change was abrupt, but Cameron was always adaptable and responsive to her immediate environment. She enjoyed the company and conversation around the formal table as much as she revelled in the quiet of the outdoors.

When she rose to speak, she informed her audience that the land over which she had just travelled stood ready to provide the country with food, lumber, and oil. There were more than forty million hectares of land ripe for tilling, oil and gas reserves that only needed to be extracted, and an abundance of natural resources like timber, salt, fish, and minerals like copper, galena, and gypsum. The land is rich with possibilities, she said. "The mind reels and the imagination staggers in thinking of the future."[97] She thought that as nature had completed its task it was time for man to take over, but she added a few caveats. Although the land through which they had travelled was vigorous and alive, it was also need of protection. She cautioned that Canada's natural resources were not inexhaustible. She pointed out that the buffalo had disappeared, seals were quickly vanishing, salmon stocks were being exhausted, and the bowhead whales were nearing extinction. She further warned that Canada's timber industry could not continue to take lumber without introducing the practice of reforestation. "It was a narrow, restricted, dishonest policy which would cause us to accumulate wealth for ourselves at the risk of the loss to our children," she said.[98]

Chapter Fourteen

INTERNATIONAL FAME

What Kipling has done for India, Agnes
Deans Cameron is doing for Canada.

—THE ILLINOIS *Rockford Republic*

Cameron returned to her home in Chicago in early October. She spent her time quietly, receiving a few friends and proudly showing them the treasures she had brought back from the north. The exuberance from travelling down rivers and over rapids, hiking, camping, and listening to many personal stories of hardship and survival in an unforgiving land, began to give way to the silence of writing. This brief respite gave her space to write articles for publication and to work on her book. There was not much time given over to idle chat and gentle reminiscing. She had over a thousand photographs to organize, long lists of flora and fauna to catalogue, interviews to give, and business that needed her attention. Invitations for speaking engagements from Canada, the United

States, and England were already lining up. Her book, *The New North: An Account of a Woman's 1908 Journey through Canada to the Arctic,* was published by D. Appleton and Company in November 1909. She told her story in twenty-four chapters illustrated with over a hundred photographs. Her book was an instant success and was received to wide acclaim.

Cameron was always newsworthy and it was not long before newspaper articles began heralding her exploits and accomplishments. The *Inter Ocean* from Chicago, the *Edmonton Bulletin,* the *Manitoba Morning Free Press,* the *Winnipeg Tribune,* the *Victoria Daily Colonist,* the *Vancouver Daily World,* the *Ottawa Journal,* the *Pittston Gazette,* the *Pittsburgh Post-Gazette* and the *Allentown Leader* of Pennsylvania, the *Dakota Country Herald* in Nebraska, the *Bakersfield Californian,* the *New York Times,* and the *Times of London* were just a few of the many papers that were writing articles about her. They featured photos of her with the moose she brought down, calling her a crack shot, photos of her posing with Inuvialuit hunters, and featured drawings of her paddling a canoe, a southern interpretation of a dugout or scow, all useful for selling newsprint. She emphasized on several occasions that the purpose of her trip and resulting book was to apprise people on the north, particularly for those contemplating a move there. In an article written about her for the November issue of the *Inter Ocean,* she was quoted as saying, "[It] is such a vast region but little is known of its present development or its possibilities. I took my trip because I wanted to throw more light on that part of the country and to secure material which will be of use to those who contemplate going into the North."[1] She repeatedly stated that she did not take her journey nor write her book to "court the spectacular."

With her book finished Cameron began preparing for a demanding lecture tour. She had reams of paper with ideas for topics and hundreds of photos with which to illustrate her presentations. After due consideration she decided on five different themes, one of which featured her beloved Vancouver Island even though it bore no relation to her recent trip. The thread through each presentation was the promotion of Canada. She titled her talks "Between the Gates of Canada," "Wheat, the Wizard of the North," "From Wheat to Whales"—her most popular talk, "The Witchery of the Peace," and "Vancouver's Isle of Dreams." She started her lecture tour in Chicago to great acclaim. The *Manitoba Morning Free Press* likened her to the Pied Piper of Hamelin who, "with facts, figures and pictures of progress and plenty could pipe people in happy bunches and set them down, satisfied to grow wheat on Canada's fat and fecund plains."[2] She presented twenty-four lectures across the United States. Her talks roused excitement among her listeners, so much so that Canada experienced a marked increase of Americans requesting additional information and literature on Western Canada.

Cameron presented her first Canadian lecture in Winnipeg on February 4, 1909. It was held at the Central Congregational Church. Hundreds of people queued up along the street to pay fifty cents to hear the famous Agnes Deans Cameron. It was a sellout crowd with standing room only. She was used to talking to large audiences but no matter how accomplished a performer, there is always that second when questions of preparation, concern over possible technical breakdown, or just sheer size of an audience spar with one's confidence and professionalism. That aside, when Cameron walked up to the stage she was comfortable and composed. Her audience was spellbound and she finished to a thundering applause. Sellout crowds met every slide show Cameron gave, with many hundreds being turned away. At the Walker Theatre in Winnipeg, for example, she spoke to an audience of over twenty-five hundred; fifteen hundred others were turned away. Kit Colman, a star writer for the *Toronto Mail and Empire* wrote, "I have heard Agnes Deans Cameron lecture . . . she is an empire builder." It was a great compliment coming from one of the most famous female journalists in the country. The *Vancouver Daily World* added that she was a "brilliant writer" and "has no equal in the gift of descriptive narration."[3] Back in her home province Cameron presented her talk "From Wheat to Whales." A reviewer for the *Vancouver Daily World* wrote a glowing report stating that, "This lecture is living history—and is offered by a woman who is at once brave, brainy and brilliant—a pioneer—and one gifted in an unusual manner with the one great gift the gods have been chary of giving to woman—humor—that salt and pepper and all seasoning necessary to make the mess we call life worth living."[4] The accolades did not stop. The *Toronto Globe* applauded her accomplishments as legendary: "Cameron . . . has just completed what is without doubt the most remarkable journey ever accomplished by a woman of this country. We know of no one, man or woman, who in one season between ice and ice had been able to follow the Mackenzie to the sea, and to return against the current of the Peace."[5]

It is not known how her lectures were subsidized but it is likely that those cities and organizations wishing to hear her speak were the ones who hosted her. The Winnipeg Women's Canadian Club sponsored her talks in Manitoba and when she went to Ottawa she travelled under the patronage of His Excellency Earl Grey, Governor General of Canada. She became such a valuable asset for Canada that a public request was directed to businessmen as well as the federal government to subsidize her talks across Canada, the United States, and England. Cameron had put Canada forefront in the minds of Americans and Britons and awakened thousands of Canadians as to the vastness and richness of their country. The *Rockford Republic* of Illinois wrote a praiseworthy report saying, "What Kipling has done for India, Agnes Deans Cameron is doing for Canada."[6] All the while Cameron was travelling across Canada and the United States she was still busy filling in those rare free moments by writing articles for national and international magazines and newspapers. She wrote "Alluring Alberta" in July, "Silhouette of the Northern Trapper" in August, and "Sentinels of Silence" in November.

Perhaps her most rewarding lectures were in her hometown of Victoria. In late September of 1909 Cameron spent a little over three weeks on the west coast giving a series of talks to sellout audiences, both in Victoria and Vancouver. The *Daily Colonist* paid tribute to her and offered her vindication over the Royal Commission incident. "How many people foresaw at the time of the lady's difficulty with the School Board that the situation was loaded with such possibilities as have arisen out of it . . . She is a teacher still, but a teacher whose schoolroom is a continent, whose pupils are numbered by hundreds of thousands. Her success is a conspicuous triumph of merit. She has brought to bear upon her special line of work an originality and force which are almost unique . . . The *Colonist* extends to her its heartiest congratulations upon what she has so far accomplished and expresses the hope that her future career may be in keeping with what she has already achieved."[7] The Sisters of St. Ann's wrote a public letter to the *Daily Colonist* saying they considered her a powerful proponent in the cause of education and how much they thought her presence had brought great joy to the city. They hoped that she would continue with her work, as it allowed her to accomplish much good.

Before she left Victoria for the east coast and then on to London, her family gave a home reception in her honour. It was the event in the city to be invited to. Around two hundred people attended, including some of her former students as well as many of Victoria's dignitaries. It was interesting that none of the school trustees or Department of Education officials who had spearheaded the move to remove her teaching certificate were in attendance. Some of the mementos she brought with her were put on display, including the collection of Arctic and sub-Arctic flora she had gathered. Each room in her brother's house was decorated with large bouquets of fragrant flowers; the reception table was adorned with trailing smilax and golden yellow chrysanthemums. An air of informal friendliness and conviviality set the tone. Throughout the afternoon and evening violin selections were rendered by a number of musicians.

After the reception, she said goodbye to her family as she, Jessie, and another niece, Gladys Cameron, travelled on to central and eastern Canada, where they had a very tight schedule of presentations. On Christmas Eve Cameron and her nieces boarded a ship at the port of Saint John, New Brunswick, and set sail across the Atlantic to London for a two-year stay. Although the *Pittsburgh Post-Gazette* of Pennsylvania wrote that Cameron travelled to London with two of her nieces, the British media almost always only mentioned Jessie Cameron Brown as her companion.[8] There was never any indication made of Gladys. Cameron, now forty-six, had been commissioned by Lord Northcliffe to write a daily column on Canadian and American subjects for the *London Daily Mail*. Lord Northcliffe was a newspaper mogul who was a pioneer in popular journalism. Although Cameron had written for many of the biggest and most prestigious magazines, and vied in popularity with the world's most read and popular writers, it was still a coup for her. The *London Daily Mail* was the biggest selling newspaper in the world, with a readership of well over a million. In addition to writing for Lord Northcliffe, Cameron was hired by the Canadian government to promote Canada and its products, as well as encourage potential emigrants to come to Western Canada. The London media loved this energetic, well-spoken woman, writing that she was "One of the most interesting visitors to London just now . . . Miss Agnes Deans Cameron, a Canadian with a magnetic personality and a wonderful flow of language. Miss Cameron is one of the few women who have explored the Arctic Ocean, and not long ago she published a book entitled 'The New North.' She has lectured in all the principal cities of Canada and the United States, her lectures being distinguished by a wonderful use of slang."[9]

Cameron and her nieces eventually settled in one of the well-appointed row houses at 10 Montague Street, located in the elegant residential enclave of Russell Square. Directly across from them was the British Museum and on the western side of the square was the University of London, where Cameron gave several talks. Although very different from the space and solitude of the Arctic, they enjoyed living in one of the great cities of the world. While there they had the good fortune to take part in the pomp and ceremony surrounding the coronation of King George V and Queen Mary.

Almost immediately Cameron set to work writing articles for the *London Daily Mail* as well as organizing her lecture tour. Her fame preceded her and people clamoured to attend her talks. At the impressive Imperial Institute in South Kensington, Cameron drew an audience of over one thousand people. The Duke of Argyle introduced her and after her slideshow said what many in the audience were thinking: "Miss Cameron, the feeling left in my mind after listening to your travels is one of unadulterated envy."[10] She gave presentations in the largest cities in England, including at the Royal Geographical Society at Burlington House, the Victoria League of London, the University of Oxford, St. Andrew's University, and Winchester College, one of the most prestigious private schools in England. His Royal Highness, Prince Arthur, Duke of Connaught and Strathearn and the future viceroy to Canada attended one of her talks. Cameron became one of his favourite authors. She not only spoke at events populated by lords and ladies, she also presented her slide shows to people in some of the poorest quarters of London. Nothing seemed to daunt her. She worked through one of the hottest summers on record and gave over two hundred talks while in London, a formidable undertaking even for this dynamic but soft-spoken woman.

The stage was her natural habitat but no matter how relaxed she may have been in front of a large crowd, she needed to be at the top of her game for each talk—she had to arouse excitement, keep her audience interested, and project her voice to audiences of over a thousand. She took it all in stride. She loved it and became one of the most in-demand speakers of her time. She did, however, admit to feeling weary at times: "In one month I gave twenty-three lectures, and each in a different town."[11]

Her home province of British Columbia was very proud of their native daughter and was boastful of her fame. The *Vancouver Daily World* wrote, "We may safely claim Agnes Deans Cameron, the versatile writer, whose book, 'The New North,' has attracted so much attention, as a Vancouverite, as she taught school here in the early days and has never lost touch with the city. The industry, the versatility of this gifted writer, the 'strength' of her work, are qualities which have won her world-wide admiration."[12]

Toward the end of 1911 Cameron's time in England came to a close. She boarded a ship to Canada arriving in Victoria on January 5, 1912. Cameron was planning on making Victoria her home once again. Rumour had it that she had purchased land that overlooked the city. In the interim she moved into the Empress Hotel, an impressive château-style edifice that had a panoramic view the Inner Harbour. Designed by the noted architect Francis Mawson Rattenbury, the Empress emulated its name. It was built for the Canadian Pacific Railway as part of their pan-Canadian chain of resort hotels catering to wealthy clients. Every aspect of the hotel conveyed a sense of luxury and beauty. When Cameron sat down for supper in the elegant dining room she could not have helped being impressed with the intricately carved beams of Australian rosewood and luxurious tables set with silver and cut glass.

She had much to contemplate: she had signed contracts with English publishers to write two books, one on England and another on British Columbia, and there were speaking engagements in Vancouver and Victoria as well as other parts of the country for which to prepare. She was invited by many organizations to appear at their events as the star attraction. One such event that she enjoyed was as an honoured guest for an upcoming car rally to be held May 4. Organized by the Canadian Highway

Association, the plan was for a hundred or so cars from Victoria, Vancouver, and Seattle to drive from Nanaimo to Alberni to plant the first post of the Canadian highway. She was looking forward to the event, as it reminded her of the excitement of her bicycling days.

Chapter Fifteen

An Untimely Death

Life is real. Five minutes now are as valuable as five minutes of eternity and as potent of possibility.

—AGNES DEANS CAMERON

A few days after the car rally Cameron began to feel unwell—a digestive upset perhaps? It was sure to go away, she thought; she didn't take it seriously. However, as the pain and nausea began to increase in tenor she realized that there was something vitally wrong. She went to see her physician who diagnosed her as having acute appendicitis. She was sent immediately to St. Joseph's Hospital to await surgery. Appendicitis was considered a grievous ailment in 1912. Cameron was taken in for surgery in the evening and, although her situation was serious, she was otherwise healthy and expected to make a full recovery. Looking on the bright side of things, a period of post-surgical convalescence would at least give her time to gather her thoughts about her next books.

The operation was successful and the hospital broadcast positive reports on her progress, to the relief of her family and friends. Their elation was short lived. By five o'clock the next morning Cameron had taken a turn for the worse; her fever spiked and her breathing became laboured. She was suffering from pneumonia, a not uncommon complication post abdominal surgery in 1912. Realizing that she was dying she had her will drawn up. She left everything to her sister Jessie Cameron with instructions to use her estate to help her nieces and nephews if they so needed it. As the hours ticked away her body struggled with the infection, and by Monday, May 13, at ten-thirty in the morning, just as the sun burst through the window embracing everyone within, Cameron's journey had come to an end. That evening the *Vancouver Daily World* had as its headline "Agnes Deans Cameron Noted Writer, Dead." Similar captions were front-page news in papers across Canada, the United States, and England.

Everyone was stunned. Telegrams from Chicago, London, Toronto, Edmonton, and Winnipeg spoke to people's shock; how could one who had so much to offer and had done so much for the country die so suddenly, they wanted to know. Tributes started flowing in. The *Edmonton Journal* wrote that Cameron was the most talked-about woman writer in Canada; another said that she was Western Canada's most impassioned publicist. The *Vancouver Daily World* extolled her passion writing, "[Her] work was by no means complete when she was called from it, and while other pens and other voices will carry it on, none among them will be impelled by a more passionate devotion to this land of mountains, lakes and fells than that which animated Agnes Deans Cameron from her earliest years."[1] The *Saturday News* of Edmonton wrote a fulsome report that talked about her charm and well-deserved celebrity: "She had an insatiable ambition, wonderful personal magnetism, and a fund of humor and capacity for fun that was boundless. As an arguer and logical thinker, she could hold her own with any man. She radiated strength. Life's goblet was always brimming over for her. She loved the world, she loved people. To be up and doing was the motto of her existence . . . As a platform speaker she had few superiors. She set many a coping stone in the Mother Land's appreciation of Canada."[2]

A pall fell over her hometown. The Victoria Local Council of Women cancelled their annual general meeting out of respect for her. Victoria City Council voted for a special tribute to Cameron, stating that the city had suffered a severe loss. They praised her service to the country. The Alexandra Club, a popular women's organization in Victoria, flew the Royal Union flag at half-mast. The *Daily Colonist* predicted that her name would come to be inscribed in the annals of history as an outstanding citizen and supporter of her province. "It is possible that when the history of British Columbia comes to be written, the name of Agnes Deans Cameron will be inscribed therein as the most remarkable woman citizen of the province, and her story will stand out all the more prominently in as much as her death occurred when she appeared to be at the very zenith of her career, with a brilliant future ahead of her."[3]

Two days after her death Cameron's body was taken to her sister's house on Collinson Street for a short service. Jessie Cameron Brown, who had been an indispensable part of Cameron's life, was deeply saddened by her aunt's death. After the family paid their respects they walked to St. Andrew's Presbyterian church. Her funeral was one of the largest the city had seen for a long time. Fortunately, the weather had cooled from a high of 27°Celcius the previous day to 16°Celcius. At exactly two-thirty in the afternoon six pallbearers, including Victoria City School Superintendent E. B. Paul, carried her flower-laden coffin into the church.[4] They were accompanied by Chopin's dramatic and haunting "Funeral March" from his *Sonata No. 2 in B-flat minor*, followed by the beautifully melodic song from Felix Mendelssohn's *Elijah*, "O Rest in the Lord." It was a fitting song, for Cameron was steadfast in her religion and knew the Bible like few others. The church was overflowing with flower wreaths and supporters, all a testament to a woman who was greatly admired and respected.

In addition to family and friends, most of the elite in the city were in attendance—among them, the mayor of the city, Beckwith, and his council; the members of the Victoria School Board, the principal and staff from the Girl's Central School, many of her past students from South Park School, the Vancouver branches of the Canadian Women's Press Club, the Women's Canadian Club, and the Daughters of the Empire, the Canadian Highway Association of Vancouver, the Local Council of Women, the Native Sons, Post 1, the Provincial WCTU, and St. Andrew's Young People's Society. They all sat in solemnity as three officiating ministers and the full choir bade her on her way. The service ended with Handel's masterful and hopeful "Dead March" from *Saul*. After the service her brother, W. G. Cameron, took her on one last trip, aboard the *Princess Charlotte* bound for Seattle. It was there that her body would be cremated. Flowers were laid at the family memorial in Ross Bay Cemetery in Victoria, but her ashes were scattered in the Strait of Georgia, setting her free to float in the ebb and flow of the current.

Eight months after Cameron's death, the case for the return of her teaching certificate came up once again. A letter to the editor of the *Vancouver Daily World* brought attention to the fact that even though the late Agnes Deans Cameron had been reinstated as a certified teacher in the province of British Columbia her name had not been listed in the annual school report of certified teachers for 1910 or 1911. Other accolades came to her posthumously. To honour her contributions to writing, the Imperial Daughters of the Empire formed an Agnes Deans Cameron Chapter whose focus, among other things, was providing books for libraries. *The New North* was still exceptionally popular and was being promoted by the media as a must read. In 1935 the Canadian Women's Press Club instituted an annual award in memory of the great journalists of their time, which included Cameron, to commemorate outstanding members of the Press Club. The award was to be presented to a Canadian woman who published an exceptional work in a newspaper or magazine. On the one hundredth anniversary of her death, Agnes Deans Cameron was featured as part of a tapestry representing the Scottish diaspora. The tapestry portrayed Cameron as a young woman wearing a long pleated skirt and flat-brimmed Stetson striding across the landscape carrying paper, pencil, and briefcase. The idea for the tapestry originated from the Prestoungrange Arts Festival in Scotland. Similar in idea to the Bayeux tapestry, the Scottish tapestry consists of 305 panels that depict Scottish history and settlement in countries around the world. Cameron was also named as one of the 150 distinguished British Columbians in celebration of Canada's 150th birthday.

Because of Cameron, England and the United States, along with the rest of Canada, leaned about the western and northern part of the Dominion, showcasing a complex and varied geography and population. Her accomplishments in this area were a real boon to the project of nation building and put Western Canada on the map. Her experiences are significant because they present us with an important piece of our history, reminding us that we are all part of the broader story.

While statues of her have never been erected, something that in the main is un-Canadian, Cameron also never received her due recognition in the history books, perhaps because she was a woman or maybe because she focused so much on the west in a country that is eastern focused. However, her name and exploits do crop up in various writings; feminists have honoured her, academics have written analytical articles about her, she has been the subject of papers and chapters about Canadian heroines, Scots in British Columbia, and early educators who were instrumental in setting standards for the professionalism of teaching and education, and she almost always is featured in articles written about women northern explorers. In 1986 a partial reprint of *The New North* opened her exploits to a new audience. A simple search on the Internet yields pages and pages of information about her. The collective consciousness of the world has since moved on, and though her time has passed into distant memory, the name Agnes Deans Cameron has never been forgotten.

ACKNOWLEDGEMENTS

I am always humbled by the enthusiastic support and assistance I receive when I approach people for information, whether it is helping find obscure bits of information, rummaging through photographs, responding to my last-minute requests with grace, helping me through the endless morass of style, or editing my work to make it presentable. I am profoundly thankful to the following people: Scott Munro of the Greater Victoria Public Library came to my aid when I asked if he could help me find Agnes Deans Cameron's address for her residence in Chicago, something I had spent weeks pursuing. There was the day I walked into the Victoria High School Archives to search for photographs of Cameron, only to realize that it was the last day of school before the summer break. Nonetheless, Deb Blackie put some of her valuable time aside for me and found many wonderful photos that I could use. Cameron was dedicated to her students and would be proud to see that the level of excellence and professionalism she demanded continues to this day. In another instance, I contacted Judi Stevensen of the Greater Victoria School District Archives who rummaged through packed boxes that were in the process of being moved to another location, to look for the files on South Park School.

"Against the Current" is a title that first appeared as the chapter heading of a discussion about Agnes Deans Cameron for *In Her Own Right*, a book Barbara Latham and I edited in 1980. I owe a great debt to Roberta Pazdro for letting me use the title of her article for this book. The inspiration and original source of the phrase is Agnes Deans Cameron's book, *The New North*, and it refers to the direction of the flow of the Mackenzie River upon her return trip from the Western Arctic. Writing of that time she explained, "We now travel against current." It is an axiom that is an exposé of her entire life.

Images are vital for a biography. Unfortunately, it is very expensive for authors to purchase a licensing fee to use them for publication in their works, so I greatly appreciate it whenever I can find photos that are in the public domain. I would like to thank Victoria High School Archives, the City of Victoria Archives, the Vancouver City Archives, and the Winnipeg Public Library for making their photos accessible and for granting me permission for their use. I would also like to thank Bruce McKenzie of the *Times Colonist* newspaper who allowed me to quote passages from the early *Daily British Colonist* and its variants. My intent was to use the original words of some of the people and events in this work. I find eyewitness accounts personalize history and help to create a bond with people and act as a link across time. I would also like to acknowledge the incredible work that the University of Victoria Archives has accomplished in putting the *British Colonist* online. It is an invaluable source of historical goings-on in the city, province, country, and the world from 1858 through to 1951.

Writing seems like a physically benign activity; however, sitting long hours bent over a keyboard takes its toll. Without the incredible support of Marita Middleton, who patched up pinched nerves, fixed various limbs that quit working, and eased back spasms, this book would never have been finished.

Importantly, I would like to thank my wonderful editor Cailey Cavallin, whose skill and attention to detail ensure my scribblings are readable and accurate. Editors are the unsung heroes of writing. I owe a great debt to my publisher Taryn Boyd and the entire team at Brindle & Glass for their interest, enthusiasm, professionalism, and guiding hand. Part of the joy of writing for me is the opportunity to be able to work with such a great group of people.

ENDNOTES

Introduction

1. Agnes Deans Cameron, *The New North: Being Some Account of a Woman's Journey Through Canada to the Arctic* (New York: D. Appleton, 1909), 61.

2. Cameron was always publically referred to as Agnes Deans Cameron, never as Agnes. For this book I have chosen to use her last name. On the other hand, I refer to her niece, Jessie Cameron Brown, and her mother, Jessie Anderson Cameron, by their first names. This is in no way meant to imply a status differential; it is simply for expediency.

3. "My Trek to the Arctic": A Chat with Miss Agnes Deans Cameron, *Daily Colonist*, February 27, 1910, Sunday Supplement, 6.

4. Ibid.

5. Cameron, *The New North*, 3.

6. "My Trek to the Arctic," *Daily Colonist*, 6.

Chapter One: The Lure of Gold

1. Ships left the Port of San Francisco to points north all year, but the best time to go northward was in winter to take advantage of the succession of low-pressure systems that create south to southwest winds and following seas.

2. From the founding of the early colony through the gold-rush period, evidence points to the fact that many of the women selling sex were Indigenous. Because the women came from diverse cultural backgrounds, it is difficult to cite any one reason as to why this was the case. Some women were slaves captured

by a particular group and had little choice in the matter. For others like the Songhees, territorial impingement of their lands, which resulted in increasing marginalization, made it difficult for them to maintain their livelihood. It was a way to bring more wealth back to their communities. Among the Tsimshian, for example, women were not chastised for selling sex for money or goods. Lamentably, they not only took home incurable venereal diseases but as the growing sexualization of Indigenous women increased, so too did violence against them, most often perpetuated by the transient gold miners. For further information see Jean Barman's essay "Aboriginal Women on the Streets of Victoria," in *Contact Zones: Aboriginal and Settler Women in Canada's Colonial Past*, eds. Myra Rutherdale and Katie Pickles (Vancouver: UBC Press, 2007), 205–227; Patrick Dunae, "Geographies of Sexual Commerce in Victoria British Columbia, 1862–1912," http://www.cliomedia.ca/Dunae-CHA60.pdf; Penelope Edmonds, *Urbanizing Frontiers: Indigenous Peoples and Settlers in 19th-Century Pacific Rim Cities* (Vancouver: UBC Press, 2010), 220–226.

3 Terry Reksten, *More English than the English: A Very Social History of Victoria* (Victoria: Orca, 1986), 73.

4 Emily Carr was later deemed one of Canada's most famous post-impressionist painters.

5 J. K. Nesbitt, "Old Homes and Families," *Daily Colonist*, June 18, 1950, Magazine Section, 11.

6 Ibid.

7 The *Daily British Colonist* and the *Daily Colonist* are the same newspaper. The *Daily British Colonist* changed its masthead to the *Daily Colonist* in 1887.

8 "The Old and The New," *Daily British Colonist*, January 2, 1865, 2.

Chapter Two: The Early Years for Cameron and for Public Education

1 Barbara completed classes at Mrs. Wilson Brown's Church Bank House Academy. She chose a course in dressmaking, apprenticing with a Mrs. Halpenny. She was later persuaded by Mrs. Edward Cridge to become matron of the Orphans' Home, which she ran very successfully for a number of years.

2 Over the years Victoria High School would graduate two premiers of British Columbia, several cabinet ministers, mayors, famous lawyers, artists, and historians. Emily Carr also graduated from Victoria High School.

3 Early in the settlement of the Colony of Vancouver Island Governor James Douglas set aside property on behalf of the Hudson's Bay Company to be developed for a boys' school.

4 John Teague, a noted architect in the city, designed the new school.

5 John Jessop, superintendent of education, *Fifth Annual Report of the Public Schools of the Province of British Columbia, 1875–76*, 90.

6 Cameron, "Posers from Children," *Chicago Daily Tribune*, February 2, 1907, 8.

7 Ibid.

8 Bronze was awarded for the secondary level, silver for the undergraduate level, and gold for the postgraduate level.

9 Newbury lived up to his award, eventually becoming a well-known and respected member of the community. To honour his contributions to the city, two streets near Victoria's Gorge area were named after him: Newbury Street and Cowper Street.

10 "The Public Schools," *Daily British Colonist*, August 8, 1876, 3.

11 Paterfamilias, "Prayer in Public Schools," *Daily British Colonist*, September 9, 1876, 3.

12 "The High School," *Daily British Colonist*, September 7, 1876, 2.

13 Alex B. Nicholson, "Reverend Nicholson's Letter of Resignation September 9, 1876," *Fifth Annual Report of the Public Schools of the Province of British Columbia, 1875–76*, Appendix H, 158.

14 Ibid, 48.

15 *Sixth Annual Report of the Public Schools of the Province of British Columbia 1876–1877*, Appendix C, Teachers' Examination Papers.

Chapter Three: The Young Teacher

1 Angela College was named after Baroness Angela Burdett-Coutts, a well-known philanthropist from a wealthy banking family in London. She was keen to spread Protestantism to the New World, and to that end she provided five thousand pounds to establish an Anglican archdiocese on Vancouver Island along with funding for the building of the school. For her service to the new diocese, Burdett Avenue, Coutts Street, and Columbia Square were named in her honour.

2 "Collegiate School for Girls," *Daily British Colonist*, October 13, 1865, 3.

3 Ibid.

4 High operating costs, lack of funding from London, years of mismanagement, and the growing popularity of public schools overtook Angela College. In 1908, after forty-three years of service, the once proud school that had educated hundreds of young students was slated to become a hotel. Angela College has had many incarnations since it was sold in 1908. It was operated for years as the Angela Hotel, changing hands a few times. In 1959 the Sisters of St. Ann

purchased the hotel and converted it into Mount St. Angela, which they ran as a semi-retirement home for their order. Its current future is unknown, but it is protected by its heritage designation.

5   Port Augusta was renamed Comox in 1893.

6   In 1875 the E & N Railway Act expropriated a large section of land for a thoroughfare up the coast. The land was part of the traditional territory of the K'ómoks First Nation who were not only not accredited as owning the land, but were never compensated for the use of their land.

7   Ben Hughes, *History of the Comox Valley* (Comox Valley: Evergreen Press, 1962), 16.

8   By the following year in 1884, the school at Port Augusta was closed. Two new schools took its place, one built in South Comox and the other in North Comox.

9   The *Wilson G. Hunt* was one of the early American steamers that plied the Sacramento, Columbia, and Fraser Rivers as a transport during the heady days of the California and British Columbia gold rushes. In 1883, after breaking a shaft, it was decided to retire the ship that had served so many for so long.

10 City of Vancouver Archives, Major James Skitt Matthews, *Early Vancouver*, vol. 4, 33.

11 Jean Barman, "Schooled for Inequality," *Children, Teachers and Schools: In the History of British Columbia*, 2nd ed. (Edmonton: Brush Education, 2003), 59.

12 "To gas" was a colloquialism that meant talking a lot.

13 "Miss Willard," *Daily British Colonist*, July 1, 1883, 3.

14 "The Schools Enemy," *Daily British Colonist*, July 13, 1885, 3.

15 The first provincial normal school opened in Vancouver in 1901 and in Victoria in 1915.

Chapter Four: A Very Public Scuffle

1   "The Past Year," *Daily Colonist*, January 1, 1890, 2.

2   Cameron, "Corporal Punishment," *Daily Colonist*, May 23, 1890, 6.

3   Ibid.

4   The issue of suspension is still being debated. In the summer of 2014 the BC Confederation of Parent Advisory Councils passed a resolution requesting schools to use alternative methods to suspension. Punishment for breaking the rules by suspending a student is currently seen as counterproductive to helping the student deal with the causes and consequences of their behaviour.

A modern-day teacher would most likely talk to the student in private, build a rapport with them, and possibly send them to a specialized teaching assistant. In the 1890s that was not common practice.

5   *Twenty-Fourth Annual Report of the Public Schools of the Province of British Columbia, 1894–95*, 201.

6   W. H. Burkholder, "Corporal Punishment," *Daily Colonist*, May 22, 1890, 4.

7   Hayward, "A Case of Discipline," *Daily Colonist*, May 23, 1890, 6.

8   Ibid.

9   "Our Schools," *Daily Colonist*, May 20, 1890, 5.

10 "Miss Cameron's Answer," *Daily Colonist*, May 26, 1890, 6.

11 "School Discipline," *Daily Colonist*, May 30, 1890, 6.

12 C. C. Bass, "Corporal Punishment," *Daily Colonist*, May 30, 1890, 6.

13 Cameron, "Parent and Teacher," *National Council of Women of Canada Report*, 1900, 247; see also *Educational Journal of Western Canada*, August–September, 1900, 454–456.

14 Cameron, "Parent and Teacher," *Proceedings of the Dominion Education Association*, July 26–29, 1904, 249.

15 Ada Alice McGeer interview, sound recording, Reynoldston Research and Studies, 1973; see also "A Memory," *B.C. Historical News*, 8, November 1974, 16–17.

16 Cameron, "Parent and Teacher," *National Council of Women of Canada Report*, 246.

17 Cameron, "Parent and Teacher," *Proceedings of the Dominion Education Association*, 1904, 242.

Chapter Five: Noteworthy Firsts for Public Education in British Columbia

1   "Report of the Principal," *Twentieth Annual Report of the Public School of the Province of British Columbia, 1890–1891*, 187.

2   *Daily Colonist*, October 17, 1893, 1.

3   "The South Ward School," *Daily Colonist*, June 1, 1894, 3.

4   Cameron, "Report of the Principal," *Twenty-Fourth Annual Report of the Public Schools of the Province of British Columbia 1894–95*, 255.

5   The Tally-Ho Company began in 1903 as the first horse-drawn transportation system in Victoria. Today it serves as a tourist attraction and has been in operation for 115 years.

[6] Cameron, *Proceedings of the Dominion Educational Association*, July 26–29, 1904, 245.

Chapter Six: Meaningful Events

[1] Cameron, "In Lava Lands," *Victoria Daily Times*, September 5, 1895, 3.

[2] Ibid, September 10, 1895, 6.

[3] Ibid.

[4] The flag of the Kingdom of Hawai'i was allowed to stand until 1898 when the United States flag was raised, signalling annexation.

[5] *Evening Bulletin* (Honolulu, Hawaii), September 27, 1895, 5.

[6] Cameron, "The Avatar of Jack Pemberton," *Pacific Monthly*, 9, May 1903, 308.

[7] Cameron, "Through British Columbia Spectacles," *Daily Colonist*, August 2, 1904, 3.

[8] Cameron, "What Men Have Said About Women," *Manitoba Morning Free Press*, August 18, 1906, 29.

[9] M. E. Angus, "A Plea for the New Woman," *Daily Colonist*, May 28, 1895, 4.

[10] Vice President of the Council of Women in Victoria, "The National Council For Women," *Daily Colonist*, May 28, 1895, 4.

[11] Cameron, "Suffrage for Women," *Daily Colonist*, May 28, 1895, 5.

[12] Ibid.

[13] Women of Japanese, Chinese, or South Asian heritage were not allowed to vote federally until the late 1940s, while Indigenous women did not gain the franchise until 1960 in most of Canada and in 1969 in Quebec.

[14] "Home for Aged Women," *Daily Colonist*, November 9, 1895, 7.

[15] Ibid.

[16] "Kindergarten Training," *Daily Colonist*, November 12, 1895, 7.

[17] George W. Blum, *The Cyclers' Guide and Road Book of California* (San Francisco: Edward Denny, 1896), 11.

[18] "Champion of Her Sex," *New York Sunday World*, February 2, 1896, 10.

[19] *A Victorian Tapestry: Impressions of Life in Victoria BC 1880–1914* (Victoria: British Columbia Provincial Archives, 1978).

[20] Cameron, "Parent and Teacher," The Dominion Educational Association, "The Minutes of Proceedings, Addresses and Papers of the Fifth Convention," (Winnipeg, July 1904), 241.

21 Ibid, 242.

22 Ibid, 244.

23 Ibid, 242.

24 Cameron, "Bands of Mercy in Schools," *Daily Colonist*, February 1, 1899, 7.

25 Cameron, "Parent and Teacher," *Proceedings of the Dominion Educational Association*, 1904, 242.

26 "A Striking Personality," *Daily Colonist*, January 18, 1901, 5.

Chapter Seven: A Troubling Time

1 Osborne was Osborne House, Queen Victoria's family home in East Cowes, Isle of Wight.

2 "What Lady Teachers Say: Do Not Approve Discrimination as to Sex in Fixing Salaries," *Daily Colonist*, April 20, 1901, 3.

3 "Claims of British Columbia," Revenue Estimates and Expenditures presented by the Finance Minister, *Daily Colonist*, March 27, 1901, 9–12.

4 "What Lady Teachers Say," 3.

5 "Candidates Make Promises," *Daily Colonist*, January 15, 1902, 6.

6 Ibid.

7 Cameron, "The Idea of True Citizenship," *Educational Journal of Western Canada*, vol. 1, no. 8 (December 1899), 233.

8 "Requests an Investigation," *Daily Colonist*, June 23, 1901, 3.

9 *Thirty-Second Annual Report of the Public Schools of the Province of British Columbia, 1902–1903*, Appendix A, 32.

10 "South Park School: Correspondence Between the Superintendent of Education and Principal," *Daily Colonist*, June 29, 1901, 3.

11 Ibid.

Chapter Eight: An Up-and-Coming Writer

1 Cameron, "The Avatar of Jack Pemberton," *Pacific Monthly*, May 1903, 305.

2 The *Pacific Monthly* merged with *Sunset Magazine* in 1911 and became known as *Sunset: The Magazine of Western Living and The Pacific Monthly*. Today it is known simply as *Sunset*.

3 "A Wrong to Canada Righted," *Daily Colonist*, December 31, 1903, 6.

4 Cameron, "The Winnipeg Fair," *Daily Colonist*, August 16, 1904, 3.

5 "Scribes and Scribblings," *Daily Colonist*, April 2, 1905, 10.

Chapter Nine: A Long Ordeal

1 To pass, students had to have an aggregate of fifty-five marks out of 1100. The pass mark for each subject was thirty-four percent. For the drawing portion sixty-six and two-thirds marks were allotted for the workbooks and thirty-three and one-third for the exam portion for a total of one hundred points. Because of the ruling no marks were given to the workbooks. However, it was decided to pass those students who had at least 516 marks overall and thirty-four percent pass on the drawing part of the exam.

2 "The Full Text of the Finding," *Daily Colonist*, February 27, 1906, 7.

3 Ibid.

4 Ibid.

5 "Miss Cameron States Her Case," *Daily Colonist*, November 28, 1905, 3.

6 "The Trustees Talk at The City Hall," *Daily Colonist*, January 17, 1906, 8.

7 "Miss Cameron States Her Case," *Daily Colonist*, November 28, 1905, 2.

8 "Petition Prays for Reinstatement," *Daily Colonist*, November 16, 1905, 3.

9 Hibben's was a delightful store. Victorians loved their books and Hibben's did not disappoint. They sold books and well-appointed stationery, music, Admiralty charts, schoolbooks, paper, math tools, and gold pens. There was just about anything anyone could want from a book and stationery store, including concertinas. Children loved visiting the store, especially at Christmas when new children's books were displayed. Books about ducks, bears, kittens, trains, and boats were always popular.

10 "Miss Cameron States Her Case," *Daily Colonist*, November 28, 1905, 2.

Chapter Ten: A Royal Commission

1 "The Drawing Investigation," *Daily Colonist*, December 21, 1905, 3.

2 Ibid.

3 Ibid.

4 Willis later served as the province's longest acting superintendent of education and deputy minister of education. In 1905 a new junior secondary school in Victoria, British Columbia, bore the name of S. J. Willis.

5 It appears that Santa did not make it to hand out the presents to the children. It is likely that the manager of Watson's theatre, Terry McKean, had read the story in the news about Fred M. Frye, a teacher in Massachusetts who was

severely burned by the candles on a Christmas tree while portraying Santa Claus for a school event, and decided to use it as an excuse for his errant Santa.

6 "Another Day Over Drawing," *Daily Colonist*, December 28, 1905, 6.

7 "Expert Evidence at Commission," *Daily Colonist*, January 13, 1906, 3.

8 "The School Controversy," letter to the editor, *Daily Colonist*, January 18, 1906, 4.

9 "What is Insubordination," letter to the editor, *Daily Colonist*, January 18, 1906, 4.

10 Barbara Latham and Roberta Pazdro, "A Simple Matter of Justice: Agnes Deans Cameron and the British Columbia Department of Education, 1906–8," in *Atlantis: Critical Studies in Gender & Social Justice*, vol. 10, no. 1, October 1984, 115.

Chapter Eleven: Political Aspirations

1 "Frame a Ticket for School Trustees," *Daily Colonist*, January 12, 1906, 2.

2 Elector, "The Position of School Trustee Candidates," letter to the editor, *Daily Colonist*, January 17, 1906, 4.

3 Ibid.

4 "Trustees Talk at The City Hall," *Daily Colonist*, January 17, 1906, 8.

5 Ibid.

6 Ibid.

7 Ibid.

8 Ibid.

9 "Agnes Deans Cameron Heads the Poll in School Trustee Election," *Daily Colonist*, January 19, 1906, 1.

10 *Minneapolis Journal* (Minneapolis, Minnesota), July 9, 1906, 6.

11 Cameron, "Miss Cameron Replies," letter to the editor, *Daily Colonist*, January 21, 1906, 4.

12 "British Columbians Seek to Secede," *Daily Colonist*, January 21, 1906, 3.

13 The chains were two platforms on either side of the ship used by the leadsman when taking soundings.

14 Over the years the "Graveyard of the Pacific" has claimed 137 ships.

15 "Finding in the Drawing Inquiry," *Daily Colonist*, February 25, 1906, 2.

[16] Cameron, letter written to the Honourable John Sebastian Helmcken on March 2, 1908. It can be found in Barbara Latham and Roberta Pazdro, "A Simple Matter of Justice: Agnes Deans Cameron and the British Columbia Department of Education, 1906–8," in *Atlantis: Critical Studies in Gender & Social Justice*, vol. 10, no. 1, October 1984, 113–115. The original letter is from a private collection in Victoria, BC

[17] The W. G. Cameron building still stands to this day. It can be found at 581 Johnson Street in Victoria's Old Town District.

[18] William George Cameron served as a city councillor in 1895, 1896, 1899–1903, 1908, 1916, 1919, and served as a Land Commissioner for the Province of British Columbia. He married twice and lived with his mother for a time after the death of his first wife.

Chapter Twelve: A Change in Direction

[1] Herbert Vanderhoof was a representative of the Canadian Pacific, the Canadian Grand Trunk Railways, and Canadian Northern. While working for the Grand Trunk Pacific Development Company he helped to lay out the town site of Vanderhoof, British Columbia, which is named after him.

[2] *Inter Ocean* (Chicago, Illinois), July 1, 1906, 22.

[3] *Vancouver Daily World*, August 3, 1906, 6.

[4] Cameron, "Edmonton, The World's Greatest Fur-Market," *Pacific Monthly* (Portland, Oregon), February 1907, 215.

[5] The Dominion government and the Canadian Pacific Railway spared no expense and provided the organization with a grant of twenty-eight thousand dollars for its operation.

[6] Cameron, letter written to the Honourable John Sebastian Helmcken on March 2, 1908.

[7] "A Busy Authoress," *Daily Colonist*, May 30, 1908, 5.

[8] Cameron, letter written to Helmcken.

[9] "Fifty-One Bills Receive Assent: Agnes Deans Cameron," *Daily Colonist*, March 8, 1908, 15.

[10] *Vancouver Daily World*, July 13, 1906, 13.

Chapter Thirteen: To the Arctic and Back

[1] 1789 is the date when the explorer Alexander Mackenzie travelled the Mackenzie River to the Arctic Ocean.

2 Cameron was cognizant of the fact that this territory had been occupied by people before the explorations of Europeans.

3 Cameron, *The New North*, 1–2.

4 Ibid, 4.

5 Ibid, 7.

6 Ibid, 25.

7 Ibid, 14.

8 Ibid, 15.

9 The figure of 600 came from the Alberta Trail New Society and Athabasca Landing Trail Committee. www.athabascalandingtrail.com.

10 Cameron, *The New North*, 25–26.

11 Ibid, 30.

12 Rivers in Canada are referenced in statute miles, not nautical miles or kilometres.

13 *Cheechako* is a Chinook jargon word meaning "tenderfoot."

14 Cameron, *The New North*, 29.

15 Ibid, 41.

16 Ibid.

17 Ibid, 45.

18 Ibid, 48.

19 *Inter Ocean*, November 29, 1908, 29.

20 Ibid.

21 Cameron, *The New North*, 36.

22 Christina Lake and Christina River, situated between Lac La Biche and Fort McMurray in northern Alberta, are named after her. Christina Gordon Public School, which was opened in 2016, also bears her name.

23 Cameron, *The New North*, 84.

24 Ibid, 115.

25 *Nistow* is a Cree word that literally meant "brother-in-law," but was sometimes used as a term for "friends."

26 Cameron, *The New North*, 54.

27 Ibid, 56.

28 Ibid, 57.

[29] Ibid, 58.

[30] Ibid, 77.

[31] Ibid.

[32] Ibid, 61.

[33] Ibid.

[34] Ibid, 65.

[35] Ibid.

[36] Ibid, 79–80.

[37] Ibid, 81.

[38] Ibid, 82–83.

[39] The Alberta and Great Waterways Railway was incorporated in 1909, and after some political difficulty began construction in 1914. By 1928 they had laid track as far as Deep Creek (now Draper). They never did connect to Fort McMurray directly.

[40] Cameron, *The New North*, 88–89.

[41] Ibid, 89.

[42] Ibid, 90–92.

[43] Ibid, 93.

[44] Ibid, 93–94.

[45] Ibid, 104.

[46] Ibid, 105.

[47] Ibid, 97.

[48] Ibid.

[49] Treaty 8 was signed at Fond du Lac by the Dënesuliné between July 25 and 27, 1899, with adhesions occurring up to 1901. Treaty 8 encompassed 840,000 square kilometres of land, which included Lesser Slave Lake, Peace River Landing, Vermilion, Fond du Lac, Dunvegan, Fort Chipewyan, Smith's Landing, Fort McMurray, and Wapiscow Lake.

[50] Cameron, *The New North*, 135.

[51] Ibid.

[52] As least as far as Cameron's meeting with the Inuvialuit was concerned, she tended to categorize the people she met in an idealized fashion, assuming they were free of the corrupting influence of civilization and were therefore

somehow purer. The danger in this way of thinking is that it was assumed when such people met southerners and urbanites they would not be able to withstand their corrupting influence. The history of colonization is replete with this kind of thinking, which led to a government patriarchy disenfranchising Indigenous peoples, and creating systematic dispossession of their land and cultures, which is still affecting groups to this day.

53 Cameron, *The New North*, 137.

54 Smith's Landing was renamed Fort Fitzgerald in 1915.

55 Cameron, *The New North*, 140.

56 Ibid, 145–146.

57 Ibid, 156.

58 Ibid, 157.

59 Ibid, 172.

60 Father P. Duchaussois, OMI, *The Grey Nuns in the Far North, 1867–1917* (Toronto: McClelland and Stewart, 1919), 129.

61 Cameron, *The New North*, 175–176.

62 Ibid, 178.

63 Ibid, 180.

64 Ibid.

65 Ibid, 185.

66 Ibid, 199.

67 Ibid, 205–206.

68 In 1823 the Hudson's Bay Company moved the post from Manitou Island to the eastern bank of the river at Fort Good Hope.

69 Cameron, *The New North*, 207.

70 Ibid, 208.

71 Ibid, 211.

72 Formerly referred to as Arctic Red River, the community officially changed to its traditional name of Tsiigehtchic (Tsee-get-chik) in April 1994. See GTC Department of Cultural Heritage Gwich'in Social and Cultural Institute. www.gwichin.ca.

73 Cameron, *The New North*, 212–213.

74 Ibid, 221.

75 Ibid, 235–236.

[76] Ibid, 219.

[77] Ibid, 267.

[78] Ibid, 266.

[79] Cameron talked about the Richardson Mountains as being part of the northernmost extent of the Rockies. Scientists have determined that they are part of the Alaskan Brooks Range.

[80] At the beginning of the twentieth century the population of the Inuvialuit stood at around 2,500 people, and by 1910 there were only 150 left.

[81] Cameron, *The New North*, 240.

[82] Ibid, 271.

[83] Ibid, 288.

[84] Ibid, 290.

[85] Ibid, 301–302.

[86] Ibid, 305.

[87] Ibid, 319–320.

[88] Ibid.

[89] Ibid, 327.

[90] Ibid, 334.

[91] Ibid, 341.

[92] Ibid, 347.

[93] Ibid.

[94] Ibid, 348.

[95] Ibid.

[96] Ibid, 357–358.

[97] Ibid, 390.

[98] "Miss Agnes Deans Cameron Addresses Women's Canadian Club," *Daily Colonist*, October 19, 1909, 3.

Chapter Fourteen: International Fame

[1] "A Woman's Trip to the Arctic: Agnes Deans Cameron Describes Her 10,000 Mile Trip to the Farthest North," *Inter Ocean*, November 29, 1908, 29.

2   "Music and the Drama: Miss Agnes Deans Cameron's Lecture 'From Wheat to Whales,'" *Manitoba Morning Free Press* (Winnipeg, Manitoba), January 30, 1909, 14.

3   "Social and Personal," *Vancouver Daily World*, September 18, 1909, 8.

4   Ibid.

5   *Toronto Globe* (Toronto, Ontario), February 6, 1901.

6   *Rockford Republic* (Rockford, Illinois), March 6, 1909, Microfiche files, British Columbia Provincial Archives.

7   "Miss Cameron's Lectures," *Daily Colonist*, October 1, 1909, 4.

8   *Pittsburgh Post-Gazette* (Pennsylvania), February 13, 1909, 14.

9   Ibid.

10 "Canada's Northland," *Edmonton Bulletin* (Edmonton, Alberta), September 2, 1910, 8.

11 "Authoress is Honored," *Vancouver Daily World*, January 17, 1912, 18.

12 "Literature and Art in Vancouver," *Vancouver Daily World*, January 6, 1912, 13.

Chapter Fifteen: An Untimely Death

1   "Agnes Deans Cameron Noted Writer, Dead," *Vancouver Daily World*, May 13, 1912.

2   "Agnes Deans Cameron," *Saturday News* (Edmonton, Alberta), May 18, 1912, 1.

3   "Miss Cameron Passes Away," *Daily Colonist*, May 14, 1912, 1.

4   E. B. Paul was principal of Victoria College and Victoria High School. The Paul building, now part of Camosun College in Victoria, was named in his honour.

SELECTED BIBLIOGRAPHY

Adams, John. *Christmas in Old Victoria*. Duncan, BC: Firgrove, 2006.

Alexie, Robert. *Porcupines and China Dolls*. Toronto: Stoddart, 2002.

Alunik, Ishmael, Eddie Kolausok and David Morrison. *Across Time and Tundra: The Inuvialuit of the Western Arctic*. Vancouver: Raincoast Books, Seattle: University of Washington Press, Gatineau: Canadian Museum of Civilization, 2003.

Angela College for Girls, 923 Burdett Avenue. Victoria: British Columbia Provincial Archives and microfilm.

Athabasca Chipewyan First Nation. Accessed June 21, 2017. www.acfn.com.

Barman, Jean. *Growing up British in British Columbia: Boys in Private School*. Vancouver: UBC Press, 1984.

————. "Birds of Passage or Early Professionals: Teachers in Late Nineteenth-Century British Columbia." *Historical Studies in Education*, 2, no. 1 (1990): 17–36.

————. *The West Beyond the West: A History of British Columbia*. Revised ed. Toronto: University of Toronto Press, 1996.

Barman, Jean and Mona Gleason, eds. *Children, Teachers and Schools in the History of British Columbia*. 2ed. Edmonton: Brush Education, 2003.

Blum, George W. *The Cyclers' Guide and Road Book of California*. San Francisco: Edward Denny, agents, 1896.

Bowen, Lynne. "Elusive Treasure," *The Beaver: Exploring Canada's History* (February 1999): 22–27.

British Columbia, Superintendent of Education. Annual Reports of the Public Schools of the Province of British Columbia, First through Thirty-Sixth reports. Victoria: Government Printing Office, 1871–1907.

Brothers, Donald Leslie. *One Hundred Years of Education in British Columbia: Special Historical Supplement to the One Hundredth Annual Report*. Victoria: Department of Education, Queen's Printer, 1972.

Burn, Christopher R. *Herschel Island Qikiqtaryuk: A Natural and Cultural History of Yukon's Arctic Island*. Yukon: Wildlife Management Advisory Council, 2012.

Calam, John. "Teaching the Teachers: Establishment and Early Years of the BC Provincial Normal Schools." *BC Studies* 61 (Spring, 1984): 30–63.

Cameron, Agnes Deans. *The New North: Being Some Account of a Woman's Journey Through Canada to the Arctic*. New York: D. Appleton, 1909.

_____. "To Success—Walk Your Own Road." *Educational Journal of Western Canada*, 4, no. 1 (1910): 10–11.

_____. "The Arctic Host and Hostess." *Canadian Magazine* 35, no. 1 (May 1910): 3–12.

_____. "The Prince of Playgrounds: Come Home by Canada and Revel in the Rockies: Beautiful Banff." Ottawa: Department of the Interior, 1910.

_____. "Humor in School: Quizzing an Oracle." *Century Magazine* (July 1910): 477–79.

_____. "Isle of Dreams." *Canada West Magazine* (January 1908): 235–37.

_____. "Succulent Dinners That Swim the Sea." *The Saturday Evening Post* 179, no. 46 (May 18, 1907).

_____. "Parent and Teacher." *Proceedings of the Dominion Education Association Convention*. (Toronto, 1905): 249.

_____. "Kipling and the Children." *Pacific Monthly* 9 (February 1903): 109–114.

_____. "The Avatar of Jack Pemberton." *Pacific Monthly* (May 1903): 305–310.

_____. "A Jubilee Junketing." *Everybody's Magazine* 9, no. 4 (October 1903).

_____. "In the Motherland." *Educational Journal of Western Canada* 3, no. 9 (January 1902): 261.

_____. "The Idea of True Citizenship: How Shall We Develop It?" *Educational Journal of Western Canada* 4, no. 8 (1899): 229–235.

_____. "Report of the Principal, June 30, 1895." *Twenty-Fourth Annual Report of the Public Schools of the Province of British Columbia, 1894–1895*. Victoria: Province of British Columbia: 255

_____. "Report of the Principal, July 6, 1891." *Twentieth Annual Report of the Public School of the Province of British Columbia, 1890–1891*. Victoria: Province of British Columbia: 87.

Cameron, Agnes Deans Fonds. British Columbia Provincial Archives: PR-1365.

_____. (AR-023) University of Victoria Special Collections.

Canadian Power and Sail Squadrons. *MAREP Hydrographic Manual*. Ottawa: Fisheries and Oceans, 1996.

Chalmers, Graeme. "Canada's Drawing Book Scandal: A Storm in a Victorian Teacup." *Canadian Review of Art Education: Research and Issues* 28, no. 1 (2001): 41–59.

_____. "South Kensington and the Colonies: David Blair of New Zealand and Canada." *Studies in Art Education* 26, no. 2 (Winter, 1985): 69–74.

Chastko, Paul Anthony. *Developing Alberta's Oil Sands: From Karl Clark to Kyoto*. Calgary: University of Calgary Press, 2004.

Choquette, Robert. *The Oblate Assault on Canada's Northwest*. Ottawa: University of Ottawa, 1995.

Clark, Cecil George. *The Best of Victoria, Yesterday & Today: A Nostalgic 115 Year Pictorial History of Victoria*. Victoria: *Victorian Weekly*, 1973.

Clay, Margaret, interview by Imbert Orchard 1974–75. Canadian Broadcasting Corporation.

Clearihue, Joseph Badenoch, interview by Imbert Orchard 1974–75. Canadian Broadcasting Corporation.

Converse, Cathy. *MainStays: Women Who Shaped BC*. Victoria: Horsdal and Schubart, 1998.

Covello, Elizabeth Jonquil. "The Northwest Territories Reconstruction Project: Telling Our Stories." PhD diss., University of British Columbia, 2009.

Darling, Olivia Grace, interview, July 19, 1984. Oral History, Project Behind the Kitchen Door. Modern History Division of the British Columbia Provincial Museum.

Dene Nation. Last modified July 2016, accessed June 21, 2017. denenation.ca.

Dominion Educational Association. *Proceedings of the Convention Held at Winnipeg, July 26–9, 1904*. Toronto: Murray Printing, 1905.

Donnelley, Reuben H., compiler. The Lakeside Annual Directory of the City of Chicago. Chicago: Lakeside Press, 1910.

Duchaussois, Rev. Father P., OMI. *The Grey Nuns in the Far North, 1867–1917*. Toronto: McClelland and Stewart, 1919.

Duff, Wilson. "The Fort Victoria Treaties." *BC Studies*, no. 3 (Autumn 1969): 3–57.

Fawcett, Edgar. *Some Reminiscences of Old Victoria*. Toronto: William Briggs, 1912.

Fleming, Thomas, ed. *Schooling in British Columbia 1849–2005*. Mill Bay, BC: Bendall Books, 2010.

Forster, Merna. *100 Canadian Heroines: Famous and Forgotten Faces*. Toronto: Dundurn Group, 2004.

Giles, Valerie M. E. *An Annotated Bibliography of Education History in British Columbia*. Ministry of Tourism and Ministry Responsible for Culture in association with Ministry of Education and Ministry Responsible for Multiculturalism and Human Rights. Victoria: Province of British Columbia, 1992.

Gough, Lyn. *As Wise as Serpents: 1883–1939 Five Women and an Organization that Changed British Columbia*. Victoria: Swan Lake Publishing, 1988.

Grant, Peter. *Victoria: A History Photographs*. Vancouver: Altitude Publishing, 1995.

GTC Department of Cultural Heritage: Gwich'in Social and Cultural Institute. www.gwichin.ca.

Gwich'in Tribal Council, Executive and Indigenous Affairs, Government of the Northwest Territories. Accessed June 21, 2017. www.eia.gov.nt.ca/en/directory/gwichin-tribal-council.

Hacking, Norman R. "British Columbia Steamboat Days, 1870–1883." *British Columbia Historical Quarterly*, April 1947. Victoria: Archives of British Columbia in cooperation with the British Columbia Historical Association, 1947.

Heeney, Canon Bertal. *Leaders of the Canadian Church*. Toronto: Ryerson, 1943.

Hessing, Melody, Rebecca Raglon, and Catriona Sandilands, eds. *This Elusive Land: Women and the Canadian Environment*. Vancouver: UBC Press, 2006.

Historic Buildings Committee. "181 Higgins Avenue: Canadian Pacific Railway Station." (June 1981).

Hughes, Ben. *History of the Comox Valley, 1862–1945*. Nanaimo, BC: Evergreen Press, 1962.

Humphreys, Danda. *Pioneer Pathways of Early Victoria*. Surrey: Heritage House, 1999.

_____. *On the Street Where You Live*. Surrey: Heritage House, 2000.

_____. *Sailors, Solicitors, and Stargazers of Early Victoria*. Surrey: Heritage House, 2001.

_____. *Government Street: Victoria's Heritage Mile*. Surrey: Heritage House, 2012.

Johnson, Francis Henry. *A History of Public Education in British Columbia*. Vancouver: UBC, 1964.

Johnson, Hugh J., ed. *The Pacific Province: A History of British Columbia*. Vancouver: Douglas and McIntyre, 1996.

Johnstone, Tiffany. "Seeing for Oneself: Agnes Deans Cameron's Ironic Critique of American Literary Discourse in The New North." *Nordlit* 23 (2008): 69–87. septentrio.uit.no/index.php/nordlit/article/view/1165/1107.

Kay, Linda. *Sweet Sixteen: The Journey that Inspired the Canadian Women's Press Club*. Montreal & Kingston: McGill-Queen's University Press, 2012.

Kelcey, Barbara E. *Alone in Silence: European Women in the Canadian North Before 1940*. Montreal & Kingston: McGill-Queen's University Press, 2001.

Krause, James Allan. *The Life and Times of the Comox Valley Region of Vancouver Island, British Columbia, Canada*. Courtenay, BC: Sotel, 1997.

LaFramboise, Lisa N. "Travellers in Skirts: Women and English-Language Travel Writing in Canada, 1820–1926." Ph.D diss. University of Alberta, 1977.

Lampman, Peter S. "South Park School Drawing Books." February 23, 1906. Original report on file in the Provincial Secretary's Office, Victoria, BC

Lang, Marjory. *Women Who Made the News: Female Journalists in Canada, 1880–1945*. Montreal & Kingston: McGill-Queen's University Press, 1999.

Latham, Barbara and Cathy (Converse) Kess, eds. *In Her Own Right: Selected Essays on Women's History in B.C.* Victoria: Camosun College, 1980.

Latham, Barbara and Roberta Pazdro. "A Simple Matter of Justice: Agnes Deans Cameron and the British Columbia Department of Education, 1906–8." *Atlantis: Critical Studies in Gender & Social Justice* 10, no. 1 (October 1984): 115.

Local Council of Women Fonds, 1907–1981. City of Victoria Archives: CVIC-271.

Macfie, Matthew. *Vancouver Island and British Columbia: Their History, Resources and Prospects*. London: Longman, Green, Longman, Roberts and Green, 1865.

MacGregor, J. G. *Paddle Wheels to Bucket-Wheels on the Athabasca*. Toronto: McClelland and Stewart, 1974.

MacLeod, Malcolm, Robert E. Blair. *The Canadian Education Association: The First 100 Years, 1891–1991*. Toronto: Canadian Education Association, 1992.

Marchand, Debbie and Linda Picciotto. *South Park School: Memories Through the Decades*. Victoria: South Park School, 2007.

McCormack, Patricia A. *Fort Chipewyan and the Shaping of Canadian History, 1788–1920s*. Vancouver: UBC Press, 2010.

McGeer, Ada. "A Memory." *B.C. Historical News* (November 1974): 16–17.

McLaren, I. S. and Lisa Framboise, eds. *The Ladies, the Gwich'in, and the Rat: Travels on the Athabasca, Mackenzie, Rat, Porcupine, and Yukon Rivers in 1926.* Edmonton: University of Alberta Press, 1995.

McLoone, Margo. *Women Explorers in Polar Regions: Louise Arner Boyd, Agnes Deans Cameron, Kate Marsden, Ida Pfeiffer, Helen Thayer.* Mankato, Minnesota: Capstone Press, 1997.

Mishler, Craig. "Missionaries in Collision: Anglicans and Oblates Among the Gwich'in, 1861-1865." *Arctic* (June 1990): 121–26.

Morrison, David and Georges-Hébert Germain. "Inuit: Glimpses of an Arctic Past." Canadian Museum of Civilization. 1977. www.historymuseum.ca/cmc/exhibitions/aborig/inuvial/indexe.shtml.

Morrison, William R. *Showing the Flag: The Mounted Police and Canadian Sovereignty in the North 1894–1925.* Quebec: Canadian Museum of Civilization, 1995.

"Oblates of the West—the Alberta Story," The Heritage Community Foundation and Institute pour le Patrimoine, Campus Saint-Jean, University of Alberta, 2009.

O'Leary, Daniel. "Environmentalism, Hermeneutics, and Canadian Imperialism in Agnes Deans Cameron's The New North." *This Elusive Land: Women and the Canadian Environment,* eds. Hessing, Melody, Rebecca Ragion, and Catriona Sandilands. Vancouver: UBC Press, 2005: 19–34.

Order in Council Providing for the Issue of a Commission Under the Public Inquiries Act, to P. S. Lampman, November 29, 1905. BC Laws, Orders in Council, no. 0650, 1905. www.bclaws.ca.

Pazdro, Roberta J. "Against the Current." *In Her Own Right.* Latham, Barbara and Cathy Kess, eds. Victoria: Camosun College, 1980: 101–123.

Peels Prairie Province. University of Alberta Library. peel.library.ualberta.ca.

Penne, Felix. "Hours in the Vancouver Library: The Nature Books." *Vancouver Daily World.* May 15, 1912: 6.

Pickles, Katie and Myra Rutherdale, eds. *Contact Zones: Aboriginal & Settler Women in Canada's Colonial Past.* Vancouver/Toronto: UBC Press, 2005.

Post, Yesman Rae. "A History of Art Education in British Columbia 1872–1939." Master's thesis. University of Victoria, 2005.

Provincial Council of Women: British Columbia 1894–1970. Scrapbook from Victoria and Vancouver Island Council of Women: Correspondence between Agnes Deans Cameron and L. Day. British Columbia Provincial Archives.

Public Schools of the Province of British Columbia Annual Reports. Victoria: Government Printer, 1874–1913.

Reimer, Derek and Janet Cauthers, eds. *A Victorian Tapestry: Impressions of Life in Victoria, B.C. 1880-1914.* Victoria: British Columbia Provincial Archives, 1978.

Reksten, Terry. *More English than the English.* Winlaw, BC: Sono Nis Press, 2011.

"Report of the Select Committee of the Senate of the Great Mackenzie Basin, Session 1891." Ottawa: Brown Chamberlin, 1891.

Roy, Wendy. *Maps of Difference: Canada, Women, and Travel.* Montreal & Kingston: McGill-Queen's University Press, 2005.

_____. "Primacy, Technology, and Nationalism in Agnes Deans Cameron's The New North." *Mosaic* 38, no. 2 (June 2005): 53–78.

Smith, Peter L. *Come Give a Cheer: One Hundred Years of Victoria High School 1876–1976.* Victoria: Victoria High School Centennial Celebrations Committee, 1976.

Smith, Shirleen. *People of the Lakes: Stories of Our Van Tat Gwich'in Elders.* Edmonton: University of Alberta Press, 2009.

Stefánsson, Vilhjálmur. *My Life with The Eskimo.* New York: Macmillan, 1918.

Tallenntire, Jenéa. "The Ordinary Needs of Life: Strategies of Survival for Single Women in 1901 Victoria." *BC Studies* 159 (Autumn 2008): 45–72.

Taylor, Elizabeth. "A Woman in the Mackenzie Delta." Pts 1, 2, 3, 4. *Outing* 25, October 1894–March 1895: Northward to Athabasca Lake, (October 1894): 44–55; Athabasca Landing to the Arctic Circle, (November 1894): 120–133; Homeward Bound, (November 1894): 229–235; Among the Eskimos, (January 1895): 304–311.

This Old House: James Bay, Victoria: Victoria Heritage Foundation, 1979.

"Treaty No. 8 June 21, 1899 and Adhesions, Reports, Etc." Reprinted from 1899 edition by Roger Duhamel, FRSC. Ottawa: Queen's Printer and Controller of Stationery, 1966. Also found on Government of Canada/Indigenous and Northern Affairs website, www.aadnc-aandc.gc.ca.

Trueman, Alice. "Playing the Game: The Education of Girls in Private Schools on Vancouver Island." Master's thesis, University of Victoria, 2009.

Truth and Reconciliation Commission of Canada. "Canada's Residential Schools: The Inuit and Northern Experience." Montreal & Kingston: McGill-Queen's University Press, 2015.

Vogel, Aynsley and Dana Wyse. *Vancouver: A History in Photographs*. Victoria: Heritage House Publishing, 2009.

Watts, Elsie Ina. "Attitudes of Parents Toward the Development of Public Schooling in Victoria, B.C. During the Colonial Period." Master's thesis, Simon Fraser University, 1986.

Western Canadian Immigration Association. *Peel's Bibliography of the Canadian Prairies to 1953*. Toronto: University of Toronto Press, 2003.

Woman's Christian Temperance Union of British Columbia 1883–86. Minute book, resolutions, membership list. Victoria: British Columbia Provincial Archives.

Yerbury, J. C. *The Subarctic Indians and the Fur Trade 1680–1860*. Vancouver: UBC Press, 1986.

INDEX